Globalization & Crime

Key Approaches to Criminology

The *Key Approaches to Criminology* series celebrates the removal of traditional barriers between disciplines and brings together some of the leading scholars working at the intersections of different but related fields. Each book in the series aids readers in making intellectual connections across subjects, and highlights the importance of studying crime, criminalization, justice, and punishment within a broad context. The intention, then, is that books published under the *Key Approaches* banner will be viewed as dynamic and energizing contributions to criminological debates.

Globalization & Crime – the second book in the series – is no exception in this regard. In addressing topics ranging from human trafficking and the global sex trade to the protection of identity in cyberspace and post 9/11 anxieties, Katja Franko Aas has captured some of the most controversial and pressing issues of our times. Not only does she provide a comprehensive overview of existing debates about these subjects but she moves these debates forward, offering innovative and challenging ways of thinking about familiar contemporary concerns. I believe that *Globalization & Crime* is the most important book published in this area to date and it is to the author's great credit that she explores the complexities of transnational crime and responses to it in a manner that combines sophistication of analysis with eloquence of expression. As one of the leading academics in the field – and someone who is genuinely engaged in dialogue about global 'crime' issues at an international level, Katja Franko Aas is ideally placed to write this book, and I have no doubt that it will be read and appreciated by academics around the world. In addition to garnering interest from her peers, the book's accessibility of style, together with subject matter that is both provocative and 'of the moment', and the inclusion of pedagogical features which characterize books in this series, will ensure that *Globalization & Crime* is required reading for undergraduates and postgraduates studying numerous and diverse degree modules. In short, *Globalization & Crime* is an exciting and very welcome contribution to Sage's *Key Approaches to Criminology* series.

Yvonne Jewkes
Series Editor

Other books in the series:

Media and Crime (2004) Yvonne Jewkes (Open University)

History and Crime (forthcoming) Barry Godfrey (Keele University), Paul Lawrence (Open University) and Chris Williams (Open University)

Globalization & Crime

Katja Franko Aas

SAGE Publications
Los Angeles • London • New Delhi • Singapore

First published 2007

SAGE Publications Ltd
1 Oliver's Yard
55 City Road
London EC1Y 1SP

SAGE Publications Inc.
2455 Teller Road
Thousand Oaks, California 91320

SAGE Publications India Pvt Ltd
B 1/I 1 Mohan Cooperative Industrial Area
Mathura Road
New Delhi 110 044

SAGE Publications Asia-Pacific Pte Ltd
33 Pekin Street #02-01
Far East Square
Singapore 048763

Library of Congress Control Number: 2007930469

British Library Cataloguing in Publication data

A catalogue record for this book is available
from the British Library

ISBN 978-1-4129-1289-1
ISBN 978-1-4129-1290-7   (pbk)

Typeset by C&M Digitals (P) Ltd., Chennai, India
Printed in Great Britain by TJ International Ltd, Padstow, Cornwall
Printed on paper from sustainable resources

As always,
for Eva and Maria

Contents

Acknowledgements   ix

1   Crime, Fear and Social Exclusion in the Global Village   1

2   Global Mobility and Human Traffic   27

3   Urban Criminology and the Global City   49

4   The 'Deviant Immigrant': Migration and Discourse about Crime   75

5   Transnational Crime and Crime Wars   101

6   Beyond the State: Globalization and State Sovereignty   129

7   Controlling Cyberspace?   151

8   Criminology between the National, Local and Global   171

References   191

Glossary   207

Index   214

Acknowledgements

The arguments presented in this book have benefited from comments and conversations with many colleagues and students from the Institute of Criminology and Sociology of Law in Oslo. For reading and commenting on parts or all of the manuscript I am indebted to Nils Christie, Helene Oppen Gundhus, Yvonne Jewkes, Nicolay Johansen, Per Ole Johansen, Heidi Mork Lomell, Annick Prieur, Lill Scherdin and May-Len Skilbrei. Editors and anonymous reviewers for *Theoretical Criminology* 11 (2) gave valuable feedback on early versions of my ideas.

I am also very grateful for the financial support I have received, including scholarships from the University of Oslo's CULCOM programme, and from the Norwegian Research Council's KIM programme. I could not have completed the project without this support.

Special thanks are owed to Yvonne Jewkes and Caroline Porter for their fantastic support and guidance, and to the staff at Sage for their assistance in producing this book. Working with them has been a pleasure.

Finally, my greatest debt is to my family, Slovene and Norwegian. To Per Christian for his belief in me. To my grandparents I owe a long overdue debt of gratitude. This book is dedicated to my daughters Eva and Maria.

1

Crime, Fear and Social Exclusion in the Global Village

Chapter Contents

What is globalization?   3

Criminology and the global, the local and the 'glocal'   6

The social and time–space compression   7

The network society, global economy and neo-liberalism   9

The changing role of the state   11

Towards a world risk society?   13

Fear of crime and the perilous quest for security   14

'The wasteful, rejecting logic of globalization'   17

The new penology and the 'factories of immobility'   19

Crime, wars, war crimes and crime wars   21

Summary   25

Study questions   26

Further reading   26

OVERVIEW

Chapter 1 provides:

- A definition of globalization as a phenomenon of increasing interconnectedness of societies, as well as a number of other meanings and controversies raised by the term.
- An introduction of the main topics and theoretical concepts pertaining to globalization & crime, which will be discussed in greater detail in the following chapters.
- An introduction of the various aspects of global interconnectedness (economic, communicational, risk, etc.).
- A discussion of the multiple ways in which global inequality shapes contemporary crime control strategies and notions of relative deprivation and social exclusion.
- A discussion of the contested meaning of crime and criminalization.

KEY TERMS

actuarial justice	(late) modernity	social exclusion
Americanization	neo-liberalism	space of flows
crime	neo-Marxism	time–space compression
globalism	ontological insecurity	
glocalization	relative deprivation	

'Huge trafficking organization smashed', 'Police "can't cope" as Vietnamese flood drugs trade', 'New plans to tackle online perverts', 'Protect yourself from identity theft', 'EU crackdown on people smuggling', 'Suspected terrorists given citizenship' – these are only some examples of headlines featured in the media in the past few years. The merging of global threats and local fears seems to have become a daily occurrence through milder and stronger forms of moral panics. At the same time, contemporary societies seem not only to be preoccupied with new forms of transnational threats, but are also developing new methods, new rationalities and solidarities in responding to these issues. The so far privileged position of the state and the national as the primary field of criminological reference is increasingly overshadowed by various transnational and sub-national configurations. 'Siamo tutti Londinesi' ('We are all Londoners'), said the posters on the streets of Rome the day after the July 2005 London attacks. The message was similar to the one displayed on the cover of the French Le Monde, in the aftermath of the September 11th attacks, pro   ling that 'We are all Americans now'. As well as expressing global solidarity, the messages revealed shared feelings of fear and vulnerability between the Western capitals. The threat of the 'foreign' contaminating the perceived security of the local has become a common theme on political agendas and in media debates.

However, if we are to discern any deeper criminological relevance of the above phenomena, we need to turn our attention to underlying social transformations in the emerging, deeply stratified global order. Today, globalization is shaping contemporary life more than ever, influencing our perceptions of community, identity and culture. The globalizing world has been described as a 'world in motion' (Inda and Rosaldo, 2002), permeated by transnational networks and flows of goods, capital, images and cultural symbols, as well as potentially risky individuals, goods and substances. The aim of this book is to examine the implications of these phenomena for studying crime and social control in a 'world in motion'. From the issues of organized crime, transnational policing, transfer of penal knowledge and policies, to a variety of trans-border sex industries (cyber and corporeal) – to name just a few – one could say that the criminological world is in motion as well. The purpose of this book is to go beyond the nation state and capture this emerging new level of criminological analysis – which in many ways we are only beginning to see the contours of – taking the global and transnational as the primary point of reference. My objective is to ask: what are the consequences of these transnational connections for criminology? How do we redefine and reorganize theoretical and methodological approaches in an increasingly interconnected world? The emerging global transformations have important implications, not only for what is commonly referred to as transnational crime, but also for local and national crime and security concerns. After all, globalization is 'not just an 'out there' phenomenon' but also an *'in here'* development' (Giddens, 1998), which is particularly applicable when it comes to penal policy. The events of 9/11 have highlighted and magnified the growing awareness that risk and insecurity are global, that space and national borders have a limited protective capacity, and that there is a need to address the issues of our mutual interconnectedness and vulnerability.

 ## What is globalization?

Globalization is a widely discussed topic and there are numerous definitions of the subject in the burgeoning globalization literature. In the popular imagination, the term is generally thought to describe the profound economic and technological developments which enable, for example, Western clothing manufacturers to produce their clothes using cheap labour from China, or companies to service their customers from a call centre in India. The term also refers to the politically charged issues of the great power of international corporations, privatization of state assets in order to meet IMF and World Bank requirements, the imperialist tendencies of Western media and culture, etc. The term globalization therefore relates to a wide range of topics, not all of which will be touched upon in this book. Many have also noted a discomfort with using the term, since the debates about globalization in the past decades have been highly polarized and divisive. Besides serving as a theoretical category of social science, the term globalization is also used in various contexts as a 'political category of blame', a 'cultural category of fear', and 'an economic category of opportunity and enterprise' (Ericson and Stehr, 2000: 30). Critics and proponents of globalization tend to see the phenomenon as either intrinsically bad or automatically good. Some therefore prefer not to use 'globalization' at all, and talk of transnationalization in order to avoid over-generalization and to 'suggest that transnational practices impact on human relationships in diverse ways in different places' (Sheptycki, 2005: 79).

Nevertheless, as Giddens (2000: 25) points out: 'Globalization may not be a particularly attractive or elegant word. But absolutely no one who wants to understand our prospects at century's end can ignore it.' For the purpose of this book, I shall start with a simple, yet useful, definition of globalization offered by Held, who describes globalization as 'the growing interconnectedness of states and societies' and 'the progressive enmeshment of human communities with each other' (Held, 2000: 42). 'Over the last few centuries, human communities have come into increasing contact with each other; their collective fortunes have become intertwined' (ibid.). Held's definition is useful also because it points to the long history of the globalizing processes. Even though we may like to think of the present interconnectedness of the world as something new and unique, historians have outlined numerous modalities of globalization and de-globalization through time, exemplified by ancient 'mini globalizers' such as traders 'like the Venetian Marco Polo, mobile warriors like Genghis Khan, and cross-border proselytizers like Saint Paul' (Holton, 2005: 40).

In *The Consequences of Modernity*, Anthony Giddens suggest that the globalizing process is an essential part of *late modernity*. According to Giddens (1990: 63) 'modernity is inherently globalizing'. He sees globalization primarily as a disembedding and stretching process

> in so far as the modes of connection between different social contexts or regions become networked across the earth's surface as a whole.
> Globalization can thus be defined as the intensification of worldwide social relations which link distant localities in such a way that local happenings are shaped by events occurring many miles away and vice versa. (Giddens, 1990: 64)

There have been numerous debates whether globalization can be described through the use of old terms such as *modernity*. Albrow argues that even those who recognize globalization as a profound contemporary transformation seek to assimilate it to modernity, thus 'reviving modernity's flagging hold on reality' (1996: 86). Globalization is therefore in danger of being seen as an -'ization' term associated with modernity and having inevitable and predictable consequences (ibid.).

Critics have furthermore pointed out that Giddens offers a far too abstract definition of globalization. Robertson (1995) emphasizes that global interconnectedness is a cultural process unfolding through the development of global consciousness, rather than simply being a process of global expansion of capitalism and modernity. Consequently, some authors prefer to use the term *globalism*, emphasising the 'subjective, personal awareness that many of us share common tastes and interests and we are all likely to share a common fate' (Cohen and Kennedy, 2000: 11). Furthermore, the globalist approach points out that there are many different types of globalization and that cultural globalization, for example, may unfold in different tempos and in different geographies from economic globalization (Held and McGrew, 2003). Others, by contrast, offer a much more sceptical view of globalization altogether, doubting both its novelty as well as its profound transformative impact (Hirst and Thompson, 1996). Capitalism has after all always functioned as a world economy.

This book will look at this emerging world of global interconnections and the debates surrounding it, particularly as they pertain to issues of crime, deviance and social control. Often, global interconnections and foreign influences on our local lives tend to be described as *Americanization*, 'McDonaldization' and Westernization. In many ways, these characterizations are to the point, also when it comes to the case of crime control and criminal justice. The last chapter will discuss penal policy transfers, and the spread of 'zero tolerance' policing will be named as one example of Americanization. However, we should also be aware of the fact that when describing the globalizing process as primarily a 'top down' process of Western dominance, one may be in danger of overlooking numerous 'bottom up' global initiatives and interconnections. There is therefore also a need to explore 'globalization from below' (Hall, 2006). In fact, resistance to globalization is essentially dependent on various global interconnections (Stiglitz, 2002; Polet, 2004). The anti-globalization protests in Seattle in 1999 involved 1,300 organizations from over 80 countries. On that day, there were also parallel demonstrations in many US and other cities around the world, from Paris to Manila and Seoul (Sheptycki, 2005). The global interconnections therefore offer a complex picture, involving multiple processes such as Westernization, the global spread of consumerism and the predominance of Western multinationals, as well as growth of the transnational sex industry, the popularity of Bollywood films across the globe, global resistance and political action. Furthermore, we will also look at the absence of these phenomena; the territories and social groups which have been left out and disconnected. Both the multiple and complex connections and the disconnections are an essential part of globalization and shall be a subject of our discussions.

Criminology and the global, the local and the 'glocal'

The challenges for criminology may lie not simply in mapping the emerging global interconnections, but also in examining how people and social institutions adjust to these developments locally, through culturally specific strategies. 'Zero tolerance' policing, mentioned above, is quite different in Oslo than in New York or in Mexico City, although people use the same term often without even translating it from English. The study of globalization needs to keep in mind this dialectic of the global and the local. As Giddens (1990: 64, italics original) writes:

> *Local transformation* is as much a part of globalisation as the lateral extension of social connections across time and space. Thus whoever studies cities today, in any part of the world, is aware that what happens in a local neighbourhood is likely to be influenced by factors – such as world money and commodity markets – operating at an indefinite distance away from that neighbourhood itself.

If we are to develop an adequate concept of globalization we need to take into account not only the stretching of social relations, but also the increasing intensity and speed of global interconnections as well as their increasing impact on local developments (Held et al., 2003: 67). Our lives and identities, including our values and perceptions of security, crime and punishment, are formed by a growing flow of international and global signs and activities. These flows include innumerable flows of people who are on the move; even those who have never moved beyond their local town or village are now transformed by the global flows. In a world of expanding media and communication technologies, 'the sitting room is a place where, in a variety of mediated forms, the global meets the local' (Morley, 2000: 2).

Robertson's (1995) term *glocalization* is often used to describe the intertwining of the global and the local. Seen from this perspective, they cannot be treated as two distinct entities: they are a new synthesis, involving both transnational and local elements. One such example, discussed in Chapter 5, is Hobbs and Dunnighan's (1998: 289) argument about the relevance of 'glocal organised crime', emphasising 'the importance of the local context as an environment within which criminal networks function'. As Hylland Eriksen (2003: 5) writes, global process and phenomena are only brought into being in so far as people invest them with content, [that] they are only activated through social processes. The point may seem trivial, yet it is easily overlooked if one sees 'the global' as a kind of Hegelian world spirit looming above and beyond human lives. The global only exists to the extent that it is being created through ongoing social life.

This approach may have much to offer when we look at the contemporary complexities of social action, as well as well as the modalities of cultural and penal policy transfers and other adaptations to global change.

The social and time–space compression

Globalizing processes force us to analyse society from a new perspective. Increasingly, people find out that their lives are influenced and ordered by events and social institutions spatially far removed from their local contexts. Social life takes place 'at a distance' (Giddens, 1990). In his seminal work *The Condition of Postmodernity*, David Harvey (1990) described one of the vital dimensions of globalization, the transformation of time and space through a process of **time–space compression**. Harvey points out that globalization is fuelled by the increasing speed of communication and movement of capital, resulting in the 'shrinking' of space and the shortening of time. It is not only Wall Street traders who watch and take part in events happening on the other side of the globe. Most of us, more or less frequently, follow global events 'as they happen and where they happen', to borrow CNN's catchy slogan. From the euphoria of the fall of the Berlin Wall, to the triviality of Michael Jackson's trial and, of course, the tragedies of Beslan, the London terror attacks and 9/11, 'when the whole world watched the surreal and stranger-than-Hollywood event as planes with live passengers flew into and demolished two of the largest buildings in the world' (Urry, 2002a: 57). A vital aspect of the globalizing process is therefore the movement of cultural images, information and ideas, which enable us to visit – physically or virtually – distant places almost anywhere in the world.

Consequently, there is a need to adjust our notions of society to these transformations.

> The undue reliance which sociologists have placed upon the idea of 'society', where this means a bounded system, should be replaced by a starting point that concentrates upon analysing how social life is ordered across time and space – the problematic of time–space distanciation. The conceptual framework of time–space distanciation directs our attention to the complex relations between *local involvements* (circumstances of co-presence) and *interaction across distance* (the connections of presence and absence). (Giddens, 1990: 64, italics original)

We need to acknowledge that we no longer live in discrete worlds, even though the worlds of national state societies never have been completely discrete. There is a need to challenge the 'belief that national political communities can be relatively autonomous because they have the capacity to control their own destinies' (Ericson and Stehr, 2000: 32). This belief is strong in much of the present political discourse on crime, where it seems as if politicians, having acknowledged their limited capacities to influence economy, or having given up the responsibility for doing so, are showing their determination to act by various measures to 'combat crime' (Bauman, 2002; Christie, 2004).

Global flows traverse national boundaries, creating a constant flux between the inside and the outside, resulting in hybridity of what before appeared to be relatively stable entities. Increasingly, the boundaries between the inside and outside are being blurred, and we are faced with the question of how to deal with the constant influx of sometimes unfamiliar and undesirable people, ideas, images, objects and activities, in our midst. The meanings of home, community, nation and citizenship become transformed beyond recognition by the global, creating hybrid identities and 'glocal' belongings. Minority youth across the world have to juggle multiple belongings, not only to the nation states they live in but also to the places of their and their parents' origin as well as other cultural and political influences. This does not mean, as anthropologist Arjun Appadurai (1996: 34) points out, that there are no relatively stable communities and networks, but that these stabilities are 'shot through with the woof of human motion, as more persons and groups deal with the realities of having to move or the fantasies of wanting to move'. Communities and societies are no longer (though they hardly ever were) systems with clear territorial and membership boundaries. The speed of contemporary communication and interaction across great distances are radically transforming the nature of almost all aspects of social life. According to Appadurai (1996: 33), modern life is lived in various transnational scapes: ethnoscapes, technoscapes, mediascapes, financescapes and ideoscapes. 'The suffix –*scape* allows us to point to the fluid, irregular shapes of these landscapes, shapes that characterize international capital as deeply as they do international clothing styles' (ibid.). The point here is that our worlds, their economic, cultural and numerous other aspects, are moving. Our jobs, friendships and family patterns, cultural symbols and leisure activities, all seem to be transformed by this mobility. We spend much of our work and leisure activities in cyberspace, we travel more than ever, consume products produced in distant places, and live increasingly surrounded by people of different nationalities, ethnicity and race.

In line with other authors mentioned above, John Urry (2000) argues that sociological inquiry needs to take account of these multiple and diverse mobilities. He outlines the need to take 'sociology beyond societies'; for a sociology that goes beyond the static notion of a society and nation-state in a 'pre-global' order to examine the various mobilities of people, images, capital, objects, information and risks. Urry thus invites us to move beyond the comparative research of nation states and to look at the level of global flows and explore the 'global complexity' (Urry, 2003). However, rather than seeing the global as the new structure – an assumption frequently made by eager globalization analysts – we shall follow Urry's (2002a: 59) more modest suggestion and envision it as an unfinished process, 'which problematises the fixed, given and static notions of social order'. A global perspective can be seen as an encouragement to transcend boundaries and to expand the territorial as well as thematic scope of conventional criminology.

The network society, global economy and neo-liberalism

Looking at material aspects of the new social ordering, Manuel Castells's seminal work on the network society (1996) has established the concept of flows and networks as a central tool and metaphor of sociological inquiry. The network society is 'a new society, based upon knowledge, organized around networks, and partly made up of flows' (Castells 1996: 398). Money, information, objects and people move through flows, creating 'a society in which the material basis for all processes is made up of flows, and in which power and wealth are organized in global networks carrying information flows' (Borja and Castells, 1997: 12). These social changes have been to a large extent facilitated by the profound technological revolution in information and communication technologies, and by subsequent changes in production, employment and social organization patterns. A result is a global economy with the capacity not only to accumulate capital across the world, but also 'to work as a unit in real time on a planetary scale' (Castells, 1996: 92). Consequently, the economical and technological developments have lead to the spread of capitalism across the world. However, as we shall see later in this chapter, the rise of network society and global economy has also produced new divisions of labour (between skilled and unskilled workers, men and women, North and South, etc.), as well as new social and spatial divisions and inequalities.

The network society is a society where '[b]oth space and time are being transformed under the combined effect of the information technology paradigm' (ibid.: 376). Castells outlines a new notion of space as the *'space of flows'*, rather than a 'space of places'. The new spatial organization of society has profound consequences for how life is lived and how power is distributed in the globalizing world. We will explore the issue further in Chapter 3, where we will see how some cities and regions, due to their participation in information networks and flows of capital, gain great advantage over the disconnected, 'switched off' territories. The so-called 'information revolution' has had a profound effect on all aspects of social life. If we compare this development to the industrial revolution, the communication networks replace the factory as the main unit of production, creating new, flexible work and production models such as 'subcontracting, the decentralization of production, outworking, job sharing, part-time work, self-employment and consultancy' (Borja and Castells, 1997: 11). The new technological developments have by no means led to a decline in industrial production: quite the opposite. There has been an unprecedented wave of industrialization, particularly in the developing countries, yet 'the new industrialization already functions in accordance with the patterns of flexible model from the outset' (ibid.: 11), thus combining the older models of industrial exploitation with the new paradigms of global competition.

Looking at the working conditions in Asian factories, one is struck by the fact that the works of classic thinkers – such as Karl Marx on commodification of labour and Michel Foucault on discipline – still have much explanatory power. However, there has clearly also been a fundamental shift from the past, described by many authors in recent years as a move from industrial to post-industrial economies, or to use another term, from Fordist to post-Fordist economies (Harvey, 1990). While the Fordist economy of mass production was based on rigid arrangements between employers, workers and the state to maintain high levels of employment and stability, the post-Fordist system is unstable and rests on flexibility with respect to labour processes, labour markets, products and patterns of consumption (Harvey, 1990). Similarly, Lash and Urry (1994) describe the end of nationally focused organized capitalism, which marked most of the 20th century, and a move towards 'disorganized capitalism', characterized by global reach and flexibility at all levels.

These economic developments have been accompanied by a certain political and economic discourse, which often tends to be equated with globalization itself – namely, ***neo-liberalism***.

> [N]eoliberalism refers to an economic and political school of thought on the relations between the state on the one hand, and citizens and the world of trade and commerce on the other. Because it espouses minimal or no state interference in the market and promotes the lifting of barriers to trade and business transactions across regional and national borders, it certainly becomes a motor of globalization. (Passas, 2000: 21)

Neo-liberalism, however, can be described as more than a 'motor of globalization', or in any case, a motor of economic globalization. The word also represents the crux of the heated discussions about globalization and its consequences. Neo-liberalism is often used to denote all that is condemned by the critics of globalization: privatization of state assets, deregulation and giving free rein to market forces, greater emphasis on individual responsibility, the dismantling of welfare state systems, etc.

For the purpose of this book, the question has to be asked, of course, what kind of relevance do the above-mentioned transformations have for studies of crime and crime control? The new canon of neo-liberalism, flexibility and personal freedom has had profound implications for the nature of work, family relations and life patterns, as is powerfully described in Bauman's (2000) outline of the transformation of modernity from solid to 'liquid modernity', leading to profound conditions of insecurity. Furthermore, the neo-liberal approach to governance has had profound effects on how the state and social institutions govern and address issues of crime and crime control, a topic which will be discussed in greater detail in Chapter 6.

The changing role of the state

The changing role of the nation state is a central aspect of contemporary globalization debates. What role will and should the state have in the new world of roaming flows of capital, people, ideas and information? The changing role of the state is a central topic throughout this book, as we encounter new modalities and ideologies of state control when it comes to control of borders and migration, transnational crime, the rise of private security, cybercrime, etc. One of the main points of the debate is the argument that the globalizing process puts into question the role of the nation state as the cornerstone of political community, social theory and governance. The so-called first wave of globalization theories in particular was very sceptical about the ability of nation states to resist the 'globalization juggernaut' (see for example Ohmae, 1990; Reich, 1991). The perception was that the nation state was 'withering away' and that its sovereignty was irreversibly challenged by the powerful world of global economy (Bauman, 1998). Some saw the development as the beginning of a 'new world disorder' (ibid.), while Hardt and Negri (2000), influentially, saw the nation state order replaced by a new order of a 'global empire'.

The challenges to state sovereignty come, significantly, not only from the increasingly interconnected and autonomous global economy, but also from the global illicit economy. The growth of illegal and illicit opportunities has been, according to several observers, an essential part of globalization and the deregulation of national economies (Castells, 2004; Naim, 2006). The triumph of neo-liberalism resulted in a massive privatization of state-owned enterprises across the world. This transformation from strong state regulation to privatised market solutions has been most visible, and problematic, in the ex-socialist economies. Castells's description of the 'pillage of Russia' (2004) outlines a tragic triumph of turbo-capitalism, built on systematic illegality and a damaging lack of state regulation. The systematic weakening of state regulatory controls 'opened the way for a wild competition to grab state property by whatever means, often in association with criminal elements' (ibid.: 187). In this case, the boundaries between state institutions and illegality are increasingly hard to discern, as corruption and organized crime become pervasive aspects of social organization. The penetration of the state by the illicit and illegal economy has been described as the problem of 'failed states' (discussed further in Chapters 5 and 6). What is important at this point is that the neo-liberal tenets of state privatization and deregulation, on the one hand, and the autonomy and lack of transparency of the world financial systems, on the other, both contributed to the weakening of central state functions, particularly in the ex-socialist countries and in the developing world. The 'pillage of Russia' also reveals a more fundamental linkage between market economies and crime: an ongoing conflict that 'pits the rigidity of state-formulated rule systems against the exigencies of the market' (Whyte, 2007: 178). The market economy, and its elevation of the pursuit of self-interest, in some aspects represents an inherent threat to the legal system. (We shall discuss the issue in Chapter 6 through the concept of anomie.)

However, when it comes to issues of crime control, the role of the state seems full of contradictions which defy simple categorizations. On the one hand, the state seems to be increasingly incapable of managing the crime problem, even in the prosperous West. We have witnessed in the past three decades an unprecedented growth in private security, as well as privatization of prisons and numerous other services incorporated in penal systems, which were traditionally seen as the prerogative of state sovereignty. Crime control has become, as Nils Christie (2000) aptly put it, an industry, where most states to a varying extent leave the provision of security to market forces. State sovereignty is also increasingly eroded 'from above', by various institutions of global governance (see Chapters 6 and 8). However, while these trends may at first glance seem to be supportive of the 'withering away' thesis, they nevertheless call for a more thorough examination, since parallel with the commercialization of security we have also witnessed a striking growth in prison populations and penal systems in many parts of the world (Christie, 2000; Pratt et al., 2005; Stern, 2006). Furthermore, we have seen a renewed show of states' 'muscle power' through the so-called 'war on terror', visible in the intensification of border controls and the expansion of state surveillance and bureaucracy (see Chapter 5). It would therefore seem that far from 'withering away', the nation still has a number of tasks, particularly in the context of controlling the 'darker sides of globalization' (Urry, 2002a: 58). As Beck (2002: 47) points out, 'the seemingly irrefutable tenets of neoliberalism – that economics will supersede politics, that the role of the state will diminish – lose their force in a world of global risks'.

The above discussion about the role of the state points to the fact that globalization is by no means an either – or process, but a complex set of developments with multiple modalities. We need to be aware of the erroneous and simplistic picture of globalization, often painted by both pro- and anti-globalization analysts, as an inevitable and deterministic process. What tends to be forgotten is that there are limits and paradoxes inherent in the globalizing process. As we shall see in the next chapter, it may seem as if we live in a 'borderless' world, yet this is the case only for inhabitants of a small number of Western nations, while global mobility for others is increasingly restricted. Similarly, the new technologies, much credited with the intensification of globalization, are in fact available only to a relatively small stratum of the world population. In Chapter 5 we shall see how global surveillance practices and technologies are creating a new visibility, at the same time as the methods used in the so-called war on terror have been marked by an extreme lack of transparency. The prisoners in Guantanamo and other captives of so-called 'extraordinary renditions' could travel across the world in almost complete anonymity, exempt from surveillance measures and from the rule of law. Ordinary travellers, on the other hand, have to submit to an increasing variety of searches and body scans in order to take a commercial flight. Even in its most visible aspects, such as the international economy, the globalization of capital is concentrated in a limited number of networks and nodes, leaving some parts of the world perhaps more disconnected than ever. The study of globalization therefore needs to keep in mind not only the intensity of transnational connections, but also the paradoxes, unevenness, concrete modalities and disconnections. In fact, one is tempted to suggest that unevenness is an intrinsic aspect of the current global transformations – that we live in a world of global capital that continues to rely on nation states, in a world that is borderless for some and full of fences for others, and where the language of freedom and opportunity goes hand in hand with pervasive structural inequality. On a more positive note, we shall see in the last chapter, that although eroding the fundamentals of state sovereignty and justice, global interconnections are also creating alternative frames and forums of justice, thus revealing globalization's often forgotten potential for empowerment.

Towards a world risk society?

The transnational connections discussed in this book crucially transform the governance of what was previously designed as nation states' 'internal' security. The transnational nature of various threats which societies face today is, like global interconnections themselves, nothing new. The environmentalist movement has been among the first to put the mutual vulnerability of societies on the public agenda. The second part of this chapter presents the changing dynamics of crime control in late modern societies, particularly through the emphasis on risk, insecurity, fear and social exclusion. Some of the major theoretical contributions on the topic have come from the growing body of work on the **risk society**, strongly influenced by the work of Ulrich Beck. The German edition of Beck's book *The Risk Society* came out in 1986, providentially, only shortly after the Chernobyl catastrophe, and became an immediate success even beyond academic circles. The book describes late modern societies as risk societies, constantly debating, managing and preventing risks they have themselves produced. In fact, he argues that risks and hazards are the results of 'successful' modernization, an inevitable dark side of progress. He outlines a transition from the relative stability of the 1950s and 1960s class societies (high employment, stable family life and stable gender roles) to the instability and insecurity of *late modernity*. In risk societies social inequality is individualized, and the focus is on fear and safety rather than on issues of class and social justice. Beck (1992: 49) argues that

> Class societies remain related to the ideal of *equality* in their developmental dynamics (in its various formulations from 'equal opportunity' to the variants of socialist models of society). Not so the risk society. Its normative counter-project, which is its basis and motive force, is *safety*. The place of the value system of the 'unequal' society is taken by the value system of the 'unsafe' society. Whereas the utopia of equality contains a wealth of substantial and *positive* goals of social change, the utopia of the risk society remains peculiarly *negative* and *defensive*. (italics original).

One can think of terrorism alerts, bird flu reports, 'mad cow disease', transnational organized crime and other frequently reported transnational risks, as potent symbols of the spirit of our times. The fact that the world is in some respects becoming a 'smaller place' has been deeply connected to insecurity through the proliferation of the images of dangers which are perceived to threaten the national and the local. For example, through global media reports about crime a murder of a child in England is 'immediately flashed around the world – and at the same time turned into a local possibility' (Pratt, 2002: 175).

Beck (1999) later boldly introduced the notion of a 'world risk society' which is, with the highly publicized threat of terrorist attacks, becoming increasingly palpable. In the world risk society, the various threats such as terrorism, ecological disasters and financial crises are marked by their borderless and deterritorialized nature. The issue of mobility and globalization of risk was also acknowledged by Giddens (1990), who suggested that the globalizing process affects the nature of risk in at least two ways: in the sense of intensity of risk, exemplified by the possibility of nuclear disasters, as well as in the sense of the *'expanding number of contingent events which affect everyone or at least large numbers of people on the planet'* (1990: 124, italics original). Through the globalizing process risks are potentially magnified, as well as disembedded and taken out of the hands of individuals and local communities. One may justifiably ask though whether the idea of a world risk society simply responds to the feelings of Western citizens who are beginning to feel now the effects of global social conflicts and environmental disasters in their, previously seemingly untouched, enclaves of security?

Fear of crime and the perilous quest for security

Concerns about fear and insecurity have been central to much criminological writing in the past two decades. Our time has been described as a 'culture of fear'

(Furedi, 2002), and it has been persuasively argued that fear and insecurity have been a potent factor behind a variety of criminal justice policies and discourses (Sparks and Hope, 2000; Zedner, 2003). Sparks and Hope (2000: 5) note that the issue of fear of crime and insecurity needs to be situated within the context of wider social and cultural transformations. '"Fear of crime" thus intersects with the larger consequences of modernity, and finds its lived social meaning among people's senses of change and decay, optimism and foreboding' (ibid.). The issue relates to the aforementioned transformations towards late and 'liquid' modernity, the end of certainty and stability, the liquidity of social bonds. Some have theorized the shift as a move towards postmodernism and the end of a homogeneous and structured narrative about crime and punishment, mirrored in the present media barrage of crime news and images of violence and devastation (Jewkes, 2004; Morrison, 1995). Addressing the question of terrorism, Jewkes (2004: 28) observes:

> Terrorist attacks on 'innocent' civilians chime with the postmodernist idea that we are all potential victims. Postmodern analyses reject traditional criminological concerns with the causes and consequences of crime, pointing instead to the fragmentation of societies, the fear that paralyses many communities, the random violence that seems to erupt at all levels of society, and the apparent inability of governments to do anything about these problems. This concern with a lurking unpredictable danger is fortified by an omnipresent media.

The current concern about terrorism is only one in the array of global threats. It has been pointed out that the globalizing process fosters insecurity. The transition from relatively stable Fordist economies to flexible post-Fordist systems has, according to a number of analysts, been a breeding ground for social insecurity. Globalization and the late modern condition are frequently credited with exacerbating what is often referred to as *'ontological insecurity'*. According to Giddens, ontological insecurity refers to a lack of 'confidence that most human beings have in their self-identity and the constancy of the surrounding social and material environments of action' (1990: 92). The notion is embodied in a series of sociological and criminological explorations (see for example Sennett, 1998; Young, 1999). In the global economy, not only the working classes, but also those who seemed to have succeeded, live under a constant threat of 'flexible work' and redundancy due to downsizing and perpetual restructuring of the economy. Consequently, 'anxiety, fear and self-interest become the new emotional responses to life in advanced capitalism' (Hall and Winlow, 2005: 32).

According to Young (2003), the conditions of permanent insecurity throughout society serve as a breeding ground for many forms of crime, as well as defining the intense response of the 'discontented majority' to acts of deviance. Those sometimes referred to as the 'contented majority' are therefore far from content; instead they 'are unsure about their good fortune, unclear about their identity, uncertain about their position on the included side of the line' (Young, 2003: 399). In a somewhat nostalgic tone, global transformations tend to be blamed for the demise of the 'golden age' of the welfare state and for creating societies which are anxious about crime, lack confidence in the state, and are more punitive by nature (Baker and Roberts, 2005; Pratt, 2007). The thought is well summarized by Young when he writes that:

> whereas the Golden Age [i.e. 1950s and 1960s] granted social embeddedness, strong certainty of personal and social narrative, a desire to assimilate the deviant, the immigrant, the stranger, late modernity generated both economic and ontological insecurity , a discontinuity of personal and social narrative and an exclusionary tendency towards the deviant. (Young, 2003: 390)

Although the heightened focus on security resonates with the themes of risk society, it contradicts the idea that governments and institutions respond rationally in order to minimize risk. Several commentators have pointed out that the narrative of the risk society needs to be balanced by taking into account the more emotional aspects of social reactions to risk. As Mythen and Walkate (2006a: 388) suggest: 'Far from a global politics of risk which emphasizes responsibility and equality, what is emerging instead, it seems, is a politics of fear and vengeance.' The issue is discussed in greater detail in Chapter 4, where we shall see how the tone of contemporary penal discourse has become in many ways more emotional, vindicative and punitive. The prospect is clearly acknowledged by Beck, who argues that 'the risk society contains an inherent tendency to become a *scapegoat society*'.

> The very intangibility of the threat and people's helplessness as it grows promote *radical and fanatical reactions and political tendencies* that make social stereotypes and the groups afflicted by them into 'lightning rods' for the invisible threats which are inaccessible to direct action. (Beck, 1992: 75, italics original)

Furthermore, while security fears may be high on the present political agenda, critics of the risk society thesis have argued that people are by no means equally affected by various risks (Mythen and Walkate, 2006a: 388). Beck's statement that 'poverty is hierarchic while smog is democratic' needs to be juxtaposed with the pervasive social inequalities within risk societies. This is acknowledged by Beck (1992: 41) himself, who indicates that there 'is a systematic 'attraction' between extreme poverty and extreme risk', exemplified by the export of hazardous industries to the Third World. Therefore, while certain social risks or 'bads' may appear to threaten everybody, other 'bads' and 'goods' are clearly unequally divided – both nationally and globally.

'The wasteful, rejecting logic of globalization'

Contemporary insecurities need to be situated in the context of the deepening social divisions between the 'winners' and 'losers' in the new world order. In what follows we shall look at the social divisions and inequalities, as well as the changing dynamics of *social exclusion* caused by the emerging global transformations. The neoliberal economic model is marked not only by its great productive dynamism, but also by the way it excludes large social sectors, territories and countries. As Borja and Castells (1997: 9) point out, what characterizes the new global economic order is 'its extraordinarily – and simultaneously – inclusive and exclusive nature'. The network society is a society where the creation of value and intensive consumption are concentrated in segments that are connected throughout the world, while other populations are 'moving from the previous situation of exploitation to a new form of structural irrelevance' (ibid.). The process of exclusion, of 'switching off', takes place both on the global level, by creating regions which are disconnected from the global flows, and on the national and local levels, by creating 'switched off' regions, cities and parts of cities. Globally connected and locally disconnected, global networks and flows introduce qualitatively different experiences of social ordering and exclusion, where the dynamic territories and segments of societies anywhere in the world gain over those who have become irrelevant in the global economy. As a result, we see 'consolidation of black holes of human misery in the global economy, be it in Burkina Faso, South Bronx, Kamagasaki, Chiapas, or La Courneuve' (Castells, 1996: 2). The 'global village' is a deeply divided village.

In his extensive and critical opus, sociologist Zygmunt Bauman describes the process as 'the wasteful, rejecting logic of globalization' (2000: 205). Pessimistically, Bauman (2004) sees globalization essentially as a process of production of 'human waste', of people who have been rendered redundant by the global spread of modernity. The populations which were before marked by their condition of exploitation, such as blue-collar workers in the industrialized North, are now in many ways rendered irrelevant in the new economic order as they find themselves out-competed by far cheaper labour forces in the developing world. And while previously in history there existed lands that were able to absorb the surplus populations produced by modernization, this is no longer the case. Needless to say, these developments have had a profound social impact and are of great relevance for studies of crime and social control. As we shall see in Chapter 2, the large global inequalities have created immense pressure on the borders of the affluent world, visible for example in daily reports about desperate attempts by African migrants to enter Europe. Furthermore, we shall see in Chapter 3 how Bauman's argument resonates with Wacquant's (2001) description of the black American ghetto as a mere 'dumping ground' rather then a reservoir of disposable industrial labour.

These examples point to the criminogenic impact of globalization and neo-liberal policies. The collapse of the socialist bloc has been widely credited as the breeding ground for organized crime, and the poorest countries in Europe, such as Moldova and other ex-Soviet republics, have become major 'exporters' of prostitution. Afghanistan, one of the poorest countries in the world, derives its livelihood by providing over 90 per cent of the world opium production (UNODOC, 2007). Several critics have taken up the issue of 'globalization and its discontents' (Sassen, 1998; Stiglitz, 2002). Stiglitz, a former World Bank economist, argues that particularly in the case of the ex-Soviet bloc the new economic system has far from brought unprecedented prosperity and a 'trickle-down effect' as its neo-liberal proponents had suggested. Instead, for many of world's populations, the transformations have resulted in poverty and social and political chaos.

Others have pointed out that the issue in question is not only one of undeniable poverty, which often cannot be attributed to global transformations alone, but also a question of the growth of spatial and social global inequality. Of the world population, about a third live on incomes of less than one dollar a day. Today, the richest 1 per cent of adults in the world own 40 per cent of the planet's wealth. The richest 10 per cent of adults account for 85 per cent of the world total of global assets.[1] However, the emerging global divisions defy the simplifications of the North–South, developing–developed world divide, although they certainly are pervasive. Social polarizations are also taking place on the national, regional and urban levels between highly paid knowledge workers and low-paid industrial and service professions (Perrons, 2004). A wave of industrialization in the Third World has contributed to large-scale migrations from the countryside, creating large populations of urban poor. We shall see in Chapter 7 that global income inequalities are partly mirrored in the access that disadvantaged populations have to information and communication technologies, which are the essential element of the new economy. There is a global digital divide between the 'haves' and 'have-nots', which has profound implications for possibilities for economic, social and cultural inclusion of these populations (Castells, 2001; Perrons, 2004).

Adverse economic deprivation and inequalities of wealth and power have a long history of being studied as causes of crime, particularly by **Marxist** and **neo-Marxist** thinkers. Marx's writing on the criminality of the proletariat may still resonate with the conditions of many peasant populations living in the sprawling slums of contemporary metropolises (Davis, 2006). However, critics have often pointed out the fallacies of simple extrapolations from poverty and economic deprivation to crime. Currie (1998) proposes a distinction between the 'market economy' and the 'market society'. Market society is, according to Currie (1998: 134), a society in which 'the pursuit of private gain increasingly becomes the originating principle for all areas of social life', and where 'all other

---

[1]http://money.guardian.co.uk/print/0,,329654256-110144,00.html

principles of social or institutional organization become eroded or subordinated to the overarching one of private gain'. He argues that the spread of market societies promotes crime through a number of mechanisms, among others, by increasing inequality and concentrating economic deprivation, by eroding the capacities of local communities, by withdrawing public services from the most needy, and by glorifying a culture of 'Darwinian competition' (ibid.).

Yet other observers have noted that one should be careful to avoid economic determinism, and should show sensitivity to the cultural and value aspects of market societies, a topic explored further in Chapters 4 and 5, when we examine the notion of anomie. Furthermore, while there may be no doubt about the existence of the great structural divides pointed out by the Marxist and critical left critique, others highlight the fact that the globalizing world is not only marked by social exclusion, but simultaneously by intense forms of social and cultural inclusion. Young (1999, 2003) suggests that while late modern societies are more exclusive than the welfare states of the post-war period, the term social exclusion, although clearly palpable and real, may no longer be adequate for describing the situation of inner city youth in the West or the situation of the deprived populations of the developing world. Young thus describes late modern societies as 'bulimic': they are inclusive, they culturally absorb massive populations; however, they simultaneously reject, 'vomit up' and structurally exclude these same populations.

Since societies no longer are discrete islands, the disadvantaged populations have become more aware of their marginalization by the constant presence of wealth in their sitting rooms through television and other media. A striking sight, while driving through poor neighbourhoods in a Third World city, is not only the dilapidated houses and the density of the population, but the overwhelming presence of satellite dishes on the rooftops. Through the consumption of images of distant places, people's experience of their localities is radically changed (Morley, 2000). In Chapter 4 we shall discuss in greater detail the emergence of global consumerism, global media and the globalization of culture, in general. We shall explore how global flows influence the production of identity and how local context becomes only one of many 'channels' of identity production. Globalization is therefore not only a material force, but also a cultural one. The pervasive social inequalities are magnified by the constant display of wealth and consumer goods in the media, reflecting not only conditions of absolute but also *relative deprivation*. Global transformations create a combustive mixture of connections and disconnections.

The new penology and the 'factories of immobility'

The transformation from modernity to late modernity has received considerable attention within Western criminology, and is often described as a major paradigm shift. The demise of the welfare state and its relatively inclusive ethos has had profound effects on the nature of contemporary penality, as exemplified by the rise of mass imprisonment and of the 'super-max' prison, and the spread of numerous other control strategies. In his seminal history of Anglo-American penality Garland (2001a) outlines a shift from penal-welfarism to a more punitive penal state and a 'culture of control'. Garland situates this transformation in the context of late modernity with its changing social structures, patterns of mobility, restructuring of the labour market and consequent rise of neo-liberalism. The demise of inclusive penal strategies was also influentially outlined via Feeley and Simon's (1992) concept of **actuarial justice**. The authors powerfully argued for the emergence of a new penology, which 'divorces crime policy from concern with social welfare'. 'Increasingly, crime policy is conceived of as a process of classification and management of populations ranked by risk; in need of segregation not integration' (Simon and Feeley, 1995: 168). As a consequence, the focus of penal systems shifts from individualized justice to managing aggregates of dangerous groups and development of new surveillance technologies. Rather than being a response to individual criminal acts, the penal system is designed for management of those who are seen to be beyond inclusion and are marked by the condition of 'advanced marginality' (Wacquant, 1999).

In the discourse of the new penology, prison is designed as the main solution for 'warehousing' superfluous populations, rather than rehabilitating them and re-integrating them into society (Simon, 2000). The development seems to have been particularly pronounced in the US which is, according to Christie (2000), with more than 2 million prisoners, heading towards conditions tragically resembling the Soviet gulags of the past. The US condition has been described as the 'era of hyperincarceration' and mass imprisonment (Simon, 2000; Garland, 2001b). For certain groups in the population, particularly young, black urban males, incarceration becomes a predictable and normal part of their lives. Penal exclusion has been thus 'layered on top of economic and racial exclusion, ensuring that social divisions are deepened, and that a criminalized underclass is brought into existence and systematically perpetuated' (Garland, 2001b: 2). The sense of change is conveyed in Bauman's observations of the US maximum security Pelican Bay prison:

> Pelican Bay prison has not been designed as a factory of discipline or disciplined labour. It was designed as a *factory of exclusion* and of people habituated to their status of the *excluded*. The mark of the excluded in the era of time/space compression is *immobility*. What the Pelican Bay prison brings close to perfection is the technique of *immobilization*. (Bauman 1998: 113, italics original)

Through its extensive use of technologies of control and isolation, the objective of the maximum security prison is no longer to prepare the inmates for re-integration into society, to teach them work discipline and social skills. Rather, the 'strategy commanded is to make the labourers *forget*, not to *learn*, whatever the work ethics in the halcyon days of modern industry was meant to teach them' (Bauman, 1998: 112, italics original). However, the exclusionist modus of late modernity is reflected not only in the growth in the numbers of those 'warehoused' in penal institutions, but also in a new cultural climate, which has been described as the 'new punitiveness' (Pratt et al., 2005). Exemplified by the 'three strikes and you're out', 'life means life', 'zero tolerance', and other populist slogans, as well as by the rise of maximum security prisons and re-emergence of the death penalty in the US, the new punitiveness appears to be a sharp departure from the emotionally restrained modernist penality and its belief in the success of social engineering and correctionalism (Simon, 2000; Garland, 2001a; Pratt et al., 2005).

Critics of Garland's work have pointed out the Anglo-American focus of the 'culture of control'. Zedner (2002) observes that the old rehabilitative ideal is still alive and well, and that the popular descriptions of its demise may be questionable in the Anglo-American context, let alone outside it. The consequences of the massive industrialization and neo-liberal ideologies on penal trends in the developing world are still, theoretically and empirically, under-examined. Prison populations are growing in many parts of the world. Worldwide, there are more than 9 million people in prisons, almost half of them in the great incarcerators – the US (2.19 million), Russia (0.87 million), and China (1.55 million) (Welmsley, 2006). Their living conditions are highly diverse and sustained by different rationalities and historic developments. It is therefore essential to balance the generalist accounts with specific local studies, a topic which will be discussed further in the final chapter.

The transformations of late modern penality, the growth of imprisonment and new forms of punitiveness are stories that have been well documented and told and retold by numerous Western academic observers. However, what is important for the purpose of this book is that at the dawn of the 21st century, the 'prison industrial complex' includes new categories of excluded populations such as immigrants and asylum seekers, and the growing number of suspects in the present war on terror, a topic discussed more thoroughly in Chapters 4 and 5. Furthermore, if sociological inquiry is, as mentioned at the beginning of this chapter, turning its attention to the various aspects of global mobilities, the task of criminology may be to look at the underside of these mobilities – global immobilization strategies, such as border controls, prisons and detention centres.

Crime, wars, war crimes and crime wars

The discussion so far has broadly outlined some major themes in contemporary global transformations and their possible relevance for the field of criminology and crime control. Late modern societies have been described as exclusive societies (Young, 1999) as well as 'elusive societies' (Bauman, 2002), where the notion of strong nation states and stable social entities is destabilized by various flows and mobilities, and where boundaries between the inside and the outside become unclear. However, I shall proceed now to suggest that a student of global transformations is faced not only with the fluidity of the concept of society, culture and government, but also with the inherent fluidity and instability of the concept of *crime* itself.

The concept of crime, and its intricate and problematic nature, has been at the crux of many, or to some extent most, criminological debates. Crime is, as Zedner (2004: 69) concludes

> a problematic category used routinely to describe a set of behaviours that, beyond a central core, are highly contested. Legal definition alone cannot adequately recognize the historical development, social relationships, practices, ideologies, and interests that determine what, at any given moment, is designated criminal.

Crime therefore cannot be simply seen as an act defined as criminal by the law; it is also an act whose definition as criminal depends on a number of social, cultural and historic circumstances. A long tradition of criminologists has explored the issue of social construction of crime. From labelling theorists such as Howard Becker to critical left theorists the argument has been that crimes are not qualities inherent in certain acts, but that one should focus on the ability of the state and certain social groups to punish according to their own interests and to impose their definitions of crime and deviance on the rest of society. Hence, there has been a lack of attention to the so-called crimes of the powerful (white-collar crime, states and their military apparatus, male violence against women, etc.), and predominance of focus on the crimes of the powerless and those who are seen to be different – 'the others' – drug users, youth subcultures, immigrant youth. Others have emphasised that definitions of criminality essentially depend on types of social settings and relations between those involved in the process. Christie (2004: 3), radically, concludes that

> Crime does not exist. Only acts exist, acts often given different meanings within various social frameworks. Acts, and the meaning given them, are our data. Our challenge is to follow the destiny of acts through the universe of meanings. Particularly, what are the social conditions that encourage or prevent giving the acts the meaning of being crime.

However, while these may be well trodden paths for criminologists, and there may be no need to re-tell them again, the transnational aspects of the contemporary condition clearly add new dimensions to the topic. In a world which is increasingly shaped by transnational and non-state actors we are faced with a myriad of situations which escape clear categorizations of traditional, nation state criminal law. The difficulties of conventional concepts of criminality and deviance become even more apparent from a global perspective and seen in the light of global social divisions. The question of accountability for abuse committed by private security personnel in the battlefields of Iraq and Afghanistan is one example. The unequal reach of criminal justice is magnified on the global scale when it comes to ensuring responsibility of global corporate and other state and non-state actors.

One of the central critiques raised by critical criminologists has been the narrowness of the concept of crime, which does not incorporate wider social injuries and harms committed by powerful social actors (Hillyard et al., 2004). Several authors have criticized criminology as a discipline for not incorporating state crime as an integral part of its subject matter, and for focusing instead on crimes and punishments within nation states (Green and Ward, 2004; Morrison, 2006). Crimes committed outside the bounded nation state territories, although enormous by comparison, do not penetrate the mainstream criminological discourse and are also seldom subjected to punishment. Morrison (2005: 290) thus concludes that

> The biggest non-punitive area we inhibit is the global inter-national system. The century just concluded perhaps saw the greatest amount of inter-human slaughter, rape, and destruction of property of any century; in partial recognition of which we even created a new crime, genocide, but in the face of which extremely few persons were ever punished.

Green and Ward (2004) argue that not only acts of genocide, but also other types of state-sponsored crime, such as corruption of state officials and elites, torture, state terror, police crime, avoidable 'natural' disasters and war crimes, should incorporated into the criminological discourse. They report, for example, the case of the late Nigerian dictator Sani Abacha, accused of stealing $4 billion from his country, which is considerably more than the annual amount stolen and damaged in all residential and commercial burglaries in England and Wales. The recent 're-construction' of Iraq, Whyte (2007: 177) suggests, can also be seen as an example of massive state-corporate criminality where

> an unknown proportion of Iraqi oil revenue has disappeared into the pockets of contractors and fixers in the form of bribery, over-charging, embezzlement, product substitution, bid ridding and false claims. At least $12 billion of the revenue appropriated by the coalition regime [i.e. the Anglo-American government] has not been adequately accounted for.

And while national prison systems are overfilled, accountability is considerably more difficult to establish on the international level and in cases when states and state actors are the culprits.

The question is, therefore, what is crime and what, after all, is the subject of this book? As boundaries between the inside and the outside become blurred, as it grows difficult to distinguish between inter-state and intra-state conflicts, it is less clear than ever what is to be the subject of criminological research and discourse. Are we only to focus on 'openly criminal' acts, represented in the popular imagination by terrorists and cynical trafficking networks, or are we also to address more ambiguous, but often no less harmful, acts of state and corporate irresponsibility and environmental damage? The Chernobyl catastrophe, for example, displaced 400,000 people and had a devastating impact on their lives and the environment (Papastergiadis, 2000). Increasingly, criminologists are beginning to turn their attention to these topics, for example, through the emerging field of green criminology.

Young (2003: 392), on the other hand, observes the 'striking similarities between the violence of conventional crime and the violence of war' and the 'parallels between the war against crime and war itself' as well as to the 'surprising ignoring of war by conventional criminology'. Throughout this book we shall see that the metaphor of war is often used in combating the crime problem and that militarization of crime control is becoming a salient aspect of several crime control measures. We shall encounter several 'crime wars' in the book: the 'war on drugs', the 'war on terror', and even the 'war on trafficking'. The terminology of war can be a dangerous metaphor in several ways, justifying extreme means in order to defend the perceived enemies of the state and therefore endangering traditional civil rights and liberties. The discussion that ensued in the aftermath of the September 11th attacks, on whether these attacks were acts of war or whether they were criminal acts, mirrors the dilemma. As Hayward and Morrison (2002: 153) observe:

> The discourse of crime and criminal justice places limits on the power of the state to investigate, and lays out rules to structure the game of investigation and proof. Some of the moves to call September 11 an act of war, and responding to it as a state of war, are designed to specifically avoid the rules of criminal justice.

Mythen and Walkate (2006a) suggest that from the present concerns around terrorism, criminologists can 'learn something about changing definitions and notions of what counts as crime, the criminal, the victim and "fear". The relativism of the concept of crime is particularly apparent when it comes to terms referring to transnational concepts, such as terrorism, transnational organized crime, the Mafia, etc. which at times become political categories of blame and are used 'more as an ideological weapon than as an analytical tool' (Ruggiero, 2003: 25). Unfortunately, this book also needs to acknowledge its limitations, since because of the lack of space it will not be able to cover a variety of acts and phenomena which due to their harmfulness could, and should, be the topic of criminological discourse. Furthermore, crime is only one in a line of circumstances affecting human security, although inevitably the one which news headlines tend to focus on. Recently, the debate has been shifting towards defining security in broader terms of human security, emphasising not the state view of security, but the security needs of people independent of the state system (Human Security Report, 2005; Wood and Shearing, 2007).

The issues of crime, insecurity and construction of crime have to be understood in the context of global interconnectedness. In the following chapters we shall see how the quest for global security is producing a variety of new surveillance measures and controls. The objective of these measures is to penetrate the vast volumes of global scapes and flows and to create more visibility. Global transformations have been accompanied by global surveillance measures, and by the growth of the less visible, global illicit flows, such as illegal migrants, drugs, illegal weapons and illegal moneys. This dynamic between the 'visibility' and 'invisibility' is one of the central topics of this book, beginning in the next chapter with the (illegal) movements of people and their control.

Summary

This chapter has provided an outline of discussions about the numerous and contested meanings of globalization. For the purpose of this book, we shall consider globalization simply as the manifold process of increasing transnational interconnectedness of societies. Globalization is not a historically new phenomenon, although it has gained powerful momentum with the progressive development of global capitalism, information and communication technologies, patterns of mobility and cultural exchange. Five aspects of global transformations were given particular consideration, as they inform our further discussions in this book:

- Disembedding of social relations refers to a process, described by Giddens (1990) as a general trait of modernity, by which social practices are ordered across space and time. The social space is no longer limited to the boundaries of physical space. Globalization intensifies the 'stretching' of social relations across time and space – the time–space compression (Harvey, 1990) – at times creating an impression of the world as a 'global village'.
- The role of the modern nation state is fundamentally transformed under the influence of global transformations. Some commentators have described the development as the 'withering of the state'. When it comes to the governance of crime and security, the picture is far more complex and contradictory. The abdication of state responsibility in some areas goes hand in hand with increased state surveillance and the expansion of the criminal justice and prison systems.
- Global inequality is a pervasive trait of the contemporary world order, which is magnified by the globalization of media and consumer culture. The global 'have nots' are incessantly bombarded with images of the lifestyles of the privileged. The development has been analysed as conducive to crime and deviance, due to the increasing feelings of relative deprivation, social exclusion, disintegration of communal life and value systems (anomie).

- The topic of the risk society marks a progressive shift in social organization towards the management and neutralization of various types of risk, rather than the achievement of more positive goals of social justice. Risk societies are prone to be scapegoat societies: this is particularly visible when it comes to political and media discourses about crime and punishment.
- The contested nature of the concept of crime is one of the central criminological topics. Crime is not an objective quality, but depends on a series of political, historic and social processes which lead to criminalization. Globalization has been a breeding ground for the new forms of criminalization that will be discussed throughout this book, such as criminalization of various aspects of migration, global resistance and Internet-related behaviour.

STUDY QUESTIONS

1   What is globalization? Discuss its negative, and potentially positive, social effects.

2   What is ontological insecurity? How does globalization in your view contribute to people's sense of insecurity?

3   Which global threats are shaping the political and media discourse in your country?

4   How are feelings of social exclusion and relative deprivation today shaped by the globalization of media and communication networks?

FURTHER READING

The production of scholarly literature about globalization is booming so it is hard to provide an easy overview. Nevertheless, David Held and Anthony McGrew's (2003) *The Global Transformations Reader* and Martin Albrow's *The Global Age* (1996) give a useful overview of the discussions. Manuel Castells's trilogy (1996, 2000, 2004) about the rise of network society gives a ground-breaking account of the economic and social aspects of global transformations. Zygmunt Bauman's extensive opus, including *Society under Siege* (2002) and *Wasted Lives* (2004), gives a valuable and critical insight into social consequences of globalization. Criminological literature on globalization is considerably scarcer; see for example Mark Findlay's (1999) *The Globalization of Crime* and Nikos Passas's (2003) edited volume *International Crimes*. For a criminological exploration of social change in late modernity see David Garland's (2001a) influential *The Culture of Control* and Jock Young's (1999) *The Exclusive Society*. The web-page of King's College in London provides a useful overview of world prison statistics and other information on prisons http://www.kcl.ac.uk/depsta/rel/icps/. The United Nations Interregional Crime and Justice Research Institute (UNICRI) regularly publishes international crime victims surveys, which provide an indication of crime and security trends as reported by victims across the world. See www.unicri.it/wwd/analysis/icvs/index.php.

2

Global Mobility and Human Traffic

Chapter Contents

Global movements of people   29

Border controls and fortress continents   31

Borders and global surveillance after 9/11   34

People smuggling and trafficking   36

On the edges of market economies   39

'Female underside of globalization'   41

The global sex trade   43

The tourist gaze   45

   Summary   47

   Study questions   48

   Further reading   48

OVERVIEW

Chapter 2 examines the following issues:

- The challenges of control presented by the global movements of people.
- The dichotomy between the imagery of unlimited mobility and a 'borderless world' and, on the other hand, a renewed emphasis on protection of borders and the rise of so-called fortress continents.
- The intensification of border controls in the post-9/11 climate.
- An analysis of people smuggling and trafficking and public discourses about them.
- Global tourism and its implications for the growth of the global sex trade and for the governance of security.

KEY TERMS

biometrics	migration	securitization
Disneyization	militarization	sex tourism
feminism	panopticon	sex work
fortress continents	people smuggling	surveillance assemblage
human trafficking	Schengen Information System (SIS)	

The image of powerful, lucrative and unscrupulous trafficking and people-smuggling criminal networks looms large in the popular imagination. The following *Guardian* (2005)[1] account is far from unusual in its gripping depiction of human misery.

> The plight of thousands of eastern European women kept as sex slaves in British brothels was highlighted yesterday as court proceedings against members of a major trafficking ring ended. Detectives believe the gang brought at least 600 illegal immigrants to the UK, many of whom were locked up, forced into prostitution, and told their families back home would be killed if they refused to obey orders. The women – the youngest known victim was 17 – were fed just one meal a day ... They were forced to have sex with up to 40 men a day for as little as £10 a time to pay off £20,000 debt each – the price for which they were 'bought'.

[1]http://www.guardian.co.uk/print/0,3858,5323763-104770,00.html

The movie industry has immortalized the phenomenon in movies such as *Dirty Pretty Things* and *Lilja 4 Ever*. Trafficking is newsworthy. It represents a combination of what Christie (1986) terms 'ideal victims' and what the media may see as the 'right sort of victims' (Jewkes, 2004) – innocent women and children who are enslaved and exploited by powerful and cruel foreign criminal networks. The discourse about trafficking also symbolically represents the popular concerns about global movements of people, and the perceived dangers of the foreign 'contaminating' the local.

This chapter examines these phenomena and situates them in a broader context of global mobility. Like movements of capital, goods, information and images, movements of people represent an essential aspect of global transformations. As the world 'becomes smaller', more people move, and more people dream of moving, than ever before. However, in the contemporary, deeply divided and stratified global order, patterns of movement also mirror pervasive global inequalities. While for some of us the world may appear to be 'smaller', 'borderless' and 'connected', for the majority of the world's population, it may appear as full of fences and dangerous obstacles.

Global movements of people

Although a constant in the world of modernity, marked by a continuous improvement of various means of transport, mobility has acquired new dimensions in the late modern context. Many of the most potent concepts and metaphors of the late modern condition have been built around the notions of movement and flow: Zygmunt Bauman's *Liquid Modernity*, Paul Virillio's (2000) analysis of speed, and Castells's 'space of flows' (1996), to name just a few. Wireless and mobile, the life of the late modern subject seems to be marked by increasing speed of movement and communication. The imagery of glossy in-flight magazines portrays modern travel as an effortless experience where our imagination is the only limit. 'Spread your wings' is the encouragement of the British Airways magazine, 'it is liberating to strive to become a global citizen' (*High Life*, 2003: 72). At work as in our leisure activities, we are living in the era of time/space compression. For Western citizens, to move is not only a privilege and a pleasure, but has become almost a compulsion (Urry, 2002b). Travel, for example, is thought to occupy 40 per cent of 'free time' in Britain (Urry, 2002b: 5). Mobility is no longer reserved for the global elites, moving between the mundane surroundings of the Swiss Alps, world capitals and exotic resorts. The flows of global nomads are increasingly joined by the less prosperous working-class migrants and travellers.

One should keep in mind though that mobility and travel take many forms, physical and virtual. Television and other media enable us daily to 'visit' faraway locations without leaving our living rooms (Morley, 2000). And although *migration* and the movement of people have always been an aspect of modern life, today there are more people living outside their homeland than at any previous time in history (Papastergiadis, 2000: 10). Movement of people has become such a pervasive aspect of contemporary life, whether related to work, pleasure, or migration, that 'it can no longer be considered as the exceptional event in the otherwise long historical process of settlement' (Papastergiadis, 2000: 24). In some countries, this mobility of people represents the main source of survival for national economies, be it money sent home by émigré workers or income from tourism. However, it is important to keep in mind that the largest part of migratory processes is internal, connected to urbanization. We shall address the issue of the growth of cities in the next chapter, and focus now on international migration.

Reliance on migration has been one of the defining aspects of developed industrial economies (Sassen, 2003). After the Second World War, the migratory flows were mostly directed from the global South to the industrialized North. However, in recent decades we have witnessed a change in the nature of migratory processes. The great Western capitals have been partly eclipsed by the global cities of the East and South as the main attractors of migrant labour. For example, over 70 per cent of the workforce in Saudi Arabia are non-nationals (Papastergiadis, 2000: 46). Castles and Miller (2003: 7) point out that there has been a 'globalization of migration'. More and more countries are crucially affected by migratory movements of all kinds, not only by labour migration, but also by refugee movements and people seeking permanent settlement (Castles and Miller, 2003). In parallel with the growth of migratory flows, most developed countries have placed greater limits on migration and permanent settlement. Consequently, there has also been an increase in illegal migration.

A variety of images and identities are used for describing the global traveller. Roughly speaking, they can be merchants, following Marco Polo's tradition, seeking to expand the scope of their trade; cosmopolitans moving between various world capitals and hot spots, ceaselessly pursuing the best weather and shopping conditions; and refugees, asylum seekers and working-class migrants, with the potential to harbour terrorists and religious fundamentalists. Historically, the plight of the Roma in Europe reveals how travelling populations have often been met with hostility and suspicion. Davidson (2005) points out that much of the existing research on migration tends to be policy-driven, and sees migration primarily as a problem for governance and national security. The focus of migration research therefore tends to be on movements of people from poor countries to affluent ones, from predominantly Muslim to Christian countries, etc., rather than on vast flows of affluent persons around the world (Davidson, 2005: 64). The question of migration is inevitably connected to issues of its control.

Border controls and fortress continents

Contemporary mobility represents an enormous challenge for the state apparatuses trying to control it. One of the traditional roles of the nation state, the maintenance of order on a certain territory, is put into question. It was argued, optimistically, particularly before the present hype of 'the war on terror', that the globalizing process would eventually lead to a borderless world (Ohmae, 1990). The new world of fluid modernity was seen as the antithesis of spatial and communal commitment. However, as much as globalization has been coupled with the images of a borderless world, it has, paradoxically, also meant introduction of ever more efficient controls of mobility. Bauman (1998) points out the importance of understanding the mutual reinforcement of globalization and mobility and, simultaneously, the renewed emphasis on territoriality. Globalization and (re)territorialization are complementary processes. While globalizing and borderless for some, the contemporary condition is increasingly localizing for others (or, one could say, for the largest part of the human population). As Bauman (1998: 88) notes:

> For the first world, the world of the globally mobile, the space has lost its constraining quality and is easily traversed in both its 'real' and 'virtual' renditions. For the second world, the world of the 'locally tied', of those barred from moving and those bound to bear passively whatever change may be visited on the locality they are tied to, the real space is fast closing up. This is a kind of deprivation which is made yet more painful by the obtrusive media display of the space conquest and of the '*virtual* accessibility' of distances that stay stubbornly unreachable in non-virtual reality.

Global mobility is an intensely stratified phenomenon. Global corporate travellers can move 'in a world of safety that extends across national boundaries' (Johnston and Shearing, 2003: 9). A large segment of the world population, on the other hand, has to rely on dangerous clandestine forms of travel. Global mobility is thus often marked with suspicion. In fact, an essential part of our globalizing condition is precisely the creation of mechanisms for distinguishing between 'good' and 'bad' mobilities, between what Bauman terms tourists and vagabonds. 'The tourists move because they find the world within their (global) reach irresistibly *attractive* – the vagabonds move because they find the world within their (local) reach unbearably *inhospitable*' (Bauman, 1998: 92–3, italics original) Freedom of movement is available to a relatively small number of highly privileged individuals, while others are doomed to various forms of clandestine and imaginary travel. The vastly stratified patterns of mobility mirror the immense inequalities of the present global order. The slogan: 'Wherever it takes you, the future takes VISA'[2] sits

---

[2]http://www.visaeurope.com/pressandmedia/imagelibrary.html (images).

painfully with images of desperate African migrants trying to climb the wire fences of Ceuta and Melilla, and images of dead bodies on the shores of southern Europe and the Mexican desert. Only in 2006, almost 30,000 African migrants in rickety boats attempted to reach the shores of the Spanish Canary Islands (BBC News, 2006).

Politicization and *securitization* of migration has been one of the defining traits of migratory movements in the past decades, evident not only in the demands for stricter border controls, but also in the discourse about the 'deviant immigrant', discussed in Chapter 4 below. America, Europe and Australia have been described as '*fortress continents*' – blocs of nations, with fortified external borders and easy internal access to cheap labour, for example, Mexican, Polish, Hungarian (Klein, 2003). While liberalizing their internal borders, fortress continents seal off their external borders, thus creating 'locked-out continents', whose residents aren't needed even for their cheap labour (ibid.). The rise of 'fortress continents' might seem strangely at odds with globalization and the spirit of free flows of capital, goods and information. Yet border controls have become in many respects stricter in the age of globalization. Since the early 1990s, most developed countries have introduced such measures as stricter border controls, visa requirements, penalties for airlines which bring in inadequately documented passengers, identity checks, workplace inspections, techniques for detection of falsified documents and more severe penalties for those caught infringing regulations (Castles and Miller, 2003: 118). The list of countries requiring a visa to enter the EU, the so-called 'black list', expanded from 70 in 1985 to over 126 in 1995 (Bigo and Guild, 2004). And while the fall of the Berlin Wall once appeared to be the defining moment of a new, 'free' world, it clearly no longer captures the spirit of the day. It has been pointed out that the dangerous clandestine routes of entry into the EU, operated by various smuggling networks, are partly created and sustained by the EU's tough immigration and asylum policy. The rise in the numbers of clandestine migrants reportedly began after the EU countries in 1995 started introducing tighter visa requirements, thus forcing Third World migrants to choose other, more dangerous routes to Europe. Climbing the walls of fortress continents is a dangerous activity for which many pay with their lives. Several thousand people are estimated to die every year while attempting to reach a new homeland. The figures, of course, are difficult to estimate.

As much as the rise of fortress continents may at first sight appear a paradox, the securitization of the border has become an intrinsinc aspect of the globalizing condition. Contemporary governments seem to be caught between two contradicting impulses: on the one hand, the urge towards increasing securitization of borders, and on the other hand, awareness of the importance of global flows for sustaining the present world economic order (Aas, 2005a). General Motors, for example, claims that 'for every minute its fleet of trucks is delayed at the

US–Canadian border, it loses about $650,000' (Klein, 2003). The objective is therefore not to seal off the border but to manage it efficiently; 'not to arrest mobility but to tame it; not to build walls, but systems capable of utilizing mobilities and in certain cases deploying them against the sedentary and ossified elements within society' (Walters, 2004: 248). Borders thus have the function of a membrane which allows global flows to get through, but which keeps the unwanted 'residue' out.

Borders establish the limits of our community and decide who is allowed inside and who is left outside. However, even though we live in 'fortress continents' whose borders are heavily militarized and daily claim numerous lives, we seldom seem to be aware of the fact that the objects of our research – often referred to as 'British society', 'American society' or the EU – are the result of intense and strict social control and selection. These processes of control and selection have clearly intensified in the past decades. The perception of illegal immigration has led to various initiatives for securitization of the border even in traditionally more open Western countries such as the US (Inda, 2006). Others, moreover, talk of **militarization** of the border (Andreas, 2000), evident for example in the increasing use of military technologies on the southern shores of Europe as well as in the building of the wall on the US–Mexico border. Some observers have appropriated Jonathan Simon's (1997) concept of 'governing through crime' and argue that there is a tendency to 'govern central aspects of global migration by strategies of criminalization and illegalization' (Walters, 2004: 247; Inda, 2006). Seen from this perspective, the notion of transnational criminal networks, although presenting a serious threat, also plays a crucial role in distinguishing between the flows of global 'goods' and 'bads'. For example, we shall see in the sections below how the measures to combat trafficking have been appropriated as immigration control measures, rather then having the sole objective of helping abused migrant women.

An important aspect of the securitzation of the border has been the expansion of international police co-operation and the deployment of new surveillance technologies. I have written elsewhere of how a wide array of technologies is used pre-emptively to prevent potentially risky individuals before they ever have a chance to enter the national territory (Aas, 2005a). Networks of airline liaison officers, employed by a number of countries, work at international airports helping airlines to prevent potentially inadmissible passengers to board planes (Bigo, 2000b). David Lyon (2003a: 123–4) points out that airports in themselves are examples of 'virtual borders, even though they are not always at the geographical edge of the territory concerned'. The airport – the symbol of contemporary mobility – is becoming an intensified focus of contemporary security strategies. The millions of people that move through most medium and large airports every year present substantial problems in terms of management and security risk. The focus on security – of both passengers and airport staff – was heightened in the aftermath of September 11th. The objective of airport controls is to check and identify travellers prior to arrival at their destination. Risk profiling of air passengers, based on extensive data gathering, is used to distinguish between safe and 'treacherous travellers' (Lyon, 2003a; Curry, 2004).

In the EU, one of the essential technologies for defending its borders has been the implementation of the ***Schengen Information System (SIS)***. SIS originated in the Schengen Agreement whose objective has been essentially to dismantle EU's internal borders while co-ordinating and strengthening its external borders, particularly through better police co-operation and exchange of information. SIS, and the Schengen Agreement itself, are today accessed by 15 states, including two non-EU states, Norway, and Iceland. Hayes (2004: 3) reports that by March 2003, the SIS had created

> [r]ecords on 877,655 people, a further 386,402 aliases, and more than 15 million objects. EU officials *estimate* that there are 125,000 access terminals to the SIS. Under finalised proposals, access to the SIS is to be extended to Europol, Eurojust, national prosecutors and vehicle licensing authorities. (2004: italics original)

Furthermore, a newly established European visa information system (VIS) will contain 'personal information supplied by people from around the world in an estimated 20 million visa applications to the EU member states every year' (Hayes, 2004). SIS is currently evolving towards SIS II where a series of additional states and information systems will be integrated – including biometric identifiers. European border security essentially depends on a variety of transnational information flows and technological zones, most notably the ones based on the Schengen Agreement as well as the so-called Dublin Convention, dealing with asylum issues. Eurodac is a database established by the Dublin Convention and is a part of the Schengen Information System; its purpose is to prevent multiple asylum applications in the EU countries. The system authorizes fingerprinting of all individuals aged over 14 who apply for asylum in an EU country, or who are found illegally present on EU borders and in EU territory. A positive fingerprint identification may result in the removal of an asylum applicant from a country (Aas, 2006).

Borders and global surveillance after 9/11

Border controls have in many ways intensified since the tragic events of September 11th. As a result of new global threats, the quest to control the mobile subject and fix him or her with a stable identity has resulted in utilization and re-utilization of a series of technologies, such as machine-readable and biometric passports, biometric visas, residence permits and ID cards, and various information systems such as Schengen and the US-VISIT program (Zureik and Salter, 2005). Several authors have pointed out how the passport, the nation state's traditional instrument for controlling mobile identities (Torpey, 2000), gained renewed salience as an instrument of social control and exclusion in the aftermath of the September 11th attacks (Adey, 2004; Lyon, 2005). As part of their measures to fight terrorism, the US government allows visa-free travel only from countries that have biometric passports. Put simply, *biometrics* is measurement, or monitoring, of parts of the body (Lyon, 2001: 72). Practically, this means that passports have a chip containing our biological data, for example fingerprints, the shape of the head or the pattern of blood vessels in the iris. After reading the chip, a machine scans the eyes, hands or measures the skull and then compares the data with the information on the chip. Furthermore, several countries are using ID cards, or are planning to use biometric ID cards (Stalder and Lyon, 2003).

The events of September 11th thus seem to have given a new impetus to state bureaucracies eager to identify their increasingly mobile populations (Lyon, 2003a). Establishing stable identities of their subjects has always been one of the central tasks of modern nation states. Every individual has to be accurately classified and connected to the state's records so that the right procedure can be applied – whether in relation to child support, a driving licence or an application for citizenship (Stalder and Lyon, 2003: 77). However, in the present world of increasing mobility the state's task of giving stable identities to the mobile and diverse populations becomes extremely difficult, if not impossible. Biometric ID cards and residence permits are part of the answer. Through the use of biometric ID cards, the practices of identifying the 'other' have the potential to proliferate and to be built into a number of automated bureaucratic systems, such as welfare and medical aid (Lyon, 2005). As a result, 'the border is everywhere' (ibid.). Consequently, Lyon (2005: 79) argues, the 'nation state's implicit definition of the "other" will be built into an automated system for determining who is and who is not a member, thus reducing dependence on face-to-face accounts of individual identity'. The trend towards increased securitization of the border has, particularly in the US, resulted in a number of surveillance practices directed towards general recording of visitors to the United States, as well as targeting specifically Arab, Muslim and other non-Western immigrant populations (Zureik and Salter, 2005). Border surveillance is only one, although an increasingly salient, aspect of the surveillance practices which have intensified after 9/11. The issue of global surveillance will be further examined in connection with the 'war on terror' and international police co-operation, discussed in Chapters 5 and 6 below.

At the same time, it would be somehow misleading to see 9/11 as a sudden change from the past. As Lyon (2003a: 4) points out, the 'attacks brought to the surface a number of surveillance trends that had been developing quietly, and largely unnoticed, for the previous decade and earlier'. The idea of a 'surveillance society' has a long history, associated particularly with the work of Michel Foucault and his explorations on the **panopticon** and panopticism (explained further in Chapter 3, below). The intensification of border controls, before and after 9/11, has to be seen as a part of a wider range of surveillance efforts, or what Haggerty and Ericson (2000) term **surveillance assemblage**. These surveillance practices

> operate[s] by abstracting human bodies from their territorial settings, and separating them into a series of discrete flows. These flows are then reassembled in different locations as discrete and virtual 'data doubles'. (Haggerty and Ericson, 2000: 605)

Through the various border surveillance practices mentioned in this chapter, such as airport profiling, Schengen Information System, the US-VISIT program and biometric passports; individuals' identities are recorded as their 'data doubles' and then communicated between various countries and agencies. We shall return to the subject of surveillance throughout this book. What is important at this point is that the vast national and global surveillance efforts to protect the border function as a form of what Lyon (2003b) terms 'social sorting' – categorizing people and assessing their risk. Various surveillance practices are essential in differentiating between 'good' and 'bad' mobilities. As Lyon (2003b: 14) writes, 'the social process occurs, as it were, on the move. Surveillance now deals in speed and mobility ... In the desire to keep track, surveillance ebbs and flows through space.'

People smuggling and trafficking

As a result of increasing securitization, the borders of the developed world are getting increasingly difficult to penetrate. Consequently, there has been a rise in clandestine migration as the Third World migrants are forced to choose other, more dangerous routes. In order to enter a Western country a Third World migrant or refugee often, or almost inevitably, needs to become an illegal migrant, relying on the services of various, more or less organized and unscrupulous, smuggling networks (Aronowitz, 2003). Organizing movements of people has become a growing industry, termed by Castles and Miller (2003: 114) the 'migration industry'. This includes numerous people who earn their living, in licit and illicit ways, by organizing global movements of people; from travel agents, labour recruiters, interpreters, banks and housing agents to human smugglers who help the migrants find their way into their guest country. And as Castles and Miller (ibid.) point out, in 'spontaneous or illegal movements, the need for agents and brokers is all the greater'.

During the past decade, trafficking and smuggling of people have become major political and crime control concerns, estimated by the United Nations to have exceeded in size the international drug trade. Heartbreaking stories about young women from the former Soviet republics (popularly referred to as 'Natashas'), lured by the vicious criminal gangs, who end up in forced prostitution without documents, money or rights, have frequently hit the headlines in the Western media. Their numbers are estimated in hundreds of thousands (Aronowitz, 2003). However, the exact figures of trafficking victims are notoriously difficult to estimate and there are great discrepancies between the estimates of various actors involved. Goodey (2005: 271) points out that one should be cautious when reading often-cited data about the enormous numbers of trafficking victims, particularly those presented by various inter-governmental organizations and NGOs, as

> one gets a sense of the same data being circulated with little reference to how this data was obtained. In turn, global figures need cautious interpretation as they often fail to distinguish between trafficking and smuggling ...

People smuggling should therefore be distinguished from *human trafficking*. While trafficking is no doubt more sinister and receives more public attention, it is also a more elusive concept. Trafficking and people smuggling are defined under the UN Convention Against Transnational Organized Crime of 2000 and its two supplementary protocols, which provide standard definitions on which UN member states can base their legislation. The so-called Palermo protocols offer the following definition of trafficking (art. 3a):

> The recruitment, transportation, transfer, harbouring or receipt of persons, by means of the threat or use of force or other forms of coercion, of abduction, of fraud, of deception, of the abuse of power or of position of vulnerability or of the giving or receiving of payments or benefits to achieve the consent of a person having control over another person, for the purpose of exploitation. Exploitation shall include, at a minimum, the exploitation of the prostitution of others or other forms of sexual exploitation, forced labour or services, slavery or practices similar to slavery, servitude or the removal of organs;

People smuggling, on the other hand, refers to cases where migrants enter a transaction with full consent and are free to leave at the end of the process.

However, in spite of the broad spectrum of behaviours which can fall into the category of, trafficking remains a somewhat elusive phenomenon. Despite frequent public outcries, and high media estimates of the numbers of victims involved, the numbers of criminal convictions for trafficking remain relatively low. Part of the reason is that the line between trafficking and smuggling is often hard to discern. In order to reach the West, migrant women as a rule acquire substantial debts which then become a source of pressure and control (Skilbrei et al., 2006). Furthermore, trafficking, like domestic violence, traditionally hasn't been strongly prioritized by a male-dominated police culture and police and judicial systems are only gradually learning to recognize the problem. Police also frequently encounter problems in getting victims' co-operation, due to victims' fear of traffickers, mistrust of the police, and fear of being expelled and sent home to the environment from which they have tried to break out. Some countries have tried to make it more attractive for trafficking victims to break out of exploitative relationships, by offering them more generous possibilities for gaining residence permits.

Researchers and human rights activists have also been pointing out that the approaches to combat trafficking tend to focus on trafficking as a form of illegal immigration and organized crime (which is reflected in the name of the convention itself: the Convention Against Transnational Organized Crime), thus treating migrant women as illegal immigrants and criminals, rather than as victims entitled to protection (Goodey, 2005). Critics have argued that the focus should be on protecting the trafficked victims' rights rather than exposing them to additional hardship (of testifying in a trial, being exposed to danger, facing the risk of being sent back to their native country and being re-trafficked). In the case of trafficking, as Goodey (2005) points out, it becomes particularly obvious how the concerns of crime control clash with those of victimology and the protection of victims. Victims tend to be treated as 'tools through which criminal justice agencies might be able to secure convictions of traffickers' (Goodey, 2005: 274).

Sanghera et al. (2005) argue that the question of trafficking and what tends to be called the 'war on trafficking', is intrinsically connected to questions of control of illegal migration. The morally charged discourse about 'sexual slavery' seeks to establish distinctions between 'innocent' and 'guilty' migrants, and while protecting the former, aims to justify stricter controls of the latter (Chapkis, 2005). The discussions about 'sexual slavery' therefore need to be situated within the context of popular concerns about migration. This however is by no means a new phenomenon. Historically, there was a great public outcry about so-called 'white slavery' in Europe and North America at the end of the 19th and the beginning of 20th centuries (Doezema, 1999). Building on depictions of the corruption of innocent young white women in the hands of Jewish, foreign and black traffickers, the 'white slavery' panic served to express wider anxieties about immigration, gender, sexuality, race and public health at the turn of the century (Doezema, 1999; Davidson, 2005).

Today, the morally charged concerns about passive and helpless women and children, who have fallen prey to cynical and unscrupulous trafficking networks have been objectified in numerous journalistic and filmic representations, most notably the influential 2002 drama *Lilja 4 Ever*. However, researchers have questioned the presumably clear categories of 'forced' and 'free' migration, and of trafficking victims as completely passive objects of exploitation (Doezema, 1999; Davidson, 2005). It has been argued that victims of trafficking may be relatively active subjects, initiating their move to the West, and to a certain extent aware that they will have to perform sexual services, although unaware of the degree of control, manipulation and exploitation involved (Aronowitz, 2003: 87). In spite of the broad UN definition of trafficking, it is not uncommon for law enforcement officials to treat these 'unclear' cases as offenders and illegal immigrants, rather than as victims in need of protection (ibid.). The intense contemporary debates about trafficking serve at some level as an attempt to create clear categories within the messy field of migration and illegal migration. As Davidson (2005: 65) puts it, 'it serves to divide the deserving "victims" from the undeserving "illegal immigrants" and to distinguish "pure" women from "impure" women' (see also Doezema, 1999). At the same time, with most of the attention focused on trafficking and 'sexual slavery', much less attention is paid to other forms of contemporary slavery, such as debt bondage and forced labour (Bales, 1999), as well as to the structural factors that underpin the presence of women and children in the global criminal economies.

On the edges of market economies

If we are to grasp the intricate dynamics of contemporary illegal migration and its control, we have to try to look at the mechanisms behind the phenomenon. Trafficking and smuggling have to be understood not only in the wider social context of wars, poverty and economic deprivation in the developing world, but also in relation to a variety of motivating factors which cause people to migrate (so-called 'push' factors') and factors that attract migration, such as the demand for services of migrant populations ('pull' factors). Reliance on economic migration has been one defining aspect of industrial economies. However, since the mid-1970s, there has also been a steady increase in the employment of immigrants in the underground economy (Castles and Miller, 2003). From Mexican farm labourers in the US to domestic workers such as maids and nannies across the world, there is a great demand for the workforce of undocumented immigrants. This, combined with the increase in state-imposed restrictions on immigration, has created ripe conditions for the growth of trafficking and human smuggling (Aronowitz, 2003). From this point of view, human trafficking and smuggling can be seen as a result of supply and demand for certain services – they are a 'global business'. 'In the receiving countries there is, and always will be a demand for cheap labour and sex. In countries of origin there is and always will be a dream of a better life and the ability to support oneself and family members at home' (Aronowitz, 2003: 89). Examination of the trafficking problem therefore necessarily needs to look into how 'the official economy benefits from goods or services provided by conventional organized crime, and vice versa' (Ruggiero, 1997: 27). This interconnection between licit and illicit economies takes place not only in the much-publicized 'sweatshops' in Asia, but also in underground economies across the developed world, where immigrants have to live and work under coercion in order to pay off their debts (Ruggiero, 1997). We also need to keep in mind that most migration takes place through personal networks of family, friends and acquaintances, rather than through engaging with organized criminal networks (Castles and Miller, 2003).

Illegal migratory processes are sustained not only by the demands of guest countries for cheap sex and labour, but also by the transnationalization of Western cultural industries, mentioned in Chapter 1. Motivation for migration is more complex than the simple question of poverty and deprivation. Parallel with the growing gap between rich and poor, globalization also brings a growing connectedness, based on the flows of cultural images, consumer products, etc. Today, poor people are constantly exposed to images of the lifestyles of the rich, which may often seem like a 'material striptease' (Ehrenreich and Hochschild, 2003: 18). These cultural interconnections are important in understanding the motives for migration; for example Dominican women who, through sexual encounters with Western tourists, dream of obtaining consumer products and living out the dreams of 'Dominicanized versions of Hollywood's *Pretty Woman*' (Brennan, 2003: 157). Similarly, Skilbrei and Polyakova (2006) report that East European women end up in sex work not necessarily because of pressing economic needs, but because they want to participate in a consumer lifestyle and actively create a better life for themselves and their families. As one of their informants put it: 'My life is too short; I want to live now.' Bales (2003) points out that this 'material striptease' can also function as a 'push factor' on poor rural families, for example in northern Thailand, which traditionally have low appreciation of women and girls, to sell them into sexual servitude.

The issues of smuggling, trafficking and slavery pose another important question: what (if any) are the limits to market economies? How can we ethically impose and enforce limits on what can be commoditized and sold on the global market? Implicitly, we are forced to question the ethical consequences of unbridled market thinking and consumerism, as well as the role of the 'contract as the guiding and universal principle of human sociality' (Davidson, 2005: 2). Global inequalities create an almost unlimited supply and demand for all kinds of 'goods' which can be bought in the global marketplace. Wealthy consumers are able to purchase from poorer countries not only a labour force, and the sexual services of men, women and children, but also art and antiques, exotic and endangered animal species as well as parts of human bodies. By seeing these activities simply as questions of controlling unscrupulous transnational organized criminal networks, we may miss important aspects of demand for these services and the willingness of well-off consumers to participate in them.

In her research about the global traffic in human organs, Scheper-Hughes (2005) describes the entry of free market thinking into provision of medicine and the resulting commodification of the human body. Due to the great global inequalities, there is no shortage of people willing to sell kidneys in particular, but also other parts of their bodies. A wealthy consumer can now purchase a new kidney in India or Pakistan for a relatively small amount of money and without needing to rely on the often overburdened public health system of his or her home country and the dwindling supply of transplant organs in an age-ing population. Even though commerce in human organs is illegal in most nations where transplant is practised, Scheper-Hughes points out that surgeons, organs brokers, and sellers and buyers of organs are generally not prosecuted, and the practice is often openly condoned by state authorities.

> [T]he spread of 'transplant tourism' has exacerbated older divisions between North and South, core and periphery, have and have-nots, spawning a new form of commodity fetishism in demands by medical con-sumers for a quality product – 'fresh' and 'healthy' kidneys purchased from living bodies. In general, the circulation of kidneys follows the established routes of capital from South to North, from poorer to more affluent bod-ies, from black and brown bodies to white ones, from females to males, or from poor males to more affluent males. (Scheper-Hughes, 2005: 150)

Scheper-Hughes describes the rise of a 'new form of globalized "apartheid med-icine" that privileges one class of patients, affluent organ recipients, over another class of invisible and unrecognized "nonpatients", about whom almost nothing is known' (2005: 149). The organ donors have virtually no access to medical help after the operations, and often find their chances of employment, marriage and normal life ruined by the operation. The author points out the invisibility of certain populations (refugees, poor peasants, the homeless, street children, prisoners, etc.), which due to their economic and political disposses-sion, do not enjoy equal protection of social institutions, including medicine. This life in the shadows is beautifully depicted in Stephen Frears's (2002) movie *Dirty Pretty Things*.

'Female underside of globalization'

To get the full picture of the 'life in the shadows' of world migrants, it is partic-ularly important to understand the specific situation of women. Today, about half of world migrants are women, which is different from the past when labour migrations and many refugee movements were male dominated (Castles and Miller, 2003: 9). Since the 1960s, there has been a feminization of migration and women have played a major role in most types of migration, including labour migration (Castles and Miller, 2003). However, most female migration is far detached from the images of female executives and professionals depicted in television commercials. There is a disturbing 'female underside of globalization' whereby millions of women from the South migrate 'to do the "women's work" of the north – work that affluent women are no longer able or willing to do' (Ehrenreich and Hochschild, 2003: 3). The immigrant labour is used to reduce the 'care deficit' in affluent societies (childcare, medical care, care of the elderly, etc.). This enormous 'care drain' is profoundly affecting migrants' local communities, especially the children of the female migrants. Many immigrant women have children; however, due to migration restriction and low wages they are unable to live with them, often for years at a time. Hochschild (2003) argues that as a consequence, children in poor countries are paying the human cost of globalization. She describes the 'care drain' as a form of imperialism and exploitation in which love is an 'unfairly distributed resource' (ibid.: 22).

The immigrant women, in their work as nannies, maids, nurses, sex workers and 'imported wives', take on the role of 'the traditional woman within the family – patient, nurturing and self-denying' (Ehrenreich and Hochschild, 2003: 12). Consequently, a division of labour between men and women, traditionally attacked by the Western feminist critiques, has now been transformed into a global power relation. From Athens, London and New York to Dubai, Hong Kong and Singapore, the lifestyles of the globally prosperous are supported by the migrant women's labour. Sassen (2003: 259) suggests that we are seeing here 'the return of the so-called serving classes in all of the global cities, and these classes are largely made up of immigrant and migrant women'. And although social class has always been an important aspect of criminological research, particularly through the influence of the various Marxist approaches to criminology, we can see that in the globalizing world the concept of class, and conflict between the classes, gains new dimensions.

The essential point here is not only that globalization changes traditional class relations across the world, but also that it is a deeply gendered phenomenon, structuring and being structured by the unequal power relations between men and women, and between poor and affluent women – a point that tends to be overlooked in the prevailing globalization theories. Therefore, like *feminist* approaches to crime and criminal justice studies, feminist studies of globalization emphasize the importance of understanding the role of gender and the specific situation of women in the process. In her critique of 'gender-blind' and 'gender-neutral' theorizing about globalization, Chow (2003: 444) points out that

> The failure to incorporate gender into the study of globalization in meaningful and systematic ways not only produces incomplete views of women's rights as fundamental human rights and inaccurate understanding of the sources of gender inequality, but also can actually undermine development

policy and practice ...Therefore, gender matters for understanding what globalization is and how it is influenced by gendered hierarchies and ideologies, which in turn shape gendered institutions, relationships, identities and experiences of women and men.

Through the great migrations of women and the industrialization of the developing world, the globalizing process has clearly created numerous employment opportunities for women across the world. While economic restructuring processes, particularly in the West, substantially reduced the numbers of male manufacturing jobs, there has been a trend towards feminization of employment. This has made women more visible and active participants in the public life of many countries and has partly destabilised traditional gender roles (Sassen, 1998). Furthermore, not only individual households, but also communities and governments increasingly depend on Third World women as the main breadwinners (Sassen, 2003). Since female labour, including migrant and sexual labour, has become a vital 'circuit of survival' in a number of developing countries, Sassen (2003: 265) points out that this has led to 'feminization of survival' in the developing world.

However, due to this economic dependence on migrant remittances, many Third World governments encourage emigration and are unwilling to take up the issues of its negative effects (Ehrenreich and Hochschild, 2003). Migrant women tend to live isolated and concealed from public view and are thus more vulnerable to exploitation. Due to their economic and social dependence on their employers they are in greater danger of becoming victims of domestic violence, sexual abuse and economic exploitation (Zarembka, 2003). If domestic violence in general tends to be an overlooked and under-reported phenomenon in most criminal justice systems, this is even more the case when it comes to domestic violence against nannies, maids, sex workers, 'imported' wives, and other migrant women and children (Ehrenreich and Hochschild, 2003). These themes, however, tend to be overlooked in the 'modern day slavery' debates, where only the 'extravagant abuses' associated with trafficking are politicised, while other aspects are 'normalized', suppressed, and made invisible (ibid.: 12).

The global sex trade

The discourse about 'modern day slavery', also presented by the newspaper article at the beginning of this chapter, has been particularly salient in connection to the so-called global sex trade. There is no doubt that the growing flows of tourists, combined with the collapse of communism and the rise of neo-liberalist policies, cultural shifts in attitudes to extramarital sex, and the Internet, have had a profound impact on the growth of commercial sex across the globe (Altman, 2001; Thorbek and Pattanaik, 2002).

> European tourists who once saw the Mediterranean as a distant luxury now holiday in the Seychelles and Phuket, while women and men from Nigeria and Brazil sell themselves on the streets of Rome and Dusseldorf, and many migrants find their jobs as entertainers, maids and nannies carry with them the expectation of sexual services. (Altman, 2001: 107)

The case of Thailand, and its burgeoning sex industry, is therefore much less exceptional than commonly believed, as commercial sex becomes an integral part of many national and city economies (Altman, 2001). The globalizing process has gone hand in hand with the growth of commercial sex. In most EU countries the market for sexual services is dominated by foreign nationals, particularly from the former Soviet bloc and Africa. One should also keep in mind the important role of the Internet as a facilitator of sex trade; a topic which shall be discussed further in Chapter 7.

Commercial sex is an extremely complex and versatile phenomenon, containing a variety of practices which sometimes tend to be confused with each other. Some countries have liberalized and regulated the sale and purchase of sexual activities; Sweden, for example, penalizes only the clients, while the majority of penal systems see the activity as illegal but often tolerate it in practice (Outshoorn, 2004). Furthermore, while media and political discourse tend to focus on the issues of trafficking and sexual slavery, researchers have been pointing out that there is a wide range of experiences within the sex trade (Thorbek and Pattanaik, 2002). Although many of them are clearly tragic, others may also offer women opportunities to better their lives in some ways. The experiences of women and girls in sexual servitude (Bales, 2003) differ greatly from, for example, Third World women and men offering sexual services to Western tourists in the hope of receiving a marriage proposal (Brennan, 2003). As McClintock points out:

> Depicting all sex workers as slaves only travesties the myriad, different experiences of sex workers around the world. At the same time it theoretically confuses social *agency* and identity with social *context*. (McClintock in Brennan, 2003: 155, italics original)

The question of agency has been a contested topic within the field of prostitution and sex work studies. Researchers and activists differ in their use of terminology. Some point out the exploitative nature and the lack of choice in any kind of commercial sex, due to gender, economic, racial and international inequalities between women and their clients. They prefer the term prostitution. Others, however, point out that 'prostitution' and 'prostitutes' are extremely morally charged terms. They emphasise women's right to choose selling sex as a profession and question the view that any kind of commercial sex involves victimization. They therefore prefer using the terms **sex work** and sex workers. Brennan (2003: 156) for example points out that sex workers can be 'at once independent and dependent, resourceful and exploited. They are local agents caught in a web of global economic relations.' While for some women (and men) sexual labour can be seen as an attempt, albeit unsuccessful, to realize their dreams of relative prosperity, there is clearly a wide range of forms of victimization they have to undergo on the journey. One particularly disturbing aspect of the contemporary global sex trade is the situation of children. The enormous threat of AIDS/HIV and other sexually transmitted diseases in some parts of the developing world has made children more exposed to risk of sexual abuse (Bales, 2003). The issue is still relatively seldom explored by Western criminological and sociological research, which tends to have a national rather than Third World focus (Davidson, 2005). We shall examine the issue further below in the discussion of so-called child sex tourism.

The tourist gaze

The figure of the tourist rarely finds its way into a criminological text. Tourism tends to be a topic overlooked by criminologists, which is certainly unwarranted by the scale of the phenomenon itself. International tourist arrivals have grown 17 times between 1950 and 1990, and tourism is now among the largest, if not the largest, legal industry in the global economy (Cohen and Kennedy, 2000: 213). Furthermore, tourism can in many ways be seen as a prime metaphor for the contemporary mobile subject. The 'looseness of attachment – being *in* but not *of* the place – makes tourism a well-aimed and pertinent metaphor for contemporary life' (Bauman in Franklin, 2003: 208, italics original). Drawing on Foucault's concept of the gaze, Urry (2002b) develops the notion of the 'tourist gaze'. Aided by guidebooks, cameras and various other practices, the tourist gaze is a certain way of relating to places, which has effects not only on the tourists themselves, but also on the places which are its objects, and on their economies.

The criminological significance of the 'tourist gaze' is yet to be properly established. However, the desire of the tourist to escape the dreary routines of everyday life and seek the 'four Ss' – sun, sand, sea and sex (Cohen and Kennedy, 2000: 218) – has had a profound impact on the growth of *sex tourism*, or so-called 'prostiturismo', across the globe (Cohen and Kennedy, 2000; Altman, 2001). Davidson (2005: 124) points out that although travel has a long history of being associated 'with a quest for sexual experience with "exotic" Others', today, commercial sex and sexual entertainment have become regular features of numerous tourist destinations all over the world. Due to this incorporation of sex into the grain of the tourist experience – think of tourist brochures praising the attractions of the 'night life'– sex tourism is difficult to define and separate from tourism in general (Davidson, 2005). Although there clearly is evidence of so-called 'organized sex tours', a majority of 'sex tourists' purchase sexual favours on 'normal' holidays (ibid.).

As noted, child sex tourism represents a particularly disturbing aspect of contemporary mobilities. Men who travel abroad in order to purchase sexual services of young boys and girls have received a considerable amount of media attention. Davidson (2005) points out that the problem appears to be difficult to combat partly due to the incorporation of child sex tourism into the 'regular' tourist industry, and partly due to the unwillingness of the governments of 'tourist sending' and 'tourist receiving' countries to take up the challenge.

> Campaigners pointed out, for example, that Western governments' *lack of interest in crimes against 'Other' children* led many sex tourist receiving countries to pursue a policy of deporting foreign nationals accused of child sexual offences rather than prosecuting them, and this, combined with the fact that offenders could often bribe their way out of trouble, meant that people who had been caught abusing children abroad could return home and continue their lives without fear of prosecution. (Davidson, 2005: 128; italics added)

The issue clearly exemplifies a number of problems that we shall encounter throughout this book: questions of national sovereignty, offences committed by foreign nationals, and questions of who receives the protection of the state in the deeply stratified world order.

Tourist flows carry important implications for the governance of security at the places of their destination. Some of the recent, highly publicized, terrorist attacks can be seen as symbolically targeting the contemporary mobile subject, by attacking tourist destinations (Egypt, Bali, Turkey), public transport systems (Madrid, London), and centres of the 'footloose economy' (the World Trade Center in New York). Egypt established its 'tourist police' force as early as in 1997, after the tragic and economically devastating massacre of 60 tourists at the Hatsheptsut temple in Luxor. Similarly, the Olympic Games have been turned into megalomaniac media and tourist events, supported by an extensive security infrastructure. Securing the Olympics in the post-9/11 world is certainly not inexpensive. The cost of the latest Olympics in Greece rose to over $1.2 billion, more than three times the amount spent in Sidney in 2000.[3] Security is of vital importance here, since it is those states, companies and destinations with the most powerful 'commercial brands' which have 'most to lose if they cannot guarantee the safety of their own citizens, companies or visitors' (Urry, 2002a: 66).

Creating sanitized environments, free of various unwanted risks, can be seen as one of the steps necessary to please the tourist gaze. However, striking 'the right balance between security of the familiar and the adventure of the strange' (Bauman in Franklin, 2003: 213) is a project fraught with difficulties and contradictions. The results are often tourist enclaves of themed environments with

---

[3]Source: www.economist.com/agenda/displayStory.cfm?story_id = 3082670.

'staged authenticity' (Urry, 2002b: 9), geared towards entertainment and consumption. The tourist also subverts the traditional notions of the 'other' (for a further discussion on 'the other' see Chapter 4). Although they are 'outsiders' in terms of membership of the nation state, tourists clearly enjoy the protection of numerous security strategies due to their power as consumers. Not only are contemporary societies making themselves 'authentic', they are also making themselves secure, for the benefit of the tourist. The position of the tourist can be contrasted with that of some other groups of global nomads – Third World migrants, asylum seekers, political dissidents – who due to their lack of purchasing power cannot claim any such protection.

Tourism is increasingly shaping contemporary landscapes; this is exemplified best by the so-called 'nowherevilles' or 'non-places' such as Holiday Inns, shopping malls, airports and Disneylands, designed to provide reassuring familiarity for the global traveller anywhere in the world (Bauman in Franklin, 2003). This adjusting of our environments to the sensibilities of the tourist gaze has been described as part of a broader trend towards the *'Disneyization'* of society (Bryman, 2004) and the deterritorialization of culture. In the next chapter, we shall see that this trend towards 'Disneyization' or 'McDisneyization' (Ritzer and Liska, 1997) is an important topic also when it comes to the transformation of city life and governance of behaviour within cities. It is not surprising then that an article by Shearing and Stenning (1985) about social control in Disneyworld has been an extremely influential contribution to the understanding of contemporary governance. A wish for highly predictable, efficient, calculable and controlled environments is something that Western consumers often demand on their 'McDonaldized' vacations, as well as in their daily lives (Ritzer and Liska, 1997: 99). In the following chapter we shall further examine the above-mentioned trends and see how they have transformed life in contemporary city environments and the mechanisms of social control.

Summary

This chapter introduced the topic of global mobility. Global movements of people are highly stratified. While the world has become smaller for the global North, citizens of the global South are faced with the closed and militarized borders of the fortress continents. As a consequence, there has been a growth in illegal forms of migration, including people smuggling and trafficking. In the past years, trafficking has received a considerable amount of media and political attention, partly because it serves as a channel for many contemporary anxieties about global mobility. Trafficking discourse has been criticized for its overly simplistic notions of organized criminal 'villains' and innocent 'ideal victims', while other, more pervasive but less dramatic aspects of migrants' victimization are under-communicated. The chapter examined 'the female underside' of globalization: the increasing employment of Third World women as maids, nannies, sweatshop workers and sex workers in the prosperous countries, as well as in tending to the local tourist industries. The demand for immigrant labour functions as a 'pull factor', attracting steady flows of migrants who often risk their lives in the process, and causes a considerable 'care drain' and 'brain drain' from their local communities.

STUDY QUESTIONS

1   How do patterns of global mobility mirror more general patterns of global inequality?

2   Discuss the criminological and wider social consequences of the militarization of the border and the rise of fortress continents.

3   Discuss media debates about human trafficking in your country. How are the victims of trafficking portrayed? Which types of victimization of migrants are invisible in media representations?

4   Globalization is also a gendered phenomenon. Discuss the impact of globalization on the lives of women in developing countries.

FURTHER READING

Stephen Castles and Mark J. Miller's (2003) *The Age of Migration* provides a good introduction and overview of the nature of contemporary migration. The International Organization for Migration runs a very useful website with a wealth of information about migration-related issues, including migration facts and figures: http://www.iom.int/jahia/jsp/index.jsp. Didier Bigo and Elspeth Guild's (2005) *Controlling Frontiers* gives an up-to-date account of European border controls, while Elia Zureik and Mark Salter's (2005) *Global Surveillance and Policing* also includes recent North American developments. The electronically available journal *Surveillance & Society* has had special issues on panopticism and surveillance of mobility (see http://www.surveillance-and-society.org/journal.htm). Barbara Ehrenreich and Ari R. Hochschild's (2003) *Global Woman* offers an accessible collection of insights into exploitation of women across the world. Sharon Pickering and Caroline Lambert's (2004) *Global Issues, Women and Justice* looks at the 'global woman' from a criminological perspective. Susanne Thorbek and Banadana Pattanaik's (2002) edited volume *Transnational Prostitution* and Kamala Kempadoo and Jo Doezema's (1998) *Global Sex Workers* give a valuable insight into the burgeoning international research on prostitution and trafficking. David Kyle and Rey Koslowski's (2001) *Global Human Smuggling* takes an informed look at human smuggling in comparative perspective. Julia O'Connell Davidson (2005) offers a sober and intriguing analysis of *Children in the Global Sex Trade*, as well as a good introduction to the debates about the nature of trafficking, prostitution and sex tourism in general.

3

Urban Criminology and the Global City

Chapter Contents

The urban explosion and the Chicago School   52

The global city as the dual city   55

The urban panopticon   59

Militarization of city life   63

The ghetto, the *banlieue* and the culture of exception   65

The fate of the local in a multicultural society   68

Gated communities and the urban 'ecology of fear'   70

Summary   73

Study questions   74

Further reading   74

OVERVIEW

Chapter 3 examines the following issues:

- The growth of cities on the global level, the emergence of so-called global cities and the trend towards urbanization of poverty.
- The impact of global inequality and consumerism on city life and on local crime control practices.
- Contemporary struggles over 'the right to the city'.
- The Chicago School of sociology and its relevance for understanding the global city.
- The ghetto and the gated community as two examples of spatial exclusion and self-exclusion.

KEY TERMS

CCTV	global city theory	social capital
Chicago School	mass–private property	urbanization of poverty
consumerism	militarization	zero tolerance policing
cultural criminology	panopticon	
gated communities	post-Fordist	

In the introductory chapter we saw that the globalizing processes have been associated with the themes of time–space compression, a declining significance of space and the emergence of the so-called 'space of flows'. However, although these themes can be used as salient explanations of numerous aspects of contemporary life, many observers have noted that space continues to matter. Social phenomena still continue to be by and large spatially situated. And although at the dawn of the information revolution some commentators predicted the demise of the city due to tele-working, tele-shopping, commuting and the like, quite the opposite has happened. The explosive growth of cities has been one of the defining traits of the contemporary world in the past decades. Today, for the first time in history, urban populations probably outnumber rural ones. By contrast, at the beginning of the last century only about 10 per cent of total world population lived in cities. Most readers of this book probably live in cities and extended metropolitan regions. In some continents such as Europe and the Americas urban dwellers represent almost 80 per cent of the population (Brenner and Keil, 2006). However, the sprawling urban world often takes a hard toll on its dwellers. Instead of the cities of light once imagined by urban futurists, today more than one billion people live in slums and shantytowns of unprecedented proportions (Davis, 2006).

Urban scholars have pointed out the profound impact that globalization has had on the spatial organization of society in general, and on city life in particular. As a result of the transformations in the nature of the global economy the city has gained a renewed, yet profoundly changed importance. In the time of global flows the city emerges as the economic and information hub and as a base for the operations of transnational corporations, global financial and political institutions, various consumer and production chains and other global actors (Sassen, 1998). Sitting in a café in the centre of London or Paris, one is struck by the extent to which global flows permeate local city life. Restaurants and shops are owned by global chains, which are frequented by masses of tourists and serviced by a predominantly foreign workforce; moving through the streets filled with the sounds of street musicians from Peru, one may be offered sexual services and illicit goods by young Africans and East Europeans. Of course, usually one need only move to the outskirts of these cities to encounter places which are so enclosed in their locality that there is not a tourist or a global chain in sight. And this too is the essence of a global city – its dividedness and its 'dual' nature, its mixture of connections and disconnections.

The globalizing process essentially reconfigures the city and the claims that various actors make about it. As Sassen points out

> The city has indeed emerged as a site for new claims: by global capital which uses the city as an 'organizational commodity', but also by disadvantaged sectors of the urban population, which in large cities are frequently as internationalized a presence as is capital. The denationalizing of urban space and the new formation of new claims by transnational actors and involving contestation, raise the question – whose city is it? (Sassen, 1998: xx)

The issues of 'whose city is it?' and who has *the right to the city* are topics frequently raised by social commentators (Ferrell, 1996, 2001; Sasssen, 1998; Høigård, 2002; Mitchell, 2003). While powerful global actors clearly make a visible imprint on the city, the global city also becomes a 'strategic site for disempowered actors because it enables them to gain presence, to emerge as subjects, even when they do not gain direct power' (Sassen, 1998: xxi). Throughout this chapter we shall see how attempts by disadvantaged groups to claim the city space often come into conflict with the interests of various commercial, private and public actors. Struggles over the rights of presence in shopping malls and on city streets, questions of graffiti, begging, homelessness and prostitution are often debated and fought in terms of criminalization. Concerns about local disorder are therefore increasingly intertwined with global transformations, such as transnational migration, global business interests, deindustrialization, consumerism, etc. Local policing and social control efforts are thus often a search for local solutions to globally produced problems. In what follows, we shall first take a look at the changing economic and social parameters of city life, and then examine the implications of these transformations for the nature of social control in the city.

The urban explosion and the Chicago School

The communities we live in are growing with unprecedented speed. Not only are more and more people living in cities – the UN estimates that about 180,000 people are being added to the urban population every day – but cities are also getting larger. While in 1950 the world had only two so-called megacities with populations over 10 million, today there are at least 20. The dream of living in a small community may gradually become a luxury enjoyed only by the privileged elite or, interestingly, by the socially marginalized. Borja and Castells point to the paradox that societies, such as China and the United States, which are 'dominated by the ideology of the rural, communal paradise – depend essentially on what their megacities do' (1997: 31).

However, rapid urbanization is by no means a novel phenomenon. The expansive growth of cities has a long history connected particularly to the 19th- and early 20th century industrialization of Europe and North America. In that respect, the recent developments described here are far from new. Nevertheless, the scale of the present urbanization dwarfs that of 19th century Europe (Davis, 2006). This development is primarily a result of massive industrialization in the developing world, particularly in Asia. The urbanization of China, for example, 'added more city-dwellers in the 1980s than did all of Europe (including Russia) in the entire nineteenth century' (Davis, 2006: 2). However, cities in other parts of the world as well have experienced an extensive influx of migrant rural populations, due to land reform, deregulation of food imports and IMF-imposed 'structural adjustment programs'. The swelling of cities is not always based on the cities' ability to sustain the newly arrived migrant populations, and leads to the **urbanization of poverty**. As the UN Secretary-General recently stated, 'the locus of global poverty is moving to the cities' (UN Habitat Report, 2003). Particularly in the developing world, rapid urbanization is a result of global forces 'pushing' people from the countryside, and so is driven by the reproduction of poverty, rather than by the supply of jobs in the cities (Davis, 2006: 16). The growth of cities carries not only serious environmental consequences, but also human ones, most visible in the exponential growth of slums and 'mega-slums' on the outskirts of numerous world cities. Moreover, the explosive urbanization of the developing world poses significant challenges for urban studies since much of urban sociology and criminology is written about European and North American cities.

The transition from small, close-knit communities to large, anonymous urban settlements has been a much-discussed topic within social sciences since the second half of the 19th century. The massive industrialization and the flight of rural populations from the countryside, the swelling of disadvantaged slum areas and, not surprisingly, crime and social disorder belong to the classic accounts of Victorian life. Numerous social observers saw the transition from rural to urban societies as a latent cause of criminality, particularly due to the alleged deterioration of social bonds holding society together. Marxist scholars, on the other hand, emphasised the exploitative nature of the industrial revolution and how the appalling living and working conditions of the urban proletariat inevitably lead to crime.

One of the most influential contributions to examining the effects of global mobility on city life, and on social life in general, came in the early decades of the 20th century from the *Chicago School* of sociology. What is usually referred to as the Chicago School is a group of sociologists and criminologists connected to the University of Chicago. Taking the sprawling, chaotic and ethnically diverse city of Chicago as a background, these scholars set out to explore the meaning and the 'urban ecology' of the industrial city. The notion of ecology in this case refers not only to the physical environment but first and foremost to the social environment, and how the combination of the two shapes the unique nature of city life. The city is seen as a product of nature and particularly of human nature; it is a natural habitat which changes with the changing trajectories of its inhabitants (Park et al., 1925). The concept of ecology also features prominently in some recent urban studies, such as for example in Mike Davis's (1999) exploration of Los Angeles and its 'ecology of fear'. Davis, like the Chicagoans, uses the concentric ring model to explain the urban decay in the heart of the city. The notion of ecology has had a profound impact in establishing the importance of spatial factors for the study of crime. Contemporary 'environmental criminology' has drawn heavily on these insights (Bottoms and Wiles, 2002). Furthermore, the linkage between space, demography and crime control is today established on the practical level in the so-called crime mapping and computerized geographic information system (GIS) which are gradually becoming standard items of police equipment in developed countries (see Chapter 7 for crime mapping).

One of the most famous, and debated, contributions of the Chicago School has been its 'concentric zone theory', first published by Park et al. in *The City* (1925). The theory was one of the earliest attempts to explain the existence of social problems based on the social differentiation of urban space. The model consisted of a set of five concentric rings: the business and administrative district in the centre of the city, surrounded by the so-called 'zone of transition' (with inner city slums, marked by decay and high density of social problems), followed by the zone of the respectable working class, a residential middle-class zone, and finally, a loosely defined suburban commuter zone. Newly arrived immigrants, it was argued, would settle first in the 'socially disorganized' zone of transition and then gradually move outwards.

Although later studies questioned the general applicability of the zone model, the Chicagoans have left a lasting imprint on urban studies and urban criminology. Chicago was at the time among the fastest growing US cities, marked by racial and ethnic diversity, and often associated with lawlessness and the reign of organized crime. Chicagoans examined the transformation of city life caused by an overwhelming influx of migrant populations, the breaking down of traditional social ties, cultural diversity and delinquency, as well as the possibilities for new forms of sociality. The relevance of the Chicago School therefore lies in its exploration of the impact of human mobility on social life – an issue which may today be more relevant than ever. The contemporary global city, like the Chicago of its time, is not only a metropolis but also an 'ethnopolis', where various nationalities and cultures mingle and melt, creating sites of 'localized globality' and 'globalized locality' (Laguerre, 2000: 19). In a modern metropolis, more than at any previous time in history, the Third World meets the First World, and is forced to share the same physical space with it. Migration is a vital aspect of contemporary urbanization since contemporary metropolises attract large global and national migrant populations. London and Paris, for example, are home to nearly 40 per cent of their nations' immigrant populations (Borja and Castells, 1997: 84). Immigrant neighbourhoods are marked by a variety of transnational cultural connections and flows to their home countries, as well as to the mainstream community and the rest of the city. Using anthropologist Arjun Appadurai's (1996) terminology, the city is a localized site of various kinds of global 'scapes', including ethnoscapes – flows of tourists, immigrants, guest workers, refugees and asylum seekers, 'denizens' (privileged foreigners) and other global nomads. Cities and their populations are in this respect mirrors of the transnational flows and global connections described throughout this book. While the glass corporate towers, and their inhabitants, represent one form of globalization, the poor migrant populations represent another type of globalization which is making its impact on city life – 'globalization from below' (Hall, 2006).

One of the central aspects of city life is the heterogeneity and mobility of its residents and the fluidity of social bonds. In cities, people live in extreme proximity with people who may otherwise be complete strangers to them. A question can therefore be asked about what kind of community can be created in this society of strangers, where people are uprooted and where, as Stuart Hall (1995) remarks, identity can better be understood in terms of individuals' *routes* rather than *roots*. The question becomes even more pressing in the contemporary context of multiculturalism, when cities are faced with the challenge of providing the basic rights of citizenship and equality to their diverse populations, while respecting the religious, cultural and lifestyle differences of these populations. The Chicago School clearly saw human mobility as a cause of the deterioration of traditional social ties and therefore of 'social disorganization' and delinquency (Shaw and McKay, 1942). The unique social conditions of urban life have been explored by a number of classical sociologists who saw the city as a breeding ground for a distinctly modern way of life and culture, marked by intense individualism, limited social involvement, but also by tolerance, diversity and sophistication. The condition was famously explored by Georg Simmel (1964) and his notion of 'the stranger' – a person simultaneously marked by spatial proximity and social distance. However, Simmel not only saw the stranger in immigrants and other marginal members of the society, but saw 'strangeness' as an inherent aspect of city life. Having the negative connotations of coldness, lack of commitment and rejection, as well as the positive potential for freedom and objectivity, 'strangeness', according to Simmel, defines the urban condition. Richard Sennett (2000) similarly describes the 'power of strangeness' and its potential to make us more complex human beings:

> In public, the urbanite may don an impassive mask, act cool and indifferent to others on the street; in private, however, he or she is aroused by these strange contacts, his or her certainties shaken by the presence of others.

Although writing at the dawn of the 20th century, Simmel's observations clearly chime with the contemporary urban condition, including his depiction of the metropolis as the seat of the money economy. Today, perhaps more than ever, cities are large conglomerations of people of different nationality, ethnic origin, skin colour and cultural belonging, as well as social class, reflecting the enormous gap between the global 'haves' and 'have-nots'. Living with social difference in spatial proximity is a project fraught with difficulties. In what follows we shall see how contemporary city life is often permeated by fear and insecurity, and shaped by numerous strategies which separate, order and control the myriad of heterogeneous city dwellers. We shall see how urban safety is a multifaceted project, having to do not only with questions of crime, but also with issues of fear, diversity and uniformity.

The global city as the dual city

Although a continuation of a long historic trend, the present surge in urbanization also has important new elements. The city analysed by the Chicago School was essentially an industrial city, marked by the demands of the burgeoning US industrial economy. Today, on the other hand, the socio-economic parameters of city life have profoundly changed. The old industrial capitals, such as Chicago, Detroit and Manchester have gone through a period of demise due to deindustrialization and the transfer of industrial production to low-cost regions of the developing world. Industrial production, which was the lifeline of the industrial city and its working class neighbourhoods, has been replaced by the informationalized, post-Fordist economy and its highly skilled workforce, supported by a vast personal-service economy, catering for their needs (Castells, 1996). As Reich (2005) illustrates this transformation:

> It used to be that about a third of the work force in advanced economies were in person-to-person jobs; now, close to half are. Today, more Americans work in laundries and dry-cleaners than in steel mills; more in hospitals and nursing homes than in banks and insurance companies. More work for Wal-Mart than for the entire U.S. automobile industry.

We can therefore begin to glimpse the extremely varied impact of global transformations on the nature of local urban environments. While the large financial centres, such as London, Frankfurt, New York and Tokyo, have expanded in size and influence (Sassen, 2001), there has been a related decline in other areas and city regions. The development is vividly described in Mike Davis's (1998) *City of Quartz*. Davis describes the structural transformation of Los Angeles during the 1980s which had a profound impact on the poor inner city black and Latino communities. Due to deindustrialization, young black working-class men saw their employment opportunities substantially diminished as jobs 'that gave their fathers and older brothers a modicum of dignity have either been replaced by imports, or relocated to white areas far out on the galactic spiral-arms of L.A.' (Davis, 1998: 305). The development was accompanied by a tragic growth in juvenile poverty and residential segregation. Not surprisingly, the minority youth have found a source of instant gratification and alternative identity in the buoyant drug economy, which has become 'the employer of last resort in the ghetto's devastated Eastside – the equivalent of several large auto plants or several hundred McDonalds' (Davis, 1998: 314; see also Bourgois, 2003 discussed later in this chapter).

The emerging global order changes the territorial organization of societies. This interplay of globalization and urban change has been most notably theorized within the so-called *global city theory*. First articulated through John Friedman's (1986) notion of a world city, the theory outlines the rise of large, highly connected metropolitan regions, which have become the centres of the 'footloose economy'. The global city is described as a financial, information and communication hub, where the most important functions of the global economy are concentrated – skills, capital, production, management, power and consumption. Global cities are not only New York, London and Tokyo, but also the rapidly expanding conglomerations in the industrializing countries such as, for example, China and India. Global cities represent the major command points in the global economy and serve as headquarters of transnational corporations and international banks, whose towers symbolically dominate the city skyline (Sassen, 2001). Furthermore, detached from the nation state, but intensely connected (by transport, information, communication and capital flows) to other global cities, the global city represents a structural background for the emerging global elite, whose cultural and economic connections may be closer to transnational spheres then to the national hinterland of the city.

Through this web of global interconnections and disconnections the global city reflects the essence of the emerging global network society and the space of flows (Castells, 1996). Here, Castells (1996: 404) points to an aspect of global cities which is of great importance for students of social control:

> [T]hey are connected externally to global networks and to segments of their own countries, while internally disconnecting local populations that are either functionally unnecessary or socially disruptive. I argue that this is true of New York as well as of Mexico or Jakarta. **It is this distinctive feature of being globally connected and locally disconnected, physically and socially, that makes megacities a new urban form** (emphasis original).

The connectivity of the network society is therefore highly selective. Global cities are marked by internal segregation and intense social stratification between those who are 'connected' to the global power networks, and those who are disconnected from them. The globalizing process crucially transforms the nature of contemporary city life, often resulting in sharp local inequalities and divisions within cities.

The global city is also a divided city or a 'dual city' (Borja and Castells, 1997; Scholar, 2006). In Mexico City, for example, a sprawling metropolis of 19 million and the second largest city in the world, 40 per cent of the population live below the poverty line and a third of its residents reside in shantytowns without basic public services. The shantytowns effectively do not play any distinctive role in the functioning of Mexico City as an international business centre (Castells, 1996: 381). Similarly, Moscow is becoming a prime example of flashy consumerism and the wealth of the Russian elite, as well as the home of several tens of thousands of homeless street children. On the other hand, the transformation of London into a global city has not necessarily meant more poverty on its streets; instead, most Londoners are poorer relative to the ultra-rich global elite which has moved into the city (Hamnett, 2003). The notion of a dual city therefore reflects the social polarization of the privileged and the marginalized city residents – the globally connected and the locally disconnected. These patterns of social inequality are also increasingly inscribed in the patterns of urban planning and spatial segregation. In *Splintering Urbanism* (2001) Graham and Marvin show how contemporary urban planning across the world has moved beyond the modernist ideal of a unitary and cohesive city towards 'splintering' and fragmentation, reflecting the highly fragmented and selectively connected nature of the network society.

> New, highly polarised urban landscapes are emerging where 'premium' infrastructure networks – high-speed telecommunications, 'smart' highways, global airline networks – selectively connect together the most favoured users and places, both within and between cities...At the same time, however, premium, and high-capability networked infrastructures often effectively bypass less favoured and intervening places and what Castells calls 'redundant' users.

Urban streets in some North American cities are no longer public spaces in the proper sense of the word, as tunnels are built below and parallel glass walkways are built above the streets, connecting office blocks, shopping malls and leisure spaces into enclosed 'skywalk cities' (Graham and Marvin, 2001). One can walk through many contemporary cities without touching public space as private space owners are building 'sanitized' pedestrian networks, enabling their clients to move without having to encounter the unpleasantness of 'street life'. Spatial segregation articulates spatially bound places dedicated to globally privileged populations. Castells (1996: 417) outlines a cultural trend towards creation of lifestyles and spatial forms 'aimed at unifying the symbolic environment of the elite around the world, thus superseding the historical spacificity of each locale'. These transnational spaces, such as airports and VIP lounges, exclusive hotels and tourist resorts, residential spaces and shopping malls, have been described as 'non-spaces' or 'nowherevilles' (Auge, 1995). They are an expression of a lifestyle where people are not linked to any specific society, but rather live life in several simultaneously. These are the 'global souls' aptly depicted in novelist Pico Iyer's (2000) novel, *The Global Soul*. The Arab city of Dubai can be seen perhaps as a paradigmatic example of this new form of sociality, symbolized by ostentatious hotels, shopping malls, tourism, simulation and exotic leisure experiences.

The developments outlined above are well expressed in Castells's (1996: 415) statement that 'elites are cosmopolitan, people are local'. However, this may be a truth with modifications. As we saw in the previous chapter, although deeply stratified, global mobility is no longer reserved for the privileged few but is a far more pervasive phenomenon. As the centres of global economy and power, the bright lights of global cities represent gravitation points for large masses of migrant and impoverished peasant populations which have become an almost unlimited source of cheap domestic, service and manufacturing labour. Cheap and flexible female migrants, for example, work as domestic servants, childcare providers, sex workers and factory workers in the so-called export processing zones. Critics have therefore pointed out that the notion of social exclusion and the 'dual city' metaphor is far from clear-cut, since these workers daily traverse the city, creating innumerable contact points between the privileged and the disadvantaged city dwellers (Young, 2003).

Earlier we saw how patterns of controlling mobility distinguish between various classes of global travellers – the tourists and the vagabonds. This global inequality also permeates city life and is evident in numerous local settings and control practices which will be addressed further in this chapter. The changing socio-economic parameters of city life are producing new geographies of social control and exclusion. Here we shall address the issues of video surveillance and the militarization of city life, as well as spatial segregation and exclusion, where gated communities and the ghetto represent two opposing poles.

The urban panopticon

Few technologies have received as much attention in recent years from criminologists, human geographers and other observers of social control as camera-based surveillance or **CCTV**. The technology was originally used for monitoring traffic flows, but has gradually become an essential item for controlling mobile and anonymous crowds in the city. As Norris and Armstrong (1999: 1) write: 'Whatever our role as we pass through the urban landscape we are subject to the presence of the cameras.' As consumers, public transport users, office workers, football supporters, residents and motorists, we are subjected to the inquisitive gaze of the camera. However, although CCTV is becoming an integral part of many city and residential landscapes across the world, there are considerable variations between various countries, particularly when it comes to surveillance of public spaces. The United Kingdom clearly stands out with what is now estimated to be almost 4.2 million cameras in operation, one for every 14 citizens (Wood, 2006). Nevertheless, there has been an expansion of CCTV surveillance across the world, particularly as big cities are stepping up surveillance in the aftermath of high-profile terrorist attacks.

Most research on CCTV situates the spread of this technology in the context of late modern consumer societies and their need to create 'purified' consumer environments. CCTV has become a standard item in shops, banks, shopping malls and other types of commercial environments. The origins of the current trend towards visual surveillance are most often theorized through the notion of the panopticon and panopticism. The **panopticon** was originally designed by the 19th century British philosopher Jeremy Bentham to be used in prisons. The word itself consists of two parts: *pan* (meaning 'all') and *optic* ('seeing'). The panoptic design was later succinctly analysed by the French philosopher Michel Foucault in his famous *Discipline and Punish* (1977). The essence of the panopticon is that it creates human conformity, not primarily by the use of physical force and restrictions, but by ensuring that its subjects are visible and feel watched at all times. As Foucault (1977: 202) points out, visibility in itself can be a trap. 'He who is subjected to a field of visibility, and who knows it, assumes responsibility for the constraints of power; he makes them play spontaneously upon himself' (ibid.). Foucault argued that the panoptic design spread from its original prison context to a number of other social settings, thus inserting 'the power to punish more deeply into the social body' (Foucault, 1977: 82). In the 19th century, the development was fuelled by rapid industrialization, the growth of mobile peasant populations, the emergence of the working classes and the challenges of their effective control.

Today, associations with the panopticon arise in a number of settings. The issue was mentioned in Chapter 2 in relation to border surveillance, and will be addressed further in Chapter 5 in relation to state surveillance and the war on terror. CCTV cameras, however, represent the paradigmatic example of panoptic surveillance in contemporary societies. CCTV surveillance is by and large mostly used on private properties, even though surveillance of public spaces is becoming increasingly common. Particularly in the UK, CCTV has often been installed as a result of partnerships between local authorities, police and retailers (Norris and Armstrong, 1999; Coleman, 2004). As such, the technology can be seen as representative of new forms of neo-liberal thinking, where the boundaries between state and private control become increasingly diffuse. Many observers therefore see CCTV as symptomatic of neo-liberal panality, of privatization of city space and of privatization of social control in general (Coleman, 2004; see also Chapter 6 below). The proliferation of CCTV has been significantly fuelled by the growth of so-called **mass–private property** in the past three decades (Shearing and Stenning, 1981; Jones and Newburn, 1998, Wakefield, 2003). Today, city life is lived to a large extent in half-public half-private spaces, such as shopping malls, transportation hubs and amusement facilities. One is usually unaware of the private nature of these spaces, since their owners generally encourage the public to frequent them and spend money in them. Private authorities are thus governing significant proportions of the totality of public space in contemporary cities, calling into question attempts to 'draw a clear line between the roles, responsibilities, functions and tasks of public and private authorities in the governance of security within liberal democratic states' (Johnston and Shearing, 2003: 32; see also Chapter 6). At this point, a question can be asked: what are the consequences of the fact that public life is increasingly conducted in private spaces?

The problematic nature of these developments may not be apparent at first-glance as the modern consumer seamlessly traverses these public/private city boundaries. Problems arise when certain social groups, such as the homeless, drug users, youth subcultures, ethnic minorities or street traders, whose social profile does not fit with the private owners' interests, claim their right of presence in these spaces. Although CCTV often tends to be publicly debated in terms of its potential for intrusion on privacy and as a symptom of the emerging 'Big Brother' society, its exclusionary and discriminatory potential is a less frequently addressed topic. Who is being watched and why? What are the results of the surveillance practices? Does CCTV, as its proponents suggest, in fact reduce crime? The answer to the last question still seems to be unclear, since despite the massive investment in the technology, there is no systematic evidence of its effectiveness as a crime prevention tool (Ditton et al., 1999; Norris and Armstrong, 1999). Rather than criminal offences, the focus of the surveillance seems to be on specific categories of people and on a diffuse category of 'undesirable behaviour', which often appears to be opposed to the commercial image of the controlled space (Norris and Armstrong, 1999; McCahill, 2002; Lomell, 2007). Norris and Armstrong (1999), for example, reveal that blacks are far more likely to be singled out for CCTV observation than whites for 'no obvious reason' (68 per cent to 35 per cent). The operators' perceptions of who does not seem to 'belong' to a particular city space influence the control practice. Surveillance practices reveal the institutional and commercial interests of the owners of the system, as well as personal biases of the CCTV operators themselves. Surveillance functions as a form of social sorting (Lyon, 2003a), distinguishing between desirable and undesirable populations.

Patterns of CCTV surveillance also reveal a more general transformation of the contemporary city towards a *post-Fordist* city, dominated by consumption, tourism and leisure experiences. Several urban scholars have pointed out the importance of this transformation for understanding the dynamics of contemporary urban social control and exclusion (Davis, 1998; Harvey, 1990). The city is not only a functional entity and a command centre in the new economy, as pointed out by the global city theory, but also a space embedded within the social production of identities. Contemporary town centres, shopping malls and tourist attractions are being transformed into 'spaces of seduction', where 'sanitized' and stylized environments are an essential part of their attractiveness

(Graham and Marvin, 2001). Sociologist Zygmunt Bauman (1997) maintains that *consumerism* represents one of the central mechanisms of establishing social order in late modern societies, as it establishes parameters for distinguishing between successful and 'flawed consumers'. While successful consumers are subtly 'seduced' to conformity, flawed consumers, who fail to keep up with the demands of the market society, need to be controlled through the use of more repressive control methods such as CCTV. While in previous epochs social conformity was defined primarily through a person's productive abilities, today, Bauman suggests, social exclusion is defined through a person's inability to consume.

The city is therefore not only a functional command centre for the global capital, but, importantly, also an entity imbued with emotional and symbolic qualities, a space of identity making and self-expression, which has recently been explored within the field of *cultural criminology* as well (Ferrell, 1996, 2001; Hayward, 2004) . In *City Limits* (2004) Hayward sees the post-Fordist city as a background for specifically modern (or better, postmodern) forms of transgression, embedded in the thrills of consumerism and a search for identity. Consequently, Hayward suggests, both shopping and shoplifting represent a specific form of identity:

> [s]treet criminals in many instances can be seen simply as consuming machines, 'urban entrepreneurs' whose primary aim is the accrual of the latest mobile phone or designer accessory – items that in today's consumer society are no longer simply desirable but are importantly perceived (especially by young people) as essential to individual identity, shifting as that may be from moment to moment. (2000: 5)

Hallsworth's (2005) study of *Street Crime*, for example, shows young, minority, robbers in a newly gentrified area of London stealing coveted consumer goods, driven by the city's fast, relentless cycle of consumption and identity seeking. For them, as one of Hallsworth's interviewees puts it, 'without these things you are nothing'.

To summarize the discussion so far, we have seen that the contemporary city is marked not only by a growing gap between the global 'haves' and 'have-nots' – where the global managerial elite shares the same urban space as impoverished third world migrants – but also by the demands of the consumer society, a constant growth in the goods on display and the cultural demands to have them. In what follows, we shall see that this co-presence of extreme wealth and poverty, and the overwhelming demands of the consumer society, create a combustive mixture and sometimes result in the use of military-style methods of social control.

Militarization of city life

According to some analysts, the proliferation of CCTV can also be seen as an example of a more general trend towards the deployment of exclusionary technologies and the **militarization** of city life (Davis, 1998; Graham and Marvin, 2001). In his influential description of 'Fortress L.A.', Mike Davis (1998: 223) describes the post-Fordist Los Angeles as a place where

> the defense of luxury lifestyles is translated into a proliferation of new repressions in space and movement, undergirded by the ubiquitous 'armed response'. This obsession with physical security systems, and, collaterally, with the architectural policing of social boundaries, has become a zeitgeist of urban restructuring, a master narrative in the emerging built environment in the 1990s.

Davis argues that technological surveillance joins other methods such as architectural and environmental features, as well as police and private security personnel, in screening undesirable elements out of urban space. Aiming to 'rejuvenate' the downtown area of the city, a variety of techniques is employed 'in a merciless struggle to make public facilities and spaces as "unliveable" as possible for the homeless and the poor' (ibid.: 232).

Spatial relations can thus be seen as a mirror of more general hierarchies of social relations and economic interests. According to French sociologist Pierre Bourdieu (1999), 'spatial profits' and the ability to dominate space represent vital aspects of the accumulation of economic and social capital. Local struggles over the use of urban space offer an important insight into general conditions of global inequality. We saw in the previous chapter how the mechanisms of global mobility are a key aspect of contemporary social stratification. Similarly, also in urban environments, restriction of movement is an important mechanism of social stratification and exclusion. One blatant example was the South African pass laws during apartheid, requiring blacks to produce documents on demand. The present proliferation of guarded gates, passes and permits has according to Davis (1998) a similar function, establishing in reality a form of 'urban apartheid'. Creating 'safe havens' for upscale tourists and privileged city dwellers, consisting of guarded office blocks and residential areas, so-called business development districts, prostitution-free zones and the like, has become a hallmark of contemporary city life (Davis, 1998; Johnston and Shearing, 2003). There has been a move towards so-called 'no-go zones' even in traditionally liberal countries such as Denmark, where drug users are fined if they move into certain central zones of Copenhagen (Frantzsen, 2006).

One of the vital models capturing the trend towards the 'militarization' of city life has been of **zero tolerance policing**. Inspired by James Q. Wilson and George L. Kelling's 'broken windows thesis', the objective of zero tolerance policing is not primarily to combat serious crime, but rather to address deviance and disorder. The authors suggested that if minor forms of social disorder in a community remain unattended, for example littering, prostitution, panhandling and graffiti, this opens the gates for more serious forms of crime. Crime prevention starts by 'fixing broken windows' (Wilson and Kelling, 1982; Kelling and Coles, 1996). Although common sense, and bordering on the obvious, zero tolerance policing has been one of the most intensely debated and controversial control strategies in the past decades, due largely to its aggressive form of enforcement. Its critics have pointed out that the strategy greatly increases the state's power of intrusion into local communities and expands its surveillance and penal apparatus (Harcourt, 2001). The lines between crime and disorder, as well as police responses to them, become increasingly blurred. 'Disorder becomes a degree of crime: breaking a window, littering, jumping a turnstile become grades along a spectrum that leads to homicide' (Harcourt, 2001: 149). We saw in Chapter 1 how the lines between crime and security are difficult, if not impossible, to draw and that crime control can be an extremely elastic concept. Similarly, we saw in this chapter how the focus of private property owners and their security personnel often seems to be on 'purifying' urban space, rather than on preventing crime. With the zero tolerance strategy too, public police forces are caught in the borderland between crime and disorder where marginal social groups, such as youth subcultures, homeless and ethnic minorities, become the object of police action due to their perceived potential for creating disorder. Zero tolerance policing was fervently promoted in the 1990s by New York City's Mayor Giuliani and Police Commissioner William Bratton and their moral crusade against so-called 'quality of life crimes'. The policy was largely credited by its proponents with the fall in the city's crime rates, although its opponents contested these claims with even greater fervour (Harcourt, 2001). Furthermore, critics have not only pointed out the policy's ineffectiveness as a crime reduction tool, but also its great ethical and financial costs. The numbers of the city's police force increased dramatically to a historical high, even as budgets for other welfare services were streamlined. Aggressive law enforcement tactics against minor offences further damaged the fragile relations between the police and the city's disadvantaged communities, escalating to several high-profile cases of police brutality against members of racial and ethnic minorities (McArdle and Erzen, 2001).

Zero tolerance policing, however, has had an impact far beyond its origin in New York City and even the United States as a whole. Several US cities have embraced the approach, along with many politicians, academics and the popular press. The policy has made an impact in several cities across the world where city and police officials often openly draw on New York's experience. 'Zero tolerance' has become a 'global export' and a case of what Jones and Newburn (2004) term 'Atlantic crossings' (for further discussion of penal policy transfers see Chapter 8 below). However, the authors are careful to point out that it is uncertain whether it is the substance of zero tolerance which is being transferred, or only its style and the rhetoric (Jones and Newburn, 2004). Although the phrase 'zero tolerance' has become popular, particularly among politicians, there is great variation in how the model is implemented in local police and penal cultures. The zero tolerance model has different connotations and modes of deployment in different places.

'Taking back the streets', which has been the objective of the model, means different things in the variety of global contexts (Johnston and Shearing, 2003). In Oslo, the relatively tranquil and prosperous Norwegian capital, a zero tolerance approach was used in an aggressive campaign against urban graffiti. Consequently, Høigård (2002) argues, the price of creating a 'pure' city has been aggressive law enforcement and criminalization of a youth culture, whose aesthetic judgements have been derided by the prevailing public discourse and power structures (see also Ferrell, 1996). The zero tolerance approach reveals similar concerns about the image of the city to those visible in the deployment of CCTV, and similarly, a question arises about who has the right to the city and who sets the rules for the use of its public space (Ferrell, 2001). Why, for example, is graffiti a criminalized form of aesthetic expression while commercials and billboards are allowed to dominate the city's visual image? Whose tastes, values and preferences are defining the various strategies for 'cleaning up' the city? Consequently, the objective of 'reclaiming the streets' has been inscribed in several subcultural movements, such as hip-hop graffiti artists, street entertainers, homeless activists, skateboarders, etc. who have tried to create alternative spaces to the consumerist notions of order and the aesthetics of Disneyfication (Ferrell, 2001). Resistance to globalization has many faces.

The ghetto, the *banlieue* and the culture of exception

Although the zero tolerance model often refers to widely diverse realities, it also unveils certain common traits within contemporary cultures of control. Not only has the 'zero tolerance' slogan travelled to European and South American cities, often together with its main architects themselves, Bratton and Giuliani, but the spread of this policy reveals some common underlying assumptions about the nature of penal policy. Instead of combating the causes of homelessness, social deprivation and social disorder, 'zero tolerance' combats their symptoms; 'it diverts attention from "causes" of crime, and from alternative "policies"' (Jones and Newburn, 2004: 133). This perspective is described by Young (1999: 130) as the 'cosmetic fallacy' which

> conceives of crime as a superficial problem of society, skin deep, which can be dealt with using the appropriate ointment, rather than as any chronic ailment of society as a whole. It engenders a cosmetic criminology which views crime as a blemish which suitable treatment can remove from a body which is, itself, otherwise healthy and in little need of reconstruction. Such criminology *distances* itself from the core institutions and proffers technical, piecemeal solutions. It, thus, reverses causality: crime causes problems for society rather than society causes the problem of crime.

The approach is by no means unique to 'zero tolerance' policies, but can be described as a trait of many governmental policies which engage in a war against the poor rather than against poverty. Nevertheless, critics have pointed out that in the context of urban environments, which are particularly fraught with violence and social deprivation, arguing for increased police intervention could have disastrous consequences for disadvantaged local communities. Looking at the case of Brazil, Wacquant (2003: 197) argues that borrowing from US-style policies would amount to a 'chaotic dictatorship over the poor', particularly because 'the Brazilian police is not a remedy against violence but a major source of violence in its own right'. 'Cleaning up' petty crime and urban disorder, such as homelessness, begging and street children, may calm down the discomfort and insecurity felt by tourists and affluent residents of the city, but would exacerbate the urban warfare taking place in the heart of the Brazilian metropolises. Hundreds, possibly thousands of people are shot by Brazilian police every year (Amnesty International, 2005). Moreover, the pervasive fear of crime exacerbates violence by legitimizing private and illegal reactions – such as hiring guards or supporting death squads and vigilantism – when institutions of order seem to fail (Caldeira, 2000).

Images of 'urban warfare' are by no means exclusive to the streets of Rio and São Paolo but at regular intervals also characterize the 'prosperous West'. The recent images of burning French *banlieues* (suburbs) clearly bear a resemblance to the 1992 Los Angeles riots, which were ignited by a similar combustive mixture of controversial police action and pervasive social exclusion of ethnic and racial minorities. The ghetto, the slum, the *banlieue* and the *favela* are contemporary connotations for spaces of urban marginality. However, they represent a far too complex issue to be addressed justly in the limited space at our disposition in this chapter. My purpose here is to look at some perspectives examining the intricate interconnections between global transformations and local patterns of social exclusion. Although the ghetto has throughout history served as a mechanism for ethnic, racial, religious and class segregation, it gains new connotations in several recent perspectives on globalization.

Global interconnections, particularly migration, have been shaping life in the ghetto for a long time. Today, however, Bauman (2004) describes the ghetto as a 'dumping ground' for the populations which have been rendered superfluous by the 'progress' of global modernity. The ghetto's function is to contain and immo-bilize in its locality the 'wasted humans' produced by modernity. Hence, his argument (1998), presented in Chapter 1, about the transformation of prisons from 'houses of correction' to 'factories of immobility', whose task is primarily to immobilize potentially risky populations. One therefore does not need pris-ons in order to be, or feel, incarcerated in the locality. The inability to move can be a result not only of technological surveillance, physical obstacles, security checkpoints and controls, but also of public transport prices and design, city planning and residential segregation. One can feel 'incarcerated' in the local community, like for example the residents of the French *banlieues* for whom, as Morley (2000) points out, the centre of Paris may feel as far as Mauritius feels for the privileged residents of the city.

Bauman's characteristically pessimistic account of the ghetto draws on the work of several critical analysts, who depict the deterioration and deepening of social marginalization in American ghettos (see for example Wilson, 1987; Davis, 1998; Wacquant, 2001). In the last decades of the 20th century, deindus-trialization took out the lifeline which sustained ghettoized populations in pre-vious epochs and gave them a minimum of decency and social cohesion. Instead, Wacquant (2001) argues, we have been witnessing the rise of the 'hyper-ghetto', which is increasingly intertwined with the growing carceral apparatus. Ghettos are enmeshed with penal institutions, and prison populations increas-ingly resemble ghetto populations. As the industrial sector and the welfare state cut down their ties to the ghetto, the penal system widens its net of control of poor urban black and minority populations. Similarly, Davis's exploration of Los Angeles (1998) depicts the growing penal system on the one hand, and the exten-sive drug economy on the other hand, as the main 'employers' of black and Latino inner-city youth. In that respect, the ghetto becomes the 'wild zone' and a space of 'exception' that escapes the 'social', as powerfully captured in Fernando Meirelles's (2002) movie *City of God*.

Although it is a common topic of political and criminological discourse, the ghetto is far less often an object of detailed empirical inquiry. A notable recent exception, Philippe Bourgois's ethnographic study *In Search of Respect* (2003), is a powerful account of the lives of young crack dealers in El Barrio, a deeply mar-ginalized immigrant neighbourhood in the midst of the wealthy Manhattan. For Bourgois's informants, the blue-collar unionized jobs that their fathers held are just a faint dream. Factory employment has been slashed by deindustrialization and replaced by a feminized service sector. The young men's tough macho cultural identity, which could function effectively on the factory shop floor, is dysfunctional in the white-collar 'yuppie' environments, which demand subservient modes of interaction. However, instead of passively accepting their structural marginalization, Bourgois's informants find themselves immersed in a violent inner city street culture, dominated by the illegal drug economy, which has become the employer of last resort for youth in El Barrio. Although the street culture offers its participants possibilities for achieving alternative forms of dignity, creativity and conspicuous consumption, Bourgois outlines how this alternative lifestyle 'ultimately becomes an active agent in personal degradation and community ruin' (2003: 9). Rather than seeing the drug economy as the *cause* of inner city decline, which can be halted by short-term policy and penal intervention, Bourgois points out that drugs are only a symptom of deeper structural problems. 'Self-destructive addiction is merely the medium for desperate people to internalize their frustration, resistance, and powerlessness' (2003: 319).

The fate of the local in a multicultural society

Ironically, the destructive drug trade simultaneously maintains the state of exception of the ghetto communities, as well as making them part of a profitable illicit global economy (see Chapter 5 on the global drug trade). The contemporary ghetto furthermore reveals not only the social damage of deindustrialization, but also the human costs of migration and the pervasive geographic inequalities between various immigrant populations and their hosts. Global cities are also multicultural cities, traversed by various types of 'ethnoscapes'. After the October 2005 riots in predominantly immigrant suburbs of Paris and other French cities, attention has been directed to the detrimental effects of much of the postwar city planning, particularly the building of large blocks of flats in the outskirts of cities, marked by a high density of people with social problems and pervasive unemployment. However, as many analysts pointed out, the outbursts of rioting in the suburbs cannot simply be understood in terms of economic deprivation and lack of opportunities; they also point to more general problems of exclusion and estrangement of minority youth within Western societies. The revolts in the suburbs have to be seen in the context of increasingly 'hostile arguments against non-European immigrants and Muslims in many Western states, including France where the *banlieues* became the spatially reified forms of such "threats"' (Dikec, 2006: 162). We shall address the questions of multiculturalism, integration, ethnic discrimination and the challenges of policing ethnically diverse societies in the next chapter. What is important here is how spatial forms can be seen as the expression of society, and how the practices of spatial exclusion are formed by the dynamics of overall social structure. Bourdieu (1999) points out that the emergence of the *banlieues*, often referred to as the 'problem suburbs', can be seen as an inscription of social inequality into spatial forms, and, ultimately, as the abdication of the welfare state in these areas (for a discussion of the changing role of the state see Chapter 6). The ghetto is therefore a social space 'defined by an *absence* – basically, that of the state and everything that comes with it, police, schools, health care institutions, associations, etc.' (ibid.: 123).

The ghetto usually tends to be described as irrational and chaotic, and fundamentally different from the rest of society (the 'state of exception' thesis). However, as William F. Whyte's (1943) classic study of the Italian ghetto in New York showed, the ghetto is structured around values and social norms which, although different from the predominant value systems, nevertheless appear rational to its members. In contrast to the predominantly pessimistic tone of the prevailing accounts of the ghetto, some authors argue that economically deprived and excluded communities may also have a lot to offer to their residents in terms of their **social capital**. Analysts such as Nils Christie (2004) and Jennifer Wood and Clifford Shearing (2007) point out the need to strengthen the local community and rebuild it with its own forces, rather then relying on 'top down' state intervention. Chicago School members were actively involved in a series of projects attempting to increase the quality of life in Chicago's disadvantaged neighbourhoods. The local can therefore emerge as a possible site for building communities around values and lifestyles other than the prevailing consumerist *Zeitgeist* of the affluent city centres. The thought was beautifully expressed by Katiuska Di Eugenio (2005: 20), who interviewed and lived among residents of the Venezuelan barrio La Vega.

> They [the residents of La Vega] also explained that life is very difficult because of the poor transportation system. They have to wake up very early to take the jeep and then wait until 9 o'clock in the evening to go back home. But they are very happy. They have discovered the dreams of building their own communities. They do not want the big malls, the big avenues or the amazing buildings. Indeed, when they go downtown they do not like it, they feel as if they asphyxiated themselves. They want their home and the basic public services.
>
> Perhaps the problem is not the Barrio, as we find in some literature. The Barrios have their lights and shadows. But the lights are not the lights of the city. The lights are the joy of living, the dreams, the breath of fresh air, and the fight for a better life, the school and the health center built by the community.

The ghetto can be seen not only as a site of optimistic potential, for local empowerment, but also as a site of new forms of sociality built on what might be called 'globalization from below', where a new multi-ethnic, multicultural reality becomes the normal form of the local (Hall, 2006).

The initiatives 'from below' have at times been criticized for not addressing larger structural problems – class and gender inequalities, social infrastructure, redistribution of wealth within society. The stress on local self-reliance in some governmental strategies may be a denial of state responsibility for these areas. Amin (2005: 630), for example, argues for the need to challenge the perception of some disadvantaged places as deserving 'only local community while other are allowed to enjoy cosmopolitan society'. We can see that the local takes on a variety of meanings. While bearing a great potential for empowerment and democracy, as well as protection from the world of speed, mobility and flow, the local is marked by marginalization due to its exclusion from the world of global flows, and therefore, power. The local is a site of new forms of cultural connections and identity, built around cultural hybridity and global interconnections, as well as a site of more intense and entrenched social divisions and spatial segregation. However, while in the case of the ghetto this segregation is something that the residents may strive to break out of, spatial and social segregation is increasingly also a lifestyle of choice for the privileged members of society, a form of escapism of the affluent.

Gated communities and the urban 'ecology of fear'

Today, the materiality of borders is revealed in a number of locations. In the previous chapter we looked more closely at the rise of Fortress Europe and Fortress America. However, the fortress continents are replicated in a number of countries and global cities, in the form of so-called *gated communities*, which guard their borders from strangers with fervour and technological savvy just as affluent states do (Blakely and Snyder, 1999; Caldeira, 2000; Graham and Marvin, 2001). The rise of gated communities in a number of countries is a potent reminder of the persistent belief that walls and fences can bring at least some kind of safety. Instead of building walls around cities, as in medieval times, contemporary members of gated communities seem to be afraid of the dangers that reside *within* the city, and so divide cities and suburbs into a number of smaller areas which are put under surveillance. In their illuminating study *Fortress America*, Blakely and Snyder (1999) show that never before in US history has 'forting up' been so widespread, not just among upper-class, but also among middle- and lower middle-class Americans. The development took off in the early 1980s and, interestingly, coincided with the massive growth of the US prison population. However, gated communities and condominium complexes are by no means a US peculiarity, but can be found in diverse settings across the world, from the crime-ridden Latin American cities to Istanbul, Mumbai, Manila, Johannesburg and Tokyo, to name just a few (Graham and Marvin, 2001).

Although often articulated through a discourse about the fear of crime, research indicates that the phenomenon of gating is not directly related to actual crime trends, nor do the gates necessarily make residents feel safer; quite the opposite – they may even create a heightened sense of fear and insecurity (Blakely and Snyder, 1999; Low, 2003). Some have argued that the rise of the gated community reveals a deeper desire and longing for community, and 'a sense of belonging and identity that counteracts the size and potential alienation of the city and globalizing world' (Low, 2003: 56). Gated communities represent 'the notion of community as an island' (Blakely and Snyder, 1999: 3), an attempt by their residents to run away from the disorder and messiness of communal life and establish some sense of control. This search for community is built around the notion of social splitting and exclusion. 'The walls and gates of the community reflect this splitting physically as well as metaphorically, with "good" people (the good part of us) inside, and the "bad" remaining outside' (Low, 2003: 139). Moreover, gating is part of a broader social process often referred to as the 'white flight' to the suburbs, where the middle classes escape intricacies of city life in order to offer their children socially (racially, ethnically, economically) homogeneous environments and where house prices function as one form of 'gate' protecting the affluent from the poor. A gated community does not need to be a suburban enclave, but can also be a guarded city condominium, a retirement community, or a community designed to provide leisure activities. Gated communities have many facets and many attractions for their members. At a time of minimal-state policies, communities are being created privately through what has been described as a 'privatopia', 'in which the dominant ideology is privatism, thus undermining the idea of public services and infrastructure (McKenzie, 1994).

Nevertheless, residents of gated communities are attracted not only to the quality of services, rising property values and the exclusiveness of their communities, but also to the social exclusion that the gates represent. They are in search of a 'perfect community' with a high level of services as well as a community without crime, without social problems and with a high level of social homogeneity. Gates help to create communities of 'insiders' where those beyond the gates are defined as 'outsiders', as strangers that represent a threat. Setha Low's ethnographic study *Behind the Gates* reveals that residents of gated communities identify ethnic changes in society as an important reason for 'gating up' and stigmatize immigrants as a source of fear. In that respect, Low points out (2003: 143), gating also involves 'racialization' of space, since the 'intruders' or deviants are often defined through visible features, particularly race and ethnicity. 'The more "purified" the environment – the more homogeneous and controlled – the greater the residents' ability to identify any deviant individuals who should not be there' (Low, 2003: 143).

Johnston and Shearing (2003: 142–3) describe how South Africa has not only adopted the concept of gated communities, but has taken it a step further by developing a 'gated town'.

> 'Heritage Park' is surrounded by an electrified fence, its perimeter being policed by forty private guards who monitor a battery of sophisticated computer equipment. Adjacent to the complex, though out of the sight-line of its residents – and in ironic invocation of the principles of 'secured by design' – the developers have built a township of 142 modest houses on land previously set aside as a squatter camp...[I]t is hoped that residents of the settlement will provide a source of labour to Heritage Park's shops and domestic premises. The parallels with the Bantustans of the old Apartheid era should be obvious.

Gated communities can be seen as a radical expression of the fragmentation of society where the solutions to the dilemmas of living with difference in modern cities are practices of social exclusion and self-exclusion. Members of gated communities can control and exclude people from their communities, and crucially, exclude themselves from city life as well. Helicopter has become elites' preferred mode of transport and a ticket to safety from urban chaos (Johnston and Shearing, 2003). The mushrooming of helipads on the roofs of global cities symbolizes the great disparities of wealth between city dwellers and the extreme mobility of the elite and its detachment from everyday city life. The new global elite, as Sennett (2000) points out, 'wants to operate in the city, but not rule it; it composes a regime of power without responsibility'.

Withdrawal from the public realm is by no means a novel phenomenon. Richard Sennett's (1974) influential study *The Fall of the Public Man* outlines how public life, a vital aspect of pre-capitalist cities, has been in decline and has gradually been surpassed by withdrawal into the private sphere. Sennett's groundbreaking book takes up the issues of living with strangers and the problematic nature of the withdrawal into the private sphere – the themes which have been central points of discussion throughout this chapter. Although still immensely vibrant and diverse, contemporary cities are often marked by an 'ecology of fear' (Davis, 1999), where 'the stranger himself is a threatening figure' (Sennett, 1974: 3). In gated communities, in guarded and 'purified' shopping malls, office buildings and residential areas, city life is marked by fear of 'the others'. As Barbara Hudson (2003: 57) points out: 'What we see today is a narrowing of the bounds of sociality to those most obviously "like us" – whether through kinship or lifestyle.' Consequently, although marked by increasing diversity and internationality of their dwellers, contemporary cities are far from being shiny examples of cosmopolitan citizenship. Quite the opposite: the tendency to create enclaves of homogeneity is increasingly creating entrenched spaces of exclusion and, on the other hand, 'safe havens of territoriality'. As Bauman (1998: 117) writes:

> In an ever more insecure and uncertain world the withdrawal into the safe haven of territoriality is an intense temptation; and so the defence of the territory – the 'safe home' – becomes the pass-key to all doors which one feels must be locked to stave off the triple threat to spiritual and material comfort.

Space therefore continues to matter, ever for those who seem to be most transnational and at home in the 'space of flows'.

Summary

Despite the salience of the transnational 'space of flows', spatial exclusion is a vital aspect of contemporary social exclusion. In this chapter we saw that the past decades have been witness to unprecedented levels of urbanization, and to the growth of vast city regions. Globalization has been analysed as a motor behind the so-called global cities. Less often discussed has been the parallel growth of slums and mega-slums and the pervasive practices of spatial segregation. Contemporary cities are a locus of concentrated global wealth and poverty, which often creates a combustive mixture in terms of social control. Another vital aspect of contemporary city life is the pervasiveness of consumer culture and the transformation from the industrial to the post-Fordist city. The impact of consumerism and widespread social inequality are felt in several aspects of contemporary crime control in the city:

- The massive growth of CCTV and other technological paraphernalia. CCTV has become a vital tool in the hands of shopping centres, business districts and municipal authorities, which aim to 'purify' city spaces of unwanted populations and make them attractive for potential consumers, tourists and clients.
- The militarization of crime control strategies, which has taken a variety of forms in the diversity of local settings – from the US-style zero tolerance policing to the outright urban warfare in the streets of Rio de Janeiro.
- The growth of ghettos and gated communities as prime examples of contemporary spatial exclusion and self-exclusion. These spaces reveal the fragmentation of societies along ethnic, class and racial lines, and the central role that experiences of crime and insecurity play in the process.

STUDY QUESTIONS

1   What are the consequences of the urbanization of poverty for city life?

2   What practices of spatial exclusion do you encounter in your city and local community?

3   How do consumerism and private business interests shape social control in the city?

4   How is life in your local neighbourhood shaped by global flows and developments? Do these global influences have any consequences on your perceptions of security?

FURTHER READING

The phenomenon of global cities has generated a wealth of literature, particularly within human geography. Neil Brenner and Roger Keil's (2006) *The Global Cities Reader* gives a useful overview of the debates. Mike Davis's extensive opus deserves to be mentioned in its own right, particularly his classic account of Los Angeles, *The City of Quartz* (1998), as well as the recent, even more disturbing, *Planet of Slums* (2006). Keith Hayward's (2004) *City Limits* takes a look at the transformation towards the post-Fordist city in a criminological perspective. CCTV is the object of numerous recent empirical and theoretical studies, particularly in the UK. Clive Norris and Gary Armstrong's (1999) *The Maximum Surveillance Society*, Roy Coleman's (2004) *Reclaiming the Streets* and Mike McCahill's (2002) *The Surveillance Web* are just some of the valuable contributions. Ben Harcourt's (2001) *Illusion of Order* critically examines 'the false promise of broken windows policing' in the US context, while Teresa Caldeira's (2000) *City of Walls* takes a look at the crime–spatial segregation nexus in São Paolo.

4

The 'Deviant Immigrant': Migration and Discourse about Crime

Chapter Contents

The dangerous migrant and criminology of the other	77
The enemy within	82
The new carceral archipelago	86
Cultural dynamics of globalization	88
'Defending our way of life'	88
'AlieNation is my nation'	91
The difficulties of living with difference and the attractions of essentialism	93
At the intersection: ethnicity, class and masculinity	95
Towards cosmopolitan citizenship?	98
Summary	98
Study questions	99
Further reading	99

OVERVIEW

Chapter 4 examines the following issues:

- The discursive linkage between migration and crime and its political implications.
- The trend towards emotive and populist discussions about crime, particularly with regard to the issue of immigrant crime.
- The nature of penal responses against immigrants and asylum seekers.
- The conflicting and contradictory nature of the cultural dynamics of globalization.
- Various forms of cultural essentialism, their drawbacks and attractions.

KEY TERMS

anomie	criminology of the other	moral panics
clash of civilizations	cultural hybridity	Orientalism
cosmopolitanism	essentialism	penal populism
criminalization	masculinity	

> The Agnelli estate in Padua is a cluster of crumbling high-rise flats. It was built in the 1980s to house the city's considerable student population. These days it is home to several hundred African immigrants. It has a reputation for crime, drugs and prostitution, and is a constant source of angry complaints from local Italian residents. This summer, after riots between opposing gangs, the left-leaning mayor of Padua took a drastic decision to seal off the estate – with a metal wall … 'It is not an instrument of segregation,' said Mayor Flavio Zanonato. 'We just want to limit the activity of the drug pushers here. This isn't a wall in Palestine. It's just something that's harder for drug dealers to jump over'… The fence has been dubbed Padua's Berlin Wall. (BBC News, 2006)[1]

This episode could very well be discussed in the context of the previous chapter, under the theme of spatial exclusion. Nevertheless, the steel wall dividing Padua also symbolically represents broader social divisions which are being articulated, justified and put in place through the discourse about immigrant crime.

---

[1]http://news.bbc.co.uk/go/pr/fr/-/2/hieurope/5385752.stm (published 28.09.2006.)

The control of national borders is, as we saw in Chapter 2, becoming a pressing task for national and international police authorities. However, protection of the national territory is not taking place only on the practical level, but also on a broader symbolic level where global movements of people have had important implications for the notions of cultural belonging, citizenship and culture. In 2006, in the majority of Western European countries, the foreign-born population accounted for between seven and 15 per cent of the total population. In the US, the newly immigrant proportion of the population is over 12 per cent and rising, compared to 5 per cent in 1970.[2] The number of foreigners in Japan has more than doubled in the past 15 years, rising to over 2 million today and transforming a once insular society. The United Kingdom is experiencing the largest wave of immigration in British history. The British government announced recently that about 600,000 migrants, most of them Poles, had registered for work in the UK since 2004. At the same time, almost one in ten British citizens is living abroad.[3]

A question can be asked about the impact of these profound global and local transformations on human subjectivity and identity, particularly when it comes to the changing perceptions of crime and deviance. In this chapter we are going to look more closely at the intricate interconnections as well as tensions that occur at various meeting points between global cultural flows and local practices. It will be suggested that the image of the 'deviant immigrant' (Melossi, 2003), and the coupling of immigration and crime, represents one of the central outlets for the articulation of the transformations of contemporary societies. International migration is increasingly defined as a question of national security, and the discourse about immigrant crime clearly exacerbates the trend. In what follows, we shall first look at the discourse about immigrant crime and at the growing 'carceral archipelago' controlling immigrant populations. We shall then examine the changing nature of cultural belonging and national culture, and their implications for understanding the concept of immigrant crime and deviance.

The dangerous migrant and criminology of the other

Discussions of the criminal nature of immigrants inevitably accompany large movements of people, when old patterns of settlement are dramatically disturbed

---

[2] http://www.guardian.co.uk/usa/story/0,,1921310,00.html
[3] http://newsvote.bbc.co.uk/mpapps/pagetools/print/news.bbc.co.uk/2/hi/uk_news/6210358.stm

by the flows of newcomers. The image of the 'deviant immigrant' has a long history and is a recurring theme in social studies, as we saw in the case of the Chicago School. In early 20th-century Chicago, '[f]oreigners were often depicted as possessing powerful criminal tendencies. For instance, fighting was seen as the national habit of the Irish, to the extent that bricks were popularly known as "Irish confetti"' (Valier, 2003: 2). Moreover, one can find numerous references to the coupling of migration and criminalization in Marx and other 19th century texts. Foucault's influential *Discipline and Punish* (1977) envisages prison as a paramount institution for disciplining and adjusting migrant populations to the needs of modernity. The issues of migration, crime, anomie and cultural conflict therefore reappear at regular intervals as a result of global and national migratory movements, such as migration across the Atlantic at the turn of the 19th century, or the south–north migrations within Europe at the end of the 1960s (Melossi, 2003). Today, the 'deviant immigrant' again features prominently in the political and media discourse in most Western countries. From violent asylum seekers, cynical smuggling and trafficking networks and Muslim terrorists to Nigerian and East European prostitutes, and ethnic youth gangs, the images of foreign criminals abound.

Representations of crime and deviance are deeply embedded in social structures and relationships within given societies. These representations mirror the inclusive and exclusive tendencies of the societies in which they emerge. In the post-war period, the image of deviants as maladjusted individuals in need of state help and intervention mirrored the predominantly inclusive modus of welfare societies (Garland, 2001a). Today, on the other hand, the images of violent and threatening asylum seekers, Muslim terrorists and immigrant youth gangs embody the protectionist and exclusionist nature of prosperous societies in an increasingly divided global order. While the welfare state discourse envisaged a world where inclusion of deviance was still possible, today the prevalent themes are those of security and protection from (presumably foreign) risks. The classic distinction between the law-abiding and the criminal, 'us' and 'them', serves to confirm and reinforce the division between the foreign and the national.

The discourse about immigration and crime can be addressed within several classical sociological and criminological perspectives, for example Erikson's *Wayward Puritans*, Howard Becker's *Outsiders* and Stan Cohen's *Folk Devils and Moral Panics*, to name just a few. These works outline how communities discuss and establish their values and norms through publicly debating cases of deviance. The classical sociological theme of fear of the stranger (discussed in Chapter 3) gains a particular salience when applied to the problem of the deviant immigrant. The immigrant and the asylum seeker represent classic examples of Simmel's figure of the stranger, marking and accentuating the 'us' and 'them' divisions within society and serving to crystallize the symbolic and cultural limits of the community. 'Indeed, the otherness of the stranger and the otherness of the deviant are collapsed in the social portrayal of the criminal immigrant' (Melossi, 2003: 376). Nevertheless, while clearly representing the figure of the stranger, the role of the deviant immigrant is a complex one at a time when a society of strangers seems to have become almost a way of life. In the globalizing world the familiar and the strange co-exist in a complex mixture in which the strange may be 'encountered in the adjoining neighbourhood, and the familiar turns up at the end of the earth' (Morley, 2000: 10).

Some authors have suggested that the discourse about the deviant immigrant can be placed in the context of what Garland (2001a) terms the **criminology of the other** (Hudson, 2003; Welch and Schuster, 2005b). Garland sees the criminology of the other as one of the dominant approaches to crime in late modern societies and a vital aspect of an emerging 'culture of control'. The criminology of the other marks the reversal of the modernist criminological project, where the punitive urge is replaced by the quest to understand and to act upon the causes of crime. The criminology of the other moves beyond the project of correction and integration of offenders into society, and serves as a justification of expanding social control and exclusion. Now, Garland argues, offenders are no longer 'like us', deserving our solidarity and the support of the penal welfare apparatus.

> They are dangerous others who threaten our safety and have no call on our fellow feeling. The appropriate reaction for society is one of social defence: we should defend ourselves against these dangerous enemies rather than concern ourselves with their welfare and prospects for rehabilitation. (Garland, 2001a: 184)

Although Garland does not address the issues of immigration and terrorism, and hardly touches upon the question of race, his outline of the criminology of the other strongly resonates with contemporary debates on these issues. Media portrayals of asylum seekers as 'bogus', 'fraudulent', 'benefit scroungers' are compounded by the heightened security concerns in the post-9/11 world (Welch and Schuster, 2005a). Similarly, in the popular terminology of 'transnational organized crime', the transnational 'suggests a crucial "otherness", an essentially alien pollutant' (Hobbs and Dunnighan, 1998: 290).

The present breach with the inclusive nature of the post-war welfare societies is perhaps most visible in the punitive turn taken by traditionally more tolerant European countries, such as Denmark and the Netherlands. The so-called 'immigrant problem' is frequently addressed through the question of their alleged criminality, ergo difference, from the native populations. Immigration and asylum are issues increasingly defined as matters of justice and domestic security, on the same level as terrorism and organized crime (Wacquant, 1999).

Reductions in asylum applications are seen as signs of governments' success, asylum seekers thus becoming populations one needs to be protected *from*, rather than people who need our protection. Allusions to a safe, mythical 'golden age', before the arrival of immigrants, have become an important aspect of contemporary European politics. The deviant immigrant seems to embody the dangers and insecurities resulting from the rapid pace of social change and the intrusion of global flows into the secure familiarity of the local (see the discussion of ontological insecurity in Chapter 1). As the British ex-prime minister Mrs Thatcher once bluntly put it, 'we joined Europe to have free movement of goods...I did not join Europe to have free movement of terrorists, criminals, drugs, plant and animal diseases and rabies and illegal immigrants' (cited in Morley, 2000: 226).

The deviant immigrant thus represents the polluting element, the quintessential other, which accompanies global transformations. Loader and Sparks (2002: 104) point out that

> It is also precisely under globalizing conditions that people's *sense of place* – and of *differences* between 'here/there', 'inside/outside', 'us/them' – takes on renewed force as a structuring feature of social relations and culture; questions of crime, danger, safety, and order often today figuring pivotally in how the quotidian life of particular neighbourhoods, towns, cities, and nations is experienced, imagined, and defended.

The debates about immigration and crime bring up the themes of declining moral standards and the threatened nature of the national. The punishment of immigrant crime (and the debates surrounding it) seems to perform a double task: on the one hand, it performs the classic Durkheimian function of strengthening social bonds and social solidarity, and on the other hand, its task is to form a sort of 'purifying filter' protecting the local and the national from threatening foreign elements. Both of these functions will be addressed in this chapter. However, while the former may be by now a classic item of criminological textbooks, the latter territory is far less explored.

In *The Division of Labor* (1933), Emile Durkheim outlines a view of punishment as an essential mechanism for maintaining social solidarity and common moral order (or what he terms 'conscience collective'). Criminal acts are an attack on society's moral norms and provoke passionate reactions on the individual and the collective level. '[T]he institutions of penality function less as a form of instrumental rationality and more as a kind of routinized expression of emotion, like the rituals and ceremonies of a religious faith' (Garland, 1990: 35). Durkheim's interpretations have been a somewhat neglected item of criminological tradition, partly due to his flawed grasp of penal history (for a useful criminological discussion of Durkheim's thesis see Garland, 1990 and Morrison,

1995). Moreover, until recently, criminological writing has primarily focused on utilitarian, reformative and crime control aspects of punishment rather than on its emotive, passionate and moralizing sides. However, this is gradually beginning to change. Several authors have pointed out the growing importance of expressive justice and of populist penal sentiments in contemporary penality (Garland, 2001a; Young, 2003; Pratt, 2007). Punishment is not only a rational instrumental activity performed by penal experts, but is increasingly (re)entering the public realm, evoking symbols and moral judgements. Punishment in late modern societies has become more vindictive, rather than simply instrumental and rational.

Although these observations may have more leverage in English-speaking countries, the emergence of **penal populism** and what is sometimes referred to as symbolic politics in punishment is a more pervasive phenomenon (Newburn and Jones, 2005; Pratt, 2007). According to Pratt (2007: 3), the rise of penal populism represents 'a fundamental shift in the axis of contemporary penal power', though the extent of this shift differs from society to society. Penal populism has given a far greater voice to those who claim to represent the public – victims' rights movements and anti-crime social movements. Political communication about punishment is increasingly evoking symbols, myths and stereotypes about the 'criminal others' in order to convey its messages effectively in the information-saturated media environments (Newburn and Jones, 2005). Furthermore, in many Western countries, the protection of borders from a perceived 'flood' of foreign populations, and the maintenance of (cultural and territorial) boundaries, has become a central aspect of symbolic politics. And while being tough on crime has for a long time been perceived as a measure of political strength and potency, being tough on *immigrant* crime may carry the promise of double rewards. For example, Hogg (2002) notes the great symbolic and political significance of the *Tampa* incident, and the subsequent draconian measures against asylum seekers in Australian politics. In August 2001, Australian troops were sent on board the Norwegian ship *Tampa* in order to prevent it from landing with 433 refugees it had saved from drowning. The Australian prime minister Howard argued that the response was aimed at preventing Australia from being a 'soft touch' on asylum, and linked the question of refugees to issues of security and terrorism – consequently also winning the national elections.

The urge to protect borders, to draw social boundaries and to 'purify' communities is, as we saw in the previous chapter, a salient aspect of contemporary social control and exclusion. Nevertheless, the drawing of moral boundaries, a traditional concern of criminal law, is today performed not only through the discourse of punishment, but also through practices of banishment and expulsion, exemplified by the *Tampa* incident. Political arguments for stringent immigration reforms regularly evoke images of 'deviant immigrants' and 'deviant asylum seekers'. The law and order discourse is thus intertwined with demands for the reinstatement of a strong nation state with clear assumptions about national identity, otherness and boundaries. As Bauman (2000: 108–9) notes:

> A united front among the 'immigrants', that fullest and most tangible embodiment of 'otherness', promises to come as near as conceivable to patching the diffuse assortment of fearful and disoriented individuals together into something vaguely reminiscent of a 'national community'; and this is one of the few jobs the governments of our times can do and be seen doing.

According to Bourdieu (1999) the opposition between 'natives' and 'immigrants' is gradually obscuring traditional class divisions within societies. The inequalities produced by the neo-liberal economic order are translated into political struggles about 'who has the right to claim all the advantages attached to membership in the national community' (ibid.: 188). Furthermore, in the context of the European Union, the talk about immigrant crime and cultural deviance serves as a vehicle for a debate about the contested nature of European identity (Melossi, 2003). Discussions about terrorism, about unscrupulous trafficking networks and honour killings, play a central role in everyday police work, as well as, on the broader level, in the resurgence of the politics of xenophobia and in renewed debates on the fate of multiculturalism.

The discourse about the deviant immigrant therefore needs to be situated within a broader context of growing global divisions and insecurities. It clearly exemplifies how globalization is not only an 'out there' phenomenon' but simultaneously an 'in here' development' (Giddens, 1998). While influenced by profound global movements and transformations, the immigrant also finds himself or herself situated at the heart of local struggles for safety and security.

The enemy within

Needless to say, the events of September 11th have brought a new dynamics to the above phenomena. The so-called 'war on terror' is a war in which the perceived enemy threat defies the state-like nature of enemies in the previous world orders. The amorphous and diffuse nature of the so-called 'new terrorism' gives rise to allusions to an 'enemy within' or a 'fifth column', thus creating innumerable points of insecurity and suspicion of foreign populations. Various governmental strategies and 'total awareness' campaigns encourage citizens to take active responsibility for managing their safety and scrutinizing their environments for risky individuals. Several highly publicized attacks and attempted attacks on European soil have led to heated discussions about the state of integration of immigrant communities, casting suspicion on whole communities and often resulting in the *'criminalization* of foreignness'. Consequently, the 'war on terror' has, according to a number of analysts, augmented the general fear of strangers and outsiders, leading to repressive measures, particularly against certain groups who are easy to identify and easy to scapegoat, such as asylum seekers, illegal immigrants, and particular ethnic and religious minorities (Welch and Schuster, 2005a).

The metaphor of the war on terrorism has become a driving force behind more restrictive national policies on immigration, detention, policing and surveillance (Cole, 2003). These developments have with renewed urgency brought up the importance of examining the nexus between criminal justice, policing, racism and ethnicity (Philipps and Bowling, 2002). Critics have pointed out the frequent racial bias of police stop and search practices. Obvious UK examples are the increase in the number of Asian people stopped by the police and the tragic incident of the police shooting of the Brazilian Jean Charles de Menezes following the July 7th London bombings. The following *Guardian* report can be seen as one example of the trend:

> The use of counter-terrorism stop and search powers has increased seven-fold since the July 7 attacks on Britain, with Asian people bearing the brunt of the increase, the Guardian has learned. People of Asian appearance were five times more likely to be stopped and searched than white people, according to the latest figures compiled by British Transport police. None of the stops have resulted in a terrorism charge, the force said...
> The force recorded 2,390 stops of Asian people, 35% of the total, and 2,168 of white people, who were 32% of the total. In London Asian people comprise 12% of the population, while white people are 63%.[4]

Through these and similar practices we are witnessing constriction of suspect populations, where innocent people are rendered risk repositories by virtue of sharing some or other of the characteristics of the 'typical terrorist' (Mythen and Walkate, 2006a). The stereotyping of minority populations therefore has an important impact on the everyday practices of social control. The purpose of combating terror can in some contexts also be used as a pretext for increased control of 'unpopular' groups, such as Chechens living in Moscow, who have been targets of aggressive stop and search tactics by the Russian police.

The perception of a non-white terrorist other has been exacerbated by the general association of terrorism with Islam. A series of mediated interpretive practices have associated the fight against terror with broader cultural conflicts

---

[4]Source: http://www.guardian.co.uk/attackonlondon/story/0,16132,1550470,00.html

between native and immigrant populations, often depicting it in terms of a *'clash of civilizations'*, and ultimately designating it as a fight between good and evil. As Mythen and Walklate (2006b: 131) argue, 'media representations of radical Islam have de-humanised and demonised in equal measure, encouraging the public to accept a separation between rational Western citizens and a monstrous terroristic Other'. In that respect, the Islamist terrorist Other represents a meeting point between Garland's criminology of the other and Edward Said's seminal analysis of the 'Oriental other' – a mirror image of the West and a prototype of all that is inferior, irrational and alien. In *Orientalism* (1978/1985) Said examines the discursive structures of language and argues that the very terms of the debate, such as for example 'the West' and 'the Orient', are charged with meanings, defining for example the West as rational and controlled and the Orient as its opposite, as the other. The discursive divisions, alas possibly used also in this book, between 'the West and the rest' and assumptions about otherness are therefore essential for understanding the materiality of global power relations and divisions.

The present suspicion of foreign and foreign-looking populations questions their membership in the communities they live in, designating them the status of outsiders. Hudson (2003: 204) sees the terrorist as a paradigmatic image of the 'monstrous other', whose 'grievance warrants no explanation; he or she is presumed immune to normal human emotions such as compassion, and is oblivious to such reasonable objections as the innocence of victims'. According to Hudson, the 'monstrous others' challenge the limits of the traditional, liberal and communitarian, notions of justice. Contemporary societies are therefore faced with a challenge of

> dealing with people who are so different that they really do seem to be beyond inclusion in the liberal community. This may be because they are literally outside, coming from other countries; or it may be that they appear to be outside our moral and imaginative community, for example serial killers, pedophiles, 'home grown' terrorists…We have to find ways of doing justice to these 'outsiders' as well as readmitting some of those we presently classify as outsiders to the status of insiders. (Hudson, 2003: 204)

In that respect, the (non-white) terrorist other represents a classic example of what Nils Christie (1986) terms a 'suitable enemy' – the kind of target which is easy to recognize, which mobilizes moral indignation and appears to be so powerful, almost satanic, that extraordinary measures are called for.

Some authors have theorized the developments by drawing on the concept of *moral panics*, most notably developed in Stanley Cohen's *Folk Devils and Moral Panics* (2002). Cohen's book offers a detailed account of how members of youth subcultures in south-east England in the 1960s were portrayed as 'folk devils' by the media and the popular press, thereby becoming an embodiment of 'deviance' and a focal point of society's moral concerns. It has been argued that the discourse about bogus asylum seekers exhibits some elements of a trans-national moral panic (Cohen, 2002). Welch and Schuster (2005a), for example, show how exaggerated claims were used to justify an official clampdown on 'bogus' asylum seekers and illegal aliens in the US and the UK, including a greater reliance on detention. The concept of moral panic is useful for revealing the unequal media representations of various social groups and events, and 'the shifting sands of audience responses, ranging from significant social reaction at one extreme to disinterest and non-intervention (or even denial) at the other' (Jewkes, 2004: 85). However, while the concept of moral panics may be useful for unveiling social constructions of 'folk devils', it does not provide the necessary insight into the underlying structural transformations of contemporary penality and its discursive and emotive aspects (see the above discussion on criminology of the other).

Furthermore, there are clearly new elements in the picture, particularly those pertaining to the transnational nature of contemporary security threats as well as the responses to them. Within the global context, racial and religious hatred, as well as fear and solidarity, transcend national boundaries and increasingly gain transnational dimensions. A murder in Netherlands can thus have an impact far beyond its immediate local and national surroundings. Nevertheless, this is still criminologically rather unexplored territory, which we are only beginning to see the contours of. Its origins lie by no means in the present security preoccupations but can be seen as gradually developing with the increasingly extensive reach of global media and communication networks and the emergence of 'transnational public spheres' – discursive arenas that overflow the boundaries of nations and states (Fraser, 2005b).

> In the United States, executions in Texas of Latin-American nationals cause riots in Mexico and South America. In Australia, death sentences for drugs in Singapore or Malaysia are a cause célèbre when Australian nationals are involved, and American media go into states of high arousal for months when an American teen is sentenced to caning [in Singapore]. (Zimring in Chan, 2005: 342)

Valier (2004) points to the emerging new forms of online community and solidarity relating to issues of crime and punishment. In highly publicized murder cases, such as the James Bulger case, these communications may achieve a global reach and form 'transnational vengeful networks' (Valier, 2004: 103). What is important here is that the extraterritorial nature of contemporary communication networks transforms the dynamics of public penal discourse and social belonging, which traditionally were connected to bounded local and national communities.

The new carceral archipelago

The blurring of lines between the foreign and the criminal is evident not only in the political and media discourse, but also in a number of practical measures. Foreign nationals and ethnic minority members constitute a growing proportion of the swelling prison populations of Europe and account for much of the surge in European prison populations since the 1990s (Albrecht, 2000; Melossi, 2003). According to the data provided by the International Centre for Prison Studies, foreigners constitute approximately 32 per cent of the total of the German prison population, 21 per cent of the French and 17 per cent of the Norwegian, whereas numbers for some other European countries are considerably higher, reaching as high as 42 per cent in Belgium and in Greece. The Albanian Ministry of Justice, for example, estimates that the number of Albanian nationals in European prisons is almost the double the Albanian national prison population. Other than indicating the deepening structural social divisions, the development opens up a number of practical problems when it comes to questions of prison governance, language barriers, difficulties in getting adequate legal help, practising religion, maintaining contact with families, etc. Wacquant (1999) goes as far as asking whether today we are witnessing a parallel development in Europe to that seen in the United States in the past three decades with the explosive growth of black and Latino prison populations: '[f]rom this point of view, foreigners and quasi-foreigners would be "the blacks" of Europe' (1999: 216). Similarly, Albrecht (2000: 144) suggests that if European countries displayed the same proportion of racial and ethnic populations as the US, 'it could be concluded on the basis of current knowledge on crime and sentencing patterns that differences in prison rates would disappear'. Looking at the UK example, Coyle (2005: 41) reports that

> [I]n 2002 for every one African Caribbean male in university there were two in prison. Between 1999 and 2002 the prison population in this country increased by 12 per cent while the number of black prisoners increased by over 54 per cent.

To the expanding prison populations one should add a wide net of detention centres for asylum seekers, 'waiting areas' and the like, in order to get a clearer picture of the growing 'carceral archipelago' of foreign populations. The numbers of immigrants and asylum seekers detained in various detention facilities are difficult to estimate. The US and many European countries have stepped up the enforcement of immigration laws and have increased their reliance on detention of illegal immigrants and asylum seekers, particularly in the aftermath of September 11th (Albrecht, 2000; Welch and Schuster, 2005a, 2005b). In the US, there are currently more than 26,000 immigrants being held in detention facilities nationwide.[5] Illegal immigrants, including asylum seekers, can be detained indefinitely if their cases present national security concerns (Welch and Schuster, 2005b). In the United Kingdom, the number of detainees increased from 250 in 1993 to 2,260 about a decade later (Welch and Schuster, 2005a). The duration, the reasons for and the nature of detention vary from country to country and have in many cases changed considerably in the past decade. What is important here is the emerging pattern of *intertwining* of penal and administrative approaches in the control of immigrant populations. Detention can be used as a short-term measure preceding immediate deportation. However, expulsion and deportation can also be used as a form of punishment which is added to, or substituted for, ordinary criminal penalties (Albrecht, 2000: 147). We are therefore witnessing expanding patterns of criminalization of migration. Looking at the US case, Cole (2004) reports that after 9/11 immigration law became a centrepiece of anti-terrorism measures. Immigration law was turned from 'an administrative mechanism for controlling entry and exit of foreign nationals into an excuse for holding suspicious persons without meeting the constitutional requirements that ordinarily apply to preventive detention'.

Although legally detention is only an administrative measure, its application often takes on characteristics of *de facto* penal incarceration, resulting in physical and mental health problems for the detainees (Weber, 2002). These measures clearly often have punitive elements, particularly as the conditions in some detention centres make them almost indistinguishable from, and sometimes worse than, prisons. As the description of one centre in Germany testifies:

> There are bars outside the windows but also inside the cells making it difficult for the detainees to open the windows themselves. Unlike in Britain, where the wardens are mostly employees of private security firms, in Kopernick they are police officers. Detainees have limited room to move and must ask the police for permission to open a window, smoke a cigarette, or fetch hot water for tea – and permission can be (and sometimes is) refused.
>
> There are no work or training possibilities in Kopernick and detainees are only allowed one hour's exercise in the yard. Visitors can be received but are separated from the detainees by Perspex, and from other visitors/detainees by a small partition ... (Welch and Schuster, 2005b: 341–2)

Since the primary purpose of detention facilities is risk-free warehousing of their inmates, rather than their rehabilitation, these institutions represent a good example of actuarial justice and its departure from the old notions of panoptic discipline.

---

[5]http://www.washingtonpost.com/wp-dyn/content/article/2007/02/14/AR2007021401777.html

The inmates of these institutions are not guilty of a crime, but are rather seen as a security risk. The so-called prison industrial complex is therefore expanding to include new categories of 'global deviants', such as immigrants and asylum seekers and the growing number of suspects in the present war on terror. And unlike in ordinary prisons, where state ownership still seems to be the general norm, detention facilities are often run by large international private security firms, such as Wackenhut and Group4Securicor, as well as by smaller local actors (see Chapter 6 for further discussion of privatization of social control). For example, Australia's largest detention centre for illegal immigrants, with 1,200 detainees, is the infamous Woomera desert centre, operated by the Wackenhut corporation.

Adverse detention conditions, combined with the pressures of legal battles to obtain residence permits, have resulted in some highly publicized cases of resistance, for example hunger strikes in Australian detention centres and a number of riots in detention centres in the UK, as well as numerous, less widely reported cases of suicide and self-mutilation. It is important to point out though that there is wide international variation in the nature of asylum and immigration facilities, as well as in the length of the detention periods. Nevertheless, the issue of asylum detention raises a number of central criminological concerns, such as the negative effects of imprisonment, the role of private security firms in the running of detention facilities, and the relationship between liberty and security (Weber, 2002). However, in spite of the fact that there is a growing body of research addressing the issues of asylum and criminalization, one could hardly claim that the issue has reached the criminological mainstream. Mainstream criminology remains preoccupied with outsiders who, at the same time, in many ways are still the 'insiders' of the privileged club of Western citizens. Critics have pointed out the need to address the plight of these 'global outsiders', who find themselves in a double bind – expelled for various reasons from their countries of origin and unwelcome in their countries of destination – thus ending up in non-spaces, such as refugee camps and detention facilities. And just as the war on terror creates its 'state of exception', globalization in general contributes to the creation of 'places in which exception becomes the rule' and which seem to be exempt from the national sphere and its universal system of human rights (Diken and Laustsen, 2005; see also the next chapter).

Cultural dynamics of globalization

'Defending our way of life'

The nature of the immigration debate reveals how the notions of culture and values play a central role in structuring the terms of the debate. Tony Blair's statement, in the aftermath of the July 7th attack in London, about 'the deter-mination to defend our values and our way of life'[6] expresses not only the wish to 'defend the sanctity of home' (Walters, 2004), but also the view of the enemy as the cultural other. However, the notion of 'defending our way of life' has a somewhat incongruous meaning in the era of 'liquid modernity'. What, after all, is 'our way of life'? Can we speak of culture and values as if they are unitary phenomena whose essence it is possible to describe and to defend? In what fol-lows, we shall examine the emerging cultural dynamics of globalization. We shall see how various global flows disturb the, until recently, relatively stable notions of home, culture, national identity and community. What constitutes a society and a community is changing and sometimes becomes unclear. As Morley suggests:

> Certainly, traditional ideas of home, homeland and nation have been destabilized, both by new patterns of physical mobility and migration and by new communication technologies which routinely transgress the sym-bolic boundaries around both the private household and the nation state. The electronic landscapes in which we now dwell are haunted by all man-ner of cultural anxieties which arise from this destabilizing flux. (Morley, 2000: 3)

The extraterritoriality of contemporary technologies and cultural transfers puts into question a number of presuppositions about life and where it is lived. Can we still talk about German, French or Moroccan culture, when the populations of these nations and their lifestyles are increasingly marked by diversity, or when large numbers of their citizens may not live in their native country? Where is the home of immigrants, who build large houses in their countries of origin yet almost never live in them (Morley, 2000)? Similarly, one may wonder where the home of the British 'home-grown terrorist' is. Today, it can no longer be taken for granted that each country embodies its own distinctive culture and that the terms 'society' and 'culture' can be simply appended to the names of nation states (Gupta and Ferguson, 2002: 66). 'The fiction of cultures as discrete, object-like phenomena occupying discrete spaces becomes implausible for those who inhabit the borderlands' (ibid.). For increasing numbers of social groups and individuals, cultural belonging is no longer tied to spatially bounded terri-tories, but follows their transnational patterns of mobility. Migrant diasporas as well as global business and professional elites are the most obvious examples. We saw in previous chapters how various movements of people traverse the planet and how cities today are not only metropolises but in many cases also 'ethnopolises'.

---

[6]Source: http://news.bbc.co.uk/1/hi/uk/4659953.stm

The development has been described by anthropologist Arjun Appadurai (1996) as de-territorialization of culture. The term denotes the 'changing social, territorial, and cultural reproduction of group identity insofar as groups no longer are 'tightly territorialized, spatially bounded, historically unselfconscious, or culturally homogeneous' (1996: 48). Just as contemporary technologies and patterns of living affect the workings of transnational corporations and money markets, so too, the 'loosening of the holds between people, wealth, and territories fundamentally alters the basis of cultural reproduction' (ibid.: 49). Furthermore, as the new channels of communication establish the possibility of having conversations across borders, new forms of cultural, political and religious belonging, as well as displacement, can occur without the physical movement of people (Appadurai, 1996). We live in a world 'where the sitting room is a place where, in a variety of mediated forms, the global meets the local' (Morley, 2000: 2). There are few places today, if any, untouched by this global interconnectedness. The satellite dish has become an essential part of urban landscapes, spreading the gospels of consumerism, youth culture and religion. We are witnessing new forms of cultural expression which are marked, as Castells (1996: 463) puts it, by

> [t]heir ideological and technological freedom to scan the planet and the whole history of humankind, and to integrate, and mix, in the supertext any sign from anywhere, from the rap culture of American ghettoes, mimicked a few months later in the pop groups of Taipei or Tokyo, to Buddhist spiritualism transformed in electronic music.

'The ghetto' is therefore not only an experience connected to physical spaces of exclusion (the 'space of places'), but also a cultural one which, through global travel of images, music and discourses, transcends spatial limits (the 'space of flows').

The role of the nation state, national culture and national belonging becomes increasingly unclear in the light of the global flows traversing its boundaries. It has been argued that the nation state has been to some extent outrivalled as the primary locus of belonging and identity making, both for the nomadic global elites and for the various immigrant diasporas (Appadurai, 1996; Bauman, 2000). 'Religions that were in the past resolutely national now pursue global missions and diasporic clienteles with vigor' (Appadurai, 1996: 22). Furthermore, the elites may identify as much with people of similar lifestyle in other global capitals as with fellow members of the nation state (Bauman, 2000). For them, Ulf Hannerz (2005: 215) points out, 'the big question would be, what can your nation do for you that a good credit card cannot do?'. Nevertheless, any conclusions about the decline of the nation state may be premature – in cultural terms as well as with regard to its potential for surveillance and control of its populace. Rather, I shall proceed to argue, we are seeing a new cultural dynamics, where cultural hybridization and homogenization of the world seem to go hand in hand with various forms of cultural essentialism.

'AlieNation is my Nation'

Crimes committed by immigrants and asylum seekers are often seen as a sign of their 'foreignness' and cultural difference from the native populations. The perception that crime committed by immigrants is somehow caused by the criminogenic traits of their cultural background, by their lack of assimilation and the lack of so-called Western values, has become a common currency of the present political and media debates. The assumption about over-representation of immigrants in crime is a deeply contested issue, particularly since official crime statistics are often unreliable in establishing the actual levels of crime, and instead indicate official reactions to certain acts and populations. However, the notion of culture as criminogenic is by no means a novel approach to explaining crime and deviance (Morrison, 1995). The view of marginalized populations as cultural others, or somehow lacking the value system of the predominant society, had a great influence on the American and British debates about the 'underclass' in the 1980s. At the time, right-wing critics saw the growing numbers of urban (mostly black) poor as marked by promiscuous self-indulgence and as lacking in the work ethic, self-control and family values. This 'breakdown of culture', it was argued, was largely created by the generous welfare provisions, which discouraged its recipients from the economic and cultural participation in mainstream society.

The subsequent critique pointed out not only the moral bias and the empirical inadequacy of the underclass thesis, but also the problematic nature of seeing 'black culture' as fundamentally different from the dominant culture, and economically marginalized ghetto populations as a cultural antithesis of mainstream society. Building on Carl Nightingale's (1993) study of the black Philadelphia ghetto, Young (1999, 2003) argues that the ghetto should not be understood as a place that is essentially different and excluded from the rest of society.

> For instead the ghetto was the apotheosis of the USA. Here is full immersion in the American Dream: a culture hooked on Gucci, BMW, Nike, watching television 11 hours per day, sharing the mainstream culture's obsession with violence, backing, at the time of the study, Bush's involvement in the Gulf War, lining up outside the cinemas, worshipping success, money, wealth and status – even sharing in a perverse way the racism of the wider society. The problem of the ghetto was not so much the process of it simply being excluded but rather one that was all too strongly included in the culture but, then, systematically excluded from its realization. (Young, 2003: 394)

Young points out the problematic nature of simplistic divisions between inclusive and exclusive societies. Rather, late modern societies are witnessing a dual process of forceful cultural engulfment of marginalized populations, as well as their pervasive exclusion ('vomiting up') because of their economic marginalization. Building on Robert Merton's (1938) notion of *anomie,* he argues that '[c]rime occurs where there is cultural inclusion and structural exclusion' (Young, 1999: 394). We shall see in the following chapters that the concept of anomie is not only relevant for understanding the perceived 'normlessness' of delinquent subcultures, but has been used as a salient explanation of globalization's impact on entire societies and social systems (see Chapter 5). Therefore, rather than seeing delinquent ethnic youth as simply under-socialized 'cultural others', their deviance needs to be understood within the context of contemporary global youth culture and its fast, relentless cycle of consumption (Hallsworth, 2005). The inability of normative systems to control the over-production of desires is, one could argue, one of the central problems of late modern consumerist societies.

While widening economic inequalities, globalization also marks the spread of global consumerism and thereby exacerbates the conditions of relative deprivation. The problem becomes acute when it comes to second and third generation immigrants. An important insight emerging from the debates about immigrant crime are the different crime patterns between the so-called first and second (third) generation of immigrant populations (Lea and Young, 1993). The relative deprivation, it is argued, is far greater in the latter group. While their parents may still measure quality of life by old-country standards, the children of immigrants come to see the world according to Western standards, and become acutely aware of their social marginalization. The main problem is therefore not the lack of assimilation into the 'Western values', but quite the opposite, the degree of assimilation (Young, 2003). These are also the populations that were disproportionately hit by the worsening economic and welfare conditions of the 1980s and 1990s. The answers are, as we saw in the previous chapter, sometimes found in the illegal drug economy and its dangerous cycle of violence and conspicuous consumption. However, as Bourgois's (2003) account of El Barrio shows, there is nothing culturally exotic about the young Puerto Rican crack dealers. 'They are not "exotic others" operating in an irrational netherworld. On the contrary, they are "made in America" – highly motivated, ambitious inner-city youths' (2003: 326).

Rather than seeing the figure of delinquent ethnic youth as essentially different from the rest of society, as under-socialized and unassimilated, these findings suggest that the question of their identity is far more complex. While undoubtedly influenced by their cultural roots in the countries of their parents' origin, they are simultaneously marked by various global cultural flows as well as by their social marginalization. The sentiment is beautifully expressed in the title of Ove Sernhede's (2002) book *AlieNation is my Nation*, depicting how Swedish immigrant youth, due to their national marginalization, create alternative identities and belongings through hip-hop and other global cultural connections. Hip-hop represents an alternative path of belonging and identity making, which is rooted neither in their parents' nor in the national culture. In that respect, the identity of immigrant youth, as well as numerous other contemporary cultural expressions, is best captured as a ***cultural hybridity*** – a kind of creolization where new, synthetic cultural forms traverse national boundaries and mix *ad infinitum*. Unlike in traditional or pre-modern societies where, it is commonly argued, identity is more or less fixed and ascribed by birth, now cultural forms are marked by a kind of disembedding similar to that analysed in Chapter 1, where the world is experienced as a 'global village'. For various diasporas and their children, identity is no longer rooted in one homeland, but is marked by a sense of 'two-ness' (Valier, 2003), of belonging to several cultural spheres simultaneously. These are the people who due to their cultural difference have to become 'balancing artists' who have to learn how to stand in two boats simultaneously (Prieur, 2004). Or, as Stuart Hall (1995: 206) writes

> who belong to more than one world, speak more than one language (literally and metaphorically) inhabit more than one identity, have more than one home; who have learned to negotiate and translate between cultures and who, because they are irrevocably the product of several interlocking histories and cultures, have learned to live with, and indeed speak from, *difference* (italics original).

The difficulties of living with difference and the attractions of essentialism

The project of living with difference, and even more so, speaking from difference, is fraught with difficulties. While late modern societies, under the banner of multiculturalism, on the surface appear to be embracing cosmopolitan lifestyles and cultural hybridity, the picture is far more complex in reality. The idea of the 'withering away' of the nation contains an increasing number of contradictions, particularly as we are witnessing a resurgence of nationalism and xenophobia in numerous nation states across the world. Although globalization seems to be a salient aspect of contemporary life, how people react to it in concrete local settings is far from clear cut and predictable. To understand the dynamics of identity constitution in contemporary societies, it should be studied in light of the effects the globalizing processes have on the concrete lives of individuals. In what follows, we shall see that the processes of 'translation' of global structural transformations into local settings often produce seemingly contradictory results. In several contexts, global transformations have met with resistance and with insistence on localism and cultural essentialism.

Globalization, as we saw in Chapter 1, is according to some analysts better understood as glocalization (Robertson, 1995). The term denotes certain reflexivity between the global and the local, between the universal and the particular. Humans are therefore active agents in adapting to and, even more importantly, resisting global change. Not surprisingly, for many groups global transformations in the form of migration, cultural hybridity and neo-liberal ideology are seen as threatening the integrity of their local communities and the survival of their cultural traditions. Consequently, we are seeing a revival of ethnicity through 'the attempt to restore strong, closed definitions of what constitutes a culture' (Hall, 1995: 200). We have seen throughout this book that the defence of the national, fortification of borders and attempts at 'purification' of local communities are taking shape through numerous forms and practices.

The revival of cultural *essentialism* has been, according to Hall (ibid.), one of the surprising responses to global transformations in a variety of cultural settings across the world; in what are usually thought of as both modern and traditional societies. Obvious examples are the revival of nationalism, the resurgence of **racism** and neo-Fascist violence across Europe (Bjørgo and White, 1993) and the massive resistance to migration. Several recent events, such as a series of lethal racist attacks (resembling pogroms) in Russia, the plight of the Roma populations in Central and Eastern Europe, and youth riots in Sydney, have called attention to the victimization of immigrant and minority populations. Nevertheless, while much of the public debates and research on ethnic and immigrant minorities has centred on the issue of their crime-proneness, far less attention has been paid to the issues of their victimization and discrimination (Albrecht, 2000). Yuval-Davis (1997: 193) describes racist discourse (which should be distinguished from various forms of racism) as

> involving the use of ethnic categorisations (which might be constructed around biological, cultural, religious, linguistic or territorially based boundaries) as signifiers of a fixed, determinist genealogical difference of 'the Other'. This 'Otherness' serves as a basis for legitimising exclusion and/or subordination and/or exploitation of the members of the collectivity thus labelled.

The figure of the 'deviant immigrant' is of central importance in the resurgence of racist discourse and the revival of essentialist notions of culture, as it represents the focal symbol of 'the other' as the polluting element in local environments. The racist notions in this context are not focused first and foremost on the perceived biological inferiority of 'the other', but rather on the security threat that he/she represents to the native community. According to Young (2003: 403), the general conditions of insecurity in late modern societies and the stereotypical projections of the minority populations can function as a 'neutralization technique' which exacerbates the use of racially motivated violence.

> The combination of material deprivation and ontological insecurity engenders attempts to secure identity by essentializing one's own culture and endeavouring to harden this identity by blaming and negatively essentializing others. Such a process of dehumanizing the other in order to secure oneself provides a major technique of neutralization with regards to the use of violence. That is if unfairness provides a rationalization for violence, dehumanization permits it.

The rise of Islamic fundamentalism can be seen as marked by an equally exclusive definition of 'culture', in this case with the focus on religion, rather than on race and ethnicity (Hall, 1995). In this perspective, some observers have argued that Islamic fundamentalism can be seen as a form of cultural essentialism emerging as a reaction and a contradiction to the colonizing nature of global flows.

> In opposition to the extraordinarily excluding nature of the system of the global economy and the flow society is the exclusion of all that excludes: concrete fundamentalism as against abstract globalization. In a society in which power and function are organized in flows, the meaning of experience is organized on the basis of potentially irreducible identities. The emergence of fundamentalisms of all kinds in our society is simply the symmetrical mirror of the gradual emptying of content, of experience, of social control, in the arena of flows in which global power networks express themselves. (Borja and Castells, 1997: 13)

Several influential social commentaries, such as Huntington's (1996) clash of civilizations thesis and Barber's (2003) thesis about the cultural clash between 'Jihad' and the 'McWorld', see globalization and various forms of resistance to it as a defining trait of contemporary identity politics. However, although the above-mentioned forms of cultural essentialism are in many ways different in nature, intensity and history – and deserve to be studied as such – they share a common feature: 'their response to globalization is to turn back to more "closed" definitions of culture, in the face of what they see as the threats to cultural identity' (Hall, 1995: 201). In that respect they also represent a collective response to the fragmentation, ambivalence and ontological insecurity of late modernity (Young, 1999).

At the intersection: ethnicity, class and masculinity

One of the main attractions of essentialism may lie in the fact that it attempts to provide ontological security and a sense of unity and superiority; particularly to otherwise marginalized social groups (Young, 1999). For these populations, relative deprivation and the lack of respect lead to an acute identity crisis, resulting in the construction of an essentialist identity based on a 'notion of hardness, a fixity, a difference of self based on gender (e.g. hypermasculinity), ethnicity, "turf" (locality) and age (e.g. gang)' (Young, 2003: 406). Groups that may find themselves stereotypically projected by the mainstream society may construct alternative, essentialized notions of the self. '[T]he othering of the poor becomes utilized by the poor to essentialize themselves' (Young, 2003: 407). An obvious example is the 'hyper-masculinity' of the ghetto youth and their 'self-referral as "nigga", the cult of "badness", the ethical inversion of "motherfucker", "pimp" or "b-boy"' (ibid.).

Bourgois's ethnographic study (2003) of Puerto Rican street-level drug dealers in East Harlem provides a valuable insight into the gender and racial dynamics of social marginalization. Drawing on Pierre Bourdieu's (1980) notion of cultural capital, the author shows how immigrant youth with low economic and cultural capital find an alternative in proudly embracing the macho street culture and the violent underground economy. Due to their, and their parents', lack of education, language and cultural skills, the oppositional street identity becomes an important source of self-respect. Physical strength and macho bravado represent valuable assets in the underground economy. However, this kind of oppositional identity appears dysfunctional and out of place in the white-collar world and in the service economy. The dealers' main problem is therefore not the lack of skills, since they manage to run a complex illegal business system, but the lack of the right kind of skills. For Bourgois's informants, the racism of mainstream society is not experienced only through the sporadic and violent police interventions, but first and foremost through how the 'professional service sector unconsciously imposes the requisites of Anglo, middle-class cultural capital' (2003: 145). The white, feminized professional sector is experienced as an assault on their sense of masculine dignity, and they are violently holding on to atavistic notions of male domination, evident in widespread sexual abuse and domestic violence.

Bourgois's account can be read as a classic example of R. W. Connell's (1995) concept of protest *masculinity*, where violence and sexuality become important sources of identity for men who are otherwise subordinated by class relations and structural inequalities. Connell's seminal work points out that there is no single concept of masculinity, but rather that there are many different masculinities, each supported by different positions of power. And just as we saw in Chapter 2 that globalization has different effects on the lives of women, depending on their social class and nationality, so too, does it have an effect on men and various constructions of masculinity. 'Globalization changes masculinities – reshaping the arena in which national and local masculinities are articulated, and transforming the shape of men's lives' (Kimmel, 2003: 603). However, according to Kimmel, globalization not only changes masculinities. Gender 'becomes one of the chief organizing principles of local, regional and national resistance to globalization, whether expressed in religious or secular, ethnic or national terms' (ibid.). We saw how essentialist notions of cultural and national belonging can be seen as a form of resistance to the global transformations; now, a similar claim is also made with regard to masculinity.

Globalization and massive migration have meant downward mobility for numerous social groups, who had built their notions of masculinity on owner-ship of land and economic independence. With their gradual proletarianization, and the greater economic independence of women from the developing world (see Chapter 2), the malcontents of globalization become also 'mal(e)contents' (Kimmel, 2003). The 'overt symbolic efforts to claim a distinct "manhood" along religious or ethnic lines to which others do not have access and which will restore manhood to the formerly privileged' can be seen as salient traits of extremist groups on the far right (white militias in the US, skinhead racists in Europe) and also in the Islamic world (Kimmel, 2003: 604). For various white extremist groups and militias, the discourses of hate (racism, homophobia, sex-ism, anti-Semitism, etc.) 'provide an explanation for the feelings of entitlement thwarted, fixing the blame squarely on "others" who the state must now serve at the expense of white men' (ibid.: 607; see also Bjørgo, 1997).

However, it may be somewhat problematic to speak of globalization and mas-culinity only when looking at the various illicit and overtly violent identities, such as hyper-masculinity of ghetto drug dealers, Islamic militants and white supremacist groups. In many ways, globalization seems to bring to light the connection between what tend to be seen as separate realms: the allegedly 'pacified' Western masculinity and the violent protest masculinity. The private security companies in the battlefields of Iraq, the conspicuous bodyguards fol-lowing members of the Russian elite and the male-dominated New York Stock Exchange may be equally salient examples. It is probably fair to say though that these topics are rather uncharted territory and are only gradually beginning to be registered on the criminological 'radar'. People's adaptation to global change in their daily lives and in their local environments is far less predictable than may transpire from the sweeping theoretical statements, and demands a thorough empirical investigation. Our purpose here has been to outline some directions that may be relevant for future discussions. We can discern multidi-mensional 'intersections' of different types of social structure having effect at the same time: issues of ethnicity, race and masculinity are simultaneously embedded within social relations of class and, on the global scale, colonialism. Large social transformations, such as globalization, deindustrialization, migra-tion and deterritorialization of culture can be seen as representing a back-ground against which people and social groups as active agents weave their own, unique patterns.

Towards cosmopolitan citizenship?

Throughout this chapter we have explored the issues of ethnicity, culture, national belonging and citizenship. Some of the developments outlined above may seem to indicate a rather pessimistic future for the possibilities of **cosmopolitan** citizenship. The idea that the manifold interconnectedness of the world and cultural globalism could contribute towards a broadening of identities, beyond national boundaries to a world community, is being put to a fundamental(ist) test with many recent developments. And as much as global media are saturated with images of cosmopolitan lifestyles and consumerism, the discourse about the deviant immigrant points to a far more complex reality. Rather than creating 'citizens of the world', the globalizing process seems to be dividing the world; creating and even deepening the 'us' and 'them' mentality – where the political and media discourse insists on the importance of protecting the national from the foreign. Of course, the notion of cosmopolitan citizenship may fit well with the lifestyles of the privileged globally mobile elites whose sense of belonging may be as much with people of similar lifestyles in other global capitals as with their fellow members of the nation state.

In the following chapter we shall see how the war on terror, and the moral panics and insecurity accompanying it, further expose the contested nature of citizenship. In the present, constantly mobile, world order the universalism of law and the Western discourse of human rights are faced not only with the problem of how to accommodate difference, but also with the constant threat of their own suspension. The 'exceptional circumstances' which in a number of cases allow for the circumscription of the rule of law also bring up the question: who are the citizens the law is trying to protect? Is the notion of citizenship flexible enough to accommodate the 'deviant immigrant', or is he/she to be faced with expulsion? Will the new global threats create conditions for cosmopolitan citizenship', or is the present condition even further deepening the 'us' and 'them' mentality?

Summary

Global transformations are contributing to a growing cultural diversity in contemporary societies. Immigrants and foreigners constitute a growing proportion of the population in most Western, as well as in numerous developing countries. In this chapter we saw that the process is at times filled with tension and anxiety, as exemplified by the politically and emotionally charged discourse about immigrant crime. It was suggested that penal discourse about immigrant crime can be seen as a symbolic protection of the national from the threatening foreign elements. The attitudes towards immigrants and immigrant crime are also shaped by the generally more punitive political climate in late modern societies and the proliferation of what Garland (2001a) terms 'criminology of the other'. Questions of migration are increasingly defined as security issues and dealt with by law enforcement and criminal justice measures; this is also evident in the detention of increasing numbers of the immigrant populations. Similarly, refugees and asylum seekers have become a security rather than a humanitarian issue. One of the main objectives of the chapter has been to explore the cultural impact and dynamics of globalization, which has been marked both by increasing cultural hybridity (exemplified by the global reach of hip-hop within minority youth cultures), and by a renewed emphasis on cultural essentialism (exemplified by various forms of nationalism, xenophobia, racism and fundamentalism).

STUDY QUESTIONS

1 In media discussions of crime, ethnicity tends to receive far more attention than other (statistically more salient) categories, such as gender, age and social class. Why are immigrants frequently defined as deviant? What are the problematic aspects of the 'deviant immigrant' construct?

2 What are the criminological consequences of the 'deviant immigrant' discourse for immigrant populations? Who are the criminal others in your country and how are their images constructed?

3 What is cultural essentialism and what are its dangers and attractions?

4 What is deterritorialization of culture and how does it influence your own identity and the patterns of cultural belonging in your country?

FURTHER READING

The notion of the 'deviant immigrant' is discussed in Dario Melossi's (2003) paper in *Punishment & Society*. John Pratt's (2007) *Penal Populism* offers an insight into the increasingly punitive tone of contemporary political, media and popular discourses about crime. European insecurities about migration and asylum are well described in Jef Huysmans's (2006) *The Politics of Insecurity*. Abdelmalek Sayad's (2004) *The Suffering of the Immigrant* represents a rare and valuable non-Western theoretical account of migration, focusing on the migrants' point of view. Sharon Pickering's (2005) *Refugees and State Crime* provides a radical and disconcerting look at the criminalization of asylum seekers. Edward W. Said's (1978/1985) *Orientalism* has become a classic reference on Western perceptions of Oriental others. Scott Poynting and Greg Noble's (2004) *Bin Laden in the Suburbs* offers an account of the Australian moral panics about immigrant crime and the construction of the 'Arab Other'. Basia Spalek's (2002) *Islam, Crime and Criminal Justice* is a comprehensive overview of criminological issues relating to Muslim populations in Britain. Tore Bjørgo and Rob White's (1993) edited volume, *Racist Violence in Europe,* also represents a valuable contribution to the field. The subject of contemporary cultural belonging is too vast to be provided with an overview. However, Pat Jess and Doreen Massey's (1995) textbook *A Place in the World?* is a useful beginning, while David Morley's (2000) *Home Territories* is a valuable read for those more advanced in the subject.

5

Transnational Crime and Crime Wars

Chapter Contents

Security in the era of time–space compression   103

The 'new terrorism'   106

'Security comes first': fear, anxiety and the dynamics
    of risk society   110

Surveillance after 9/11   113

The 'state of exception'   116

The war on drugs   120

Illicit flows and the global criminal economy   123

    Summary   126

    Study questions   127

    Further reading   127

OVERVIEW

Chapter 5 examines the following issues:

- The changing parameters of security and its perceptions in the post-9/11 climate, and the blurring lines between crime and warfare and between internal–external notions of security.
- The discourse about the 'new terrorism' and its implications for crime control.
- The criminological, ethical and humanitarian consequences of the 'war on terror'.
- The notion of risk society and some theoretical perspectives on the growth of surveillance practices.
- The concept of transnational organized crime and law enforcement responses to it.

KEY TERMS

anomie	risk society	surveillant assemblage
failed states	securitization	terrorism
illicit private authority	social construction of crime	transnational organized crime (TOC)
militarization	state of exception	viewer society

Terrorism has been described as the dark side of globalization (Powell in Urry, 2002a). However, we shall see in this chapter that globalization's darker sides are far more complex and pervasive than the popular media focus on Osama bin Laden and his alleged network suggests. Rather than simply representing the 'dark side' of globalization, illicit flows and activities are seen by some as representing its *real* nature (Naim, 2006). Transnational criminal networks have given nourishment to some of the most talked about forms of contemporary 'folk devilry' (Sheptycki, 2000b). The intensified global connectivity and the emerging world of global networks and flows are creating new challenges for the national, local and international authorities trying to control them. The chapter describes the trend towards deterritorialization of illicit activities where state borders are perceived to have an increasingly limited protective capacity. Moreover, we shall examine some broader theoretical aspects of transnational crime and governments' reactions to it. In Chapter 2 we explored the issue of human smuggling and trafficking. This chapter takes, among other subjects, a closer look at drug trafficking and terrorism. The chapter also looks at the emerging new security landscape and further explores one of the central themes of this book: the intricate relationship between freedom and security. In Chapter

3 we saw how gated communities are trading off freedoms of their residents in order to ward off insecurity. We shall extend this topic by looking at the present 'war on terror' and the issues of risk society. The globally distributed images of Guantanamo prisoners and the abuses of Abu Ghraib represent some of the most potent images of the present security climate and its consequences for the nature of social control and the state of civil liberties. They touch upon the main themes discussed in this chapter: the 'war on terror' and the trans-border strategies of combating terror, and the issues of human rights, particularly the changing attitudes towards the use of torture and the right to a fair trial.

Security in the era of time–space compression

The events of September 11th and the subsequent global 'war on terror' have produced and continue to produce innumerable narratives and analyses. They tend to be described as a paradigmatic shift on several levels, and they doubtless deserve the attention of a separate book. My ambitions are therefore far more modest: I aim primarily to discuss the intricate interconnections between 9/11 and the changing notions of globalization, security, risk and crime control. As Calhoun et al. (2002: 18) point out, globalization 'helped to create the conditions for the September 11 attacks; it shaped how people saw them, and, in turn, it will itself be influenced for decades to come not just by the attacks but by responses to them'. The attacks, and the responses to them, are essentially marked by the various forms of global connectivity and interdependence discussed throughout this book: the global media networks, the intensification of international police co-operation and global surveillance technologies, securitization of migration, and the problematization of immigrant–native relations, discussed in the previous chapter.

The events of September 11th tend to be described as global events. New York can be seen as the epitome of the global city, and the fallen twin towers as the supreme symbols of its power (Hayward and Morrison, 2002). Alluding to Castells's space of flows, Bauman (2002) sees the fallen Manhattan towers as the most potent symbolic reminder of the end of the era of space and the annihilation of the protective capacity of space. 'Places no longer protect, however strongly they are armed and fortified. Strength and weakness, threat and security have now become, essentially, *extraterritorial* (and diffuse) *issues that evade territorial* (and focused) *solutions*' (Bauman, 2002: 88; italics original). On a similar note, the National Commission on Terrorist Attacks Upon the United States (2004: 517), established in the aftermath of September 11th, pointed out that in the post-9/11 world threats are defined more by the fault lines within societies than by the territorial boundaries between them. In cases such as terrorism, as well as global disease or environmental degradation, the challenges have become transnational rather than simply international. The events of 9/11 bear according to several commentators, the hallmark of a post-Cold War development where the previous distinctions between internal and external notions of security are obsolete (Bigo, 2000a; Beck, 2002; Flyghed, 2005). The threat of terrorism is today presented as always potentially hidden inside the state, like a 'fifth column', as well as trying to enter from the outside. Speaking about the Chechen terrorist attacks, the Russian defence minister summarized the thought: 'In essence, war has been declared on us, where the enemy is unseen and there is no front.'[1] The military has therefore undergone profound transformations in the post-Cold War era:

> Since the new enemy is within the body of society, there is a need for a new strategic military line; no longer so concerned with interstate conflict, the military has a new set of jobs: anti-guerrilla tactics, prevention of terrorism, drugs prohibition enforcement, and international peace-enforcement are just some of them. (Bigo, 2000a: 83)

In the aftermath of 9/11 and the subsequent series of highly publicized terrorist attacks, such as the ones in Bali, Madrid, Beslan and London, it became obvious that territory can no longer be seen as a guarantee of security. The terrorist threat serves as a constant and potent reminder that 'the domestic populations and ways of life of Western nations in the "zones of prosperity" are no longer effectively sealed off from contemporary global disorders' (Hogg, 2002: 200). In the era of time–space compression, the 'safe' and the 'wild zones' are highly proximate, only a plane ride or an Internet connection apart (Urry, 2002a: 63). The fallen Twin Towers therefore also represent an abrupt influx of the real into the insulated world of the First World citizens. 9/11 can be seen as a violent intrusion which managed to penetrate the 'phantasmic screen' separating the digitalized First World from Third World realities (Zizek, 2002). Violence and devastation that before seemed to be banished to the outskirts of the prosperous West (or at least to the hidden pockets of its poverty-stricken ghettos), now moved inside and attacked its very symbols of power and prosperity. Morrison (2006) argues that, before 9/11, criminology inhabited a 'civilised space', where violence was an extraordinary event and where war was banished outside the boundaries of the Western world. This focus on issues of internal security is no longer sustainable. There is an immediate security interdependence between foreign policy and national and local security concerns, and vice versa. Foreign policy is thus no longer properly 'foreign', as external conflicts often have an almost immediate impact on national and local security strategies. If before the great superpowers 'exported' their conflicts to the battlefields of the developing

---

[1]Source: www.msnbs.msn.com/id/5881958/print/1/displaymode/1098/

countries, now the Third World's conflicts are being felt in the very centres of power and development. Although this, in itself, is not a new phenomenon – think of the often repeated phrase that 'the Algerian war is not over in France' – it now has a new momentum. One obvious example was the 2006 controversial publication of the prophet Muhammad cartoons in some Scandinavian newspapers, the consequence of which was painfully and immediately felt in the form of riots, boycotts, embassy attacks and protests across the world.

The new hybridity of internal and external notions of security is also connected to more profound transformations in the nature of contemporary political conflicts and warfare. According to a number of analysts the global security landscape has undergone a profound transformation in the aftermath of the fall of the Berlin Wall. Whilst during the Cold War the oppositions between the West and the Soviet bloc were clear-cut and rigid, we are now faced with much more diffuse security constellations. In his influential book, *The Transformation of War* (1991), military historian Martin van Creveld argues that we have been witnessing a transformation in the nature of warfare where wars no longer are waged by state armies, fighting for territorial control, but rather by terrorist, guerrilla and paramilitary groups and other non-state formations. The majority of armed conflicts today are fought *within* states, not between states (Human Security Report, 2005). These so-called 'low intensity conflicts', which despite their name can produce tragic consequences, are mostly fought in poor countries where weak governments confront small and ill-equipped opponents (ibid.). On the other hand, the recent wars in Iraq, Kosovo and Afghanistan have been described as 'asymmetric warfare', where high-tech armies and US-led 'coalitions of the willing' combat militarily far weaker opponents. In asymmetric warfare, a military superpower finds itself pitted against a non-state entity with modest military resources. The enemy's strength lies in its ability to merge with global civil society and to threaten state security primarily by endangering and spreading fear in the civilian population, rather than inflicting military damage. Terrorism is therefore a tactic that militarily weak political groups employ against their strong opponents.

Consequently, there has been not only a blurring of boundaries between internal and external notions of security, but the boundaries between crime and war also become increasingly hard to discern. 'Conventional resolutions of global conflict such as war state-against-state have been replaced...by crime as warfare, and warfare as crime control' (Findlay, 2003: 234). Ethnic, religious and other conflicts in places like Russia, Central Asia, West Africa and parts of Latin America are increasingly intermingled with drug trafficking, people smuggling and other forms of organized crime (Hogg, 2002: 196). If before it was still possible to distinguish between crime and war, and military and police domains (although the lines never have been clear cut), today, this distinction is becoming difficult. We have thus been witnessing a trend 'toward "criminal justice *militarization*," in which social relations are redefined through a convergence of militaristic, police, and penal contexts' (Brown, 2005: 985). 'Even while it is being argued that terrorism, organized crime and the Mafia are on the rise, which demands a reply from the armed forces, police are moving into military domains' (Bigo, 2000a: 84). The establishment of the US Department of Homeland Security can be seen as a response to the conflation of internal and external forms of security, which seeks to enhance communication and information sharing between different security agencies, including the FBI and the CIA (Ericson, 2007: 54). 'The view is that borderless threats require borderless law enforcement across organizational entities nationally and internationally, and across categories of citizens and non-citizens' (ibid.).

However, traditionally, war has received little criminological attention (for exceptions see Nikolic-Ristanovic, 1998; McLaughlin, 2001; Jamieson, 2003; Morrison, 2006). This omission becomes increasingly problematic in light of recent developments. The criminologists' unease with the language of war, international security and terrorism coincides with the conceptual placement of terrorism in the domain of warfare rather than crime control. The point here is that this conceptual placement has important political implications for state responses to acts of terror. As a crime, terrorism falls under the auspices of law enforcement agencies and the due process of law, whereas as an act of war, it merits a military response. The issue was intensely debated in the aftermath of 9/11, as is evident in the following statement by the US president:

> I know that some people question if America is really in a war at all. They view terrorism more as a crime, a problem to be solved mainly with law enforcement and indictments… [But I state] The terrorists and their supporters declared war on the United States, and war is what they got. (George Bush, cited in Morrison, 2006: 31)

The well-known results were the consequent US invasion of Afghanistan and Iraq and, recently, Somalia. Terrorist organizations have, by implication, become parties which can declare war.

The 'new terrorism'

When writing about **terrorism**, one of the first obstacles we encounter is that there is no one widely accepted definition of the phenomenon. The contested nature of the concept of crime (discussed in Chapter 1), becomes particularly evident when it comes to terrorism. Discussions about the meaning of terrorism can therefore give us a useful insight into the processes of labelling and *social construction of* *crime*. The often repeated saying that 'one man's terrorist is another man's freedom fighter' has a long historical resonance. Numerous countries, such as Israel, Kenya, Cyprus and Algeria, were founded on nationalist resistance movements which relied heavily on urban guerrilla warfare against colonial powers (Hoffman, 2005). The boundaries between terrorism and legitimate political action are therefore complex and unclear, as are the boundaries between terrorism and warfare. Civilian infrastructure was considered a legitimate target by the Allies during the Second World War, most notably during the bombings of Dresden, Nagasaki and Hiroshima. Furthermore, in the 20th century, the term terrorism came to be used to denote not only anti-state violence but also state-sponsored forms of terror such as extra-judicial executions, kidnapping, torture and violent gangs (ibid.). These historical examples tend to be overlooked today when the main focus of the terrorist discourse seems to be on 'evil' individuals and networks, rather than states terrorizing their own populations.

Generally speaking, terrorism can be described as 'the use of violence and intimidation to disrupt or coerce a government and/or an identifiable community' (Mythen and Walkate, 2006a: 381). Commonly, the creation of fear and intimidation is seen as one of its central means and objectives. However, terrorism is an extremely elusive concept and can cover a variety of activities. In the aftermath of the 9/11 attacks numerous countries expanded their legal definitions of terrorism, criminalizing a range of preparatory acts and activities. Mathiesen (2003: 447) thus points out that the EU's definition of 'terroristic purpose', which also includes 'unduly compelling governments or international organizations to execute or to abstain from executing an act', can cover a range of legitimate political protests. Are Greenpeace activists who chain themselves to nuclear power plants terrorists? The politically contested nature of the phenomenon is also revealed in the fact that the UN has consistently failed to agree on its definition (Saul, 2006). The term terrorism tends to be used as a political and an ideological weapon rather than as an analytical concept. As Hoffman (2005: 260) suggests:

> Terrorism is a pejorative term. It is a word with intrinsically negative connotations that is generally applied to one's enemies and opponents, or to those with whom one disagrees and would otherwise prefer to ignore … Hence the decision to call someone or label some organization 'terrorist' becomes almost unavoidably subjective, depending largely on whether one sympathises with or opposes the person/group/cause concerned.

Terrorist violence may be a result of domestic or international political struggles. This chapter will focus primarily on the latter, although domestic terrorism can be far deadlier. According to some estimates (and keeping the difficulties of definition and measurement in mind), 239 of the 327 terrorist attacks committed in the United States between 1980 and 1999 were perpetrated by domestic groups, most of them aligned with the extreme right (Human Security Report, 2005). The Oklahoma City bombing in 1995 was the deadliest terrorist attack committed on the US soil before 9/11, killing 168 people and injuring over 800. Nevertheless, it is international terrorism which is at present commanding an enormous amount of political and public attention and has served as a justification of two major wars. Interestingly, international terrorism has killed fewer than 1,000 people a year, on average, over the past 30 years, although there has been arguably a significant increase in serious attacks in recent years (ibid.). It may therefore appear that international terrorism is, like several other forms of crime discussed in this book, more feared and receives more media and political attention than its objective risk justifies.

One could argue that the present focus, verging at times on obsession, serves as a channel for other political debates and insecurities. Like the issue of trafficking, international terrorism seems to crystallize a series of fears and insecurities connected to globalization and modernity. Contemporary terrorism tends to be described both as a product of globalization, due to its use of global technologies, migration, communication and financial systems, as well as essentially an anti-globalization movement which aims to reinstate the importance of traditional identities. The politically charged and proliferating discourse about terrorism seems to serve as a vehicle for debating contemporary political conflicts, influentially articulated for example in Samuel Huntington's (1996) **clash of civilizations** thesis and in Benjamin Barber's (2003) McWorld vs. Jihad argument. Criminology has traditionally given little attention to the question of terrorism (see for example McLaughlin, 2001; Deflem, 2004). However, few would deny today the relevance of international terrorism for our rapidly changing notions of security, the rule of law and human rights. The pervasive climate of insecurity affects many aspects of everyday life in the Western world and is tipping the balance between state control and civil liberties not only in matters directly related to terrorism, but also in other fields of social control. As we saw in the previous chapter, the morally charged discourse about terror has been essential in constructing the terrorist as the 'monstrous other' and has been an important aspect in the construction of the 'deviant immigrant'. The dangers of labelling and strategies of exclusion through discourse become particularly apparent when discussing control measures to combat terrorism (Mythen and Walkate, 2006a).

One of the prevailing conventional wisdoms today is that we are facing a radically new kind of terrorism. Walter Laqueur (2001) influentially argues that this 'new terrorism' marks a shift from the previous terrorist organizations, such as the IRA and other nationalist movements, towards 'clusters of fanatics bent on vengeance and simple destruction'. These groups are marked not only by their alleged monstrous ruthlessness, but also by their catastrophic potential due to the ability to obtain weapons of mass destruction, their religious fervour, and the ability to act on the global rather than on the national level. They invoke a new imagery of the enemy which is transnational, redistributed, without a centre and can strike anywhere in the heart of the civil society. The terminology of global networks and fluids has been used extensively to describe contemporary terrorist threats. Urry (2002a: 66), for example, conceptualizes al-Qaeda as a global fluid, 'made up of very different self-organizing elements that regularly change their shape, form and activities'. Al-Qaeda has even been described as the 'McDonalds of terrorism' (Murdoch, 2004) – being a 'global brand', using the media to its advantage and assuming a franchise form not unlike the ones used in the contemporary business world.

The events of September 11th tend to be seen as 'global events' not only because of the trans-national perception of the emerging new threats. 'The television pictures from that day – transmitted immediately around the globe – have arguably become the most visually arresting and memorable news images ever seen, evoking countless cinematic representations' (Jewkes, 2004: 27). The events of 9/11, the Beslan tragedy, the Bali bombings and others aimed through their spectacularity to capture the attention of the global media and addressed themselves to global audiences, rather than just trying to capture the more modest national headlines. As such, these events are a product of a world of global media and information flows, where 'the camera may be the most effective weapon with which to retaliate, bringing violence of an extraordinary intensity into the living rooms of global audiences' (Ferrell et al., 2005: 8). These events clearly show how global communication networks, the so-called mediascapes, crucially shape contemporary perceptions of crime and communication about crime (see also Jewkes, 2004). The spectacular is shared across the world, which can now follow the bizarre details of Michael Jackson's, Saddam Hussein's and O.J. Simpson's trials. But to gain insight into these tragic events, one needs to be aware of the communicative aspects of these actions. These actions designate 'the world' as their audience. Although sometimes, as in the case of Beslan, the political objectives of the perpetrators may be primarily national, the spectacularity of the actions clearly aims to get the attention of the global media. Perhaps due to their exclusion from the normal channels of political action, engaging in the game of getting such attention presents itself as an answer. In that respect, the attacks can be seen as a form of political communication (Bjørgo, 2005) where, due to the extremely selective and sensationalist nature of the contemporary media landscape, only extreme events are able to capture the attention of global audiences.

Using the global media and communication networks to their advantage is therefore not only an option of the globally powerful. The globally distributed images from Abu Ghraib unveiled the brutality of a military superpower, despite its savvy in 'public relations' management. Moreover, cyberspace has become an important locus of political communication and identity formation, particularly for younger populations in developing countries as well as for various militant Islamic groups (see discussions in Chapter 7). And although various radical Muslim identities tend to be described as primitive and uncivilized by the various 'clash of civilizations' theses, they are sustained by distinctly global networks of communications (Internet, global television networks, etc.) and patterns of living (immigrant diasporas and global travel). We live at a time when the informational and mediated nature of social relations transcends the old notions of the Panopticon (Bauman, 2000). Power is about speed, lightness and distance which, as Urry (2002a: 60) notes, is true both for the global elites as well as for those trying to resist them, such as anti-globalization protesters and terror networks.

'Security comes first': fear, anxiety and the dynamics of risk society

The main criminological relevance of the present focus on terrorism lies in the changing dynamics of social control and the intensified search for security. Although the casualties of terrorist attacks may have been relatively low on a world basis, few would deny that the phenomenon has had a profound effect on the way we live our daily lives, particularly, as we saw in Chapter 2, on the way we travel. Today, an ordinary international flight almost invariably involves several types of screening, luggage checks, identity checks and even a body search. Procedures that before were designed to check particularly suspicious individuals and locations are now moving to the mainstream and becoming a common occurrence. Not only knives, explosive substances and sharp objects, but also lipsticks, baby bottles and other mundane objects have become bearers of risks which need to be neutralized.

Globalization has for a long time been associated with insecurity, due to neo-liberalism's rampant individualism, the demise of the welfare state, and the proliferation of various forms of global risks. In Chapter 1, we suggested that the narrative of the *risk society*, initially developed by Ulrich Beck (1992), can offer a useful insight into the emerging dynamics of insecurity. Beck describes contemporary societal organization as permeated by the constant awareness of various threats, which are essentially global in their nature, thus producing communities organized around the discourse of safety and fear. Beck then expanded his risk society thesis in the aftermath of the September 11th attacks and framed the issue of terrorism and responses to terrorism in terms of a 'world risk society' (2002: 41).

> [W]orld risk society does not arise from the fact that everyday life has generally become more dangerous. It is not a matter of the *increase*, but rather of *de-bounding* of uncontrollable risks. The de-bounding is three-dimensional: spatial, temporal and social.

De-bounded risks are no longer linked to specific geographic locations and national boundaries; moreover, they can have unlimited temporal dimensions (think of the future dangers of nuclear waste and global warming), and it is difficult to delineate their social dimensions in terms of causes, affectedness and responsibility.

In the context of risk society, the objective of combating possible risks, rather than more positive goals of social justice, becomes a major social factor shaping the political cultures of Western nations and their strategies of social control. Today, there seem to be almost no limits to how much security we can crave (Zedner, 2000), and consequently, how much control, crime and deviance we can produce (Christie, 2004; Ericson, 2007). The self-supporting dynamic of risk society is evident in the following report about the latest 'security strategy' by the British security services.

> A system sending email terror alerts to the public is being launched by security chiefs at MI5. People will be able to register on the MI5 website to receive updates when the threat level changes ....Plans to extend the service to sending text messages to mobile phones are also being considered ....The level of the terror threat to the UK is assessed by the government's Joint Terrorism Analysis Centre. The current threat is set at the second highest level, 'severe', which means an attack is considered 'highly likely'. In November, Dame Eliza, MI5's director general, warned the terror threat was 'serious' and 'growing', and that 1,600 individuals were being kept under surveillance. Steve Aukstakalnis works for a company in the United States, Alerts USA, which provides a similar service. (BBC, 2007)[2]

It can, of course, be asked whether this constant information flow in fact increases people's security or increases their sense of insecurity? Fear and anxiety have a surprising ability to renew themselves and to create a momentum of their own. The contemporary cultural climate has been, even before the present focus on terror, described as a 'culture of fear' (Furedi, 2002). In a world obsessed with all kinds of danger – from environmental dangers and germ warfare to health risks and risks of crime – safety comes to dominate the public discourse and the way we live our lives. Fear of crime has thus become one of the central political, media and criminological concerns in the past decades. This is by no means a development specific to the post-9/11 climate, but has rather been

---

[2]http://news.bbc.co.uk/2/hi/uk_news/6242883.stm

described as a pervasive trait of late modern societies (see the discussion of ontological insecurity in Chapter 1). Consequently, reducing fear and insecurity has become almost as important an issue as reducing crime itself, as is exemplified by various 'reassurance policing' initiatives (Zedner, 2000). This line of thought sees insecurity as a politically and socially constructed phenomenon. Fear and insecurity are not objective entities but emotional and political categories which are shaped by politicians, governments, the media and various experts. Furthermore, as we shall see in Chapter 6, risk and insecurity represent a great financial opportunity for a series of private security providers. Crime control has become a commodity, and the industry has received a great boost in the post-9/11 climate of insecurity.

According to Lucia Zedner (2000, 2003), pursuit of security, rather than more narrowly defined crime control, has become a vital justification of numerous forms of social control in contemporary societies, from the expansion of surveillance cameras, intensification of airport and border controls and extended powers of national and international security agencies to the enormous growth in the private security industry. However, the quest for security is also full of paradoxes, for example that 'security promises reassurance but in fact increases anxiety; that security is posited as a universal good but presumes social exclusion; that security promises freedom but erodes civil liberties' (Zedner, 2003: 158). Safety and insecurity are subjective phenomena, often disconnected from objective probabilities of risk and victimization. Typically, elderly women living alone feel far more insecure than young men who frequent pubs, although their objective risks of victimization are quite the opposite (Zedner, 2000). Furthermore, the prosperity and relative safety of a country do not necessarily protect its citizens from insecurity; in fact, they may feel less secure than citizens of relatively more volatile countries.

The trend towards **securitization** has become a prominent trait in several aspects of contemporary governance, including the governance of crime. We saw, for example, in Chapters 2 and 4 how issues of migration and asylum are increasingly framed as threats to national security, rather than as humanitarian problems. The burgeoning security discourse is, as Huysmans (2006: xi) points out, a 'political technique of framing policy questions in logics of survival with a capacity to mobilize politics of fear in which social relations are structured on the basis of distrust'. The rationality of risk society runs to some extent opposite to the classic neo-liberal canon of minimal state intervention and expenditure (see discussion in Chapter 6). As Beck (2002: 47) reports

> When asked whether the $40 billion that the US government requested from Congress for the war against terrorism didn't contradict the neoliberal creed to which the Bush administration subscribes, its spokesman replied laconically: 'Security comes first.'

The EU's anti-terror and other security efforts have enhanced its state-like qualities (Mathiesen, 2006) and have become a vital motor of EU integration, resulting in a number of developments, such as the European arrest warrant, European evidence warrant, the appointment of the so-called 'Terror Tsar' and the money laundering directive.

Directly related to the tendency towards securitization is the growing urge towards **criminalization** of various types of social problems and unwanted behaviour. Late modern societies are, according to Simon (1997), being 'governed through crime'. In school, family, welfare, residential and other areas, there is an increasing tendency towards government intervention and distribution of blame. Instead of seeing problematic behaviours as a question of social policy, they tend to be defined as security and criminal issues. According to Ericson (2007: 1), new laws are enacted 'to criminalize not only those who actually cause harm, but also those merely suspected of being harmful, as well as authorities who are deemed responsible for security failures'. This 'precautionary logic' is a further step in the escalation of risk thinking. While traditionally, risk management represents an acceptance of certain levels of risk, the precautionary logic no longer dares to take chances and aims to eliminate risk altogether. 'While in many contexts, including in law, uncertainty has conventionally spelled innocence, within precautionary logic uncertainty is a reason for extreme pre-emptive measures' (Ericson, 2007: 23).

Surveillance after 9/11

Contemporary counter-terrorism responses often seem to chime with George Orwell's dystopian vision of a 'Big Brother' surveillance society, as well as with the concept of panopticism, developed by Michel Foucault (see Chapters 2 and 3; Lyon, 2006). Orwell's famous novel *Nineteen Eighty-Four* portrays a society permeated by the fear of 'Big Brother'. It is a society where neighbours spy on each other and where every sound can potentially be overheard and every movement scrutinized. Published in 1949, the book was written as an allusion to the totalitarian regimes of Nazi Germany and the Soviet Union, yet it seems to retain considerable relevance for the contemporary condition. The expansion of various technologies for monitoring human behaviour, such as the widespread use of video surveillance, the Internet, geographic information and monitoring systems, and the innumerable databases and electronic trails which have become a part of our daily lives, all keep plenty of life in the 'Big Brother' metaphor. Further momentum today is gained from the intensive use of information and communication technologies and their capacity 'to combine different surveillance technologies into a *surveillant assemblage*, yielding new forms of knowledge and control' (Ericson, 2007: 52; see also Chapter 2).

However, it would be misleading to see the events of September 11th and the subsequent terrorist attacks in Europe as the main cause of the phenomenon. As Lyon (2003a: 4) points out, the 'attacks brought to the surface a number of surveillance trends that had been developing quietly, and largely unnoticed, for the previous decade and earlier'. Contemporary surveillance measures therefore have a long history, often stemming from the commercial sector rather than the state, as seemed to be Orwell's view. Surveillance is today inscribed into the very grain of our everyday lives. Perhaps a more appropriate metaphor for this development would not be 'Big Brother' but rather lots of 'little brothers' and 'sisters' who watch and record innumerable aspects of our lives. One only has to think of the personal information about us possessed by insurance companies, banks, online and off-line shops and other businesses. Commercial entities employ 'data-mining' technologies to obtain information about their customers and devise marketing campaigns. When we surf and shop on the Internet our clicks are carefully monitored as they provide valuable commercial information about our habits and preferences. Whether we are aware of the fact or not, databases create identities for each one of us – so-called 'data doubles' (Lyon, 2003a) – and in some ways, these doubles are more important than our real selves. Without the information recorded in databases, an individual could not vote, get a bank loan or a driving licence. Even more importantly, our 'data doubles' are analysed by various commercial and state authorities and are of vital consequence for the kind of treatment we receive from them. Surveillance thus functions as a form of 'social sorting', as a means of placing people into social classes and categories (Lyon, 2003a, 2006).

The state, nevertheless, retains a strong presence and has increased its appetite for information in the post-9/11 climate. According to Lyon (2003a), we have witnessed globalization, intensification and integration of surveillance practices. The integration or merging of state and commercial surveillance capabilities, always a latent possibility and a frequent dystopian vision, has recently become a more palpable reality. New European legislation on data retention, for example, requires telephone companies and Internet service providers to keep records of calls, text messages, emails and Internet connections for up to two years.[3] In the US, the Pentagon and the Department of Homeland Security created the Total Information Awareness Program, which under the slogan 'Knowledge is power', aimed to extend the commercial data-mining techniques to encompass almost every conceivable aspect of life and communication (Lyon, 2003a; Ericson, 2007). The electronic trails, to which we usually attach little

---

[3]http://news.bbc.co.uk/2/hi/europe/4527840.stm

importance, thus gain a sinister potential in the present security climate. However, although the events of 9/11 have served as a catalyst for the introduction of new surveillance technologies across the world (Zureik and Salter, 2005) there are nevertheless considerable national differences in the developments, which merit detailed comparative analysis. There are also substantial differences between countries with regard to the attitudes towards, and the regulation of, surveillance practices. At one point, a data-sharing agreement that provided US authorities with 34 pieces of information on airline passengers coming from Europe was declared illegal by the European Supreme Court due to the inadequate US privacy regulation. The argument that 'data protection is offender protection' at the moment appears to have less resonance in the European climate, although the boundaries of privacy are constantly moving.

Some critics have tried to moderate the dystopian visions of the Big Brother society by arguing that the perception of gradual erosion of civil liberties may be exaggerated and overly pessimistic (Waddington, 2005), while others have pointed out that people are not simply passive objects of the surveillant gaze, but often actively participate in the process. The Big Brother metaphor becomes somewhat inapt in societies where, on a TV show with the same name, individuals willingly put themselves under the 24-hour observation of global audiences, and the global audiences seem to cherish the occasion. Contemporary society has been described as a '*viewer society*', fostered by the culture of television, cinema and the Internet (Mathiesen, 1997; Lyon, 2006). As things once kept private become open to the public gaze – think of MySpace and YouTube – so it 'seems of less consequence that this or that bit of once-protected personal data is disclosed' (Lyon, 2006: 36). The erosion of privacy is therefore not only a result of repressive government intervention in the lives of its citizens, but also a result of a cultural change through which citizens themselves willingly give up their privacy (see the discussion on the Internet and the 'synopticon' in Chapter 7).

Furthermore, individual citizens and the private sector are being actively enlisted in the task of combating contemporary global risks. A Texas governor has for example proposed using remote surveillance cameras that would be connected to the Internet, allowing US citizens the opportunity to help the state in border surveillance.[4] US citizens are also actively encouraged by their government to take part in efforts to combat terror and to 'become the eyes and ears' of law enforcement agencies (Andrejevic, 2006). The Department of Homeland Security has published a 200-page manual entitled *Are You Ready? An In-Depth Guide to Citizen Preparedness* (see Ericson, 2007). The department also sponsors an Internet site www.ready.gov which provides risk information for citizens, children and businesses. We are not

---

[4]http://news.bbc.co.uk/2/hi/world/americas/5040372.stm

only being watched, as the Big Brother and panopticon metaphors would have it, but are also actively watching ourselves (Yesil, 2006). The development is a good example of the so-called responsibilization strategy (discussed further in Chapter 6) and it resonates with Foucault's (1977) argument that those who are under surveillance may internalize that knowledge and through self-governance conform to social norms. The development is therefore also a question of cultural change, where citizens internalize the norms of surveillance society. Perhaps one day we might even feel unsafe when moving in places without CCTV cameras and mobile phones? Perhaps some of us already do?

The 'state of exception'

The present 'war on terror', and its climate of insecurity, clearly shows us that globalization is first and foremost an ethical challenge (Bauman, 2002: 17). The surveillance practices which have arisen in the shadow of the war on terror raise a number of ethical issues regarding how far a society can go in the name of security and how much liberty it is prepared to sacrifice. How much intrusion into the lives of its citizens is justifiable in order to preserve the stability of the social order? Should the information about what kind of books we borrow from our libraries be used for intelligence purposes, or are there limits which cannot be crossed in the name of security? Discussion of security and its justifications has been a recurring theme for students of crime control and criminal justice, but the dilemma gains new dimensions and immediacy in the present cultural climate. As Hudson (2003) points out: 'In contemporary Western societies adherence to long-held principles of justice is endangered by excessive concern with safety'. In *Justice in the Risk Society* (2003), the author takes up a number of central ethical dilemmas regarding the dichotomy between risk and justice, some of which have emerged throughout this book: zero tolerance policing, the extensive use of video surveillance and, not least, the various methods currently used in the war on terror. The goal of security has become a public good which seems to need almost no justification (Zedner, 2003) and penal policy seems to be increasingly dominated by the theme of public protection, rather than the aim of enhancing social justice.

I argued previously that the language of war, and the perception of terrorists as warring parties, in itself carries a conceptual shift away from traditional principles of criminal justice and due process of law. The trend towards securitization and precautionary logic have been particularly pronounced in relation to the fight against the 'new terrorism'. The war on terror has been described as a 'stateless war' (Bauman, 2002) where both sides 'militate against the imposition of constraints on the newly gained extraterritoriality of the skies or the freedom to ignore or push aside the "laws of nations" where such laws feel inconvenient for the purpose at hand' (ibid.: 93). In the aftermath of 9/11 numerous countries not only intensified their surveillance measures, but also enacted more severe legislation on immigration and on the detention of terrorist suspects, and gave greater powers to the police, thus tipping the balance between civil liberties and the power of the state in favour of the latter. It is important to keep in mind that this erosion of civil liberties and the proliferation of surveillance practices has disproportionately targeted certain minority groups, as pointed out by Cole (2004: 5) in his account of the US developments:

> Since September 11, we have repeatedly [done precisely the opposite], sacrificing the rights of minority groups – noncitizens, and especially Arab and Muslim noncitizens – in the name of majority's security interests. The government has selectively subjected foreign nationals to interviews, registration, automatic detention, and deportation based on their Arab or Muslim national origin ...

According to Ericson (2007: 24), 'new laws are enacted and new uses of existing laws are invented to erode or eliminate traditional principles, standards, and procedures of criminal law that get in the way of pre-empting imagined sources of harm'. The rationality behind the development is that the 'legal order must be broken to save the social order' (ibid.: 26). Assertions of the links 'between international terrorism and conventional transnational crime, and that, for example, drug traffickers and distributors support terrorists, makes increased severity all the more justifiable' (Ruggiero, 2003: 32).

Analysing the changing legal landscape, Italian philosopher Giorgio Agamben (2005) has provided an influential reference by describing it as a *'state of exception'*. Drawing heavily on the work of Michel Foucault and Carl Schmitt, Agamben argues that the state of exception has become a normal paradigm of contemporary government. The concept of the 'state of exception' has enjoyed a remarkable popularity in the post-9/11 security climate as it can obviously cover a number of recent phenomena, such as the issue of extraordinary renditions, the concept of 'enemy aliens', detention of terror suspects without trial and the use of torture, to name just a few. Guantanamo Bay has perhaps more than any other institution come to exemplify the meaning of exceptionalism. The geographical placement of the camp and the language of 'enemy combatants', coined by the US government, have all served to bend the ordinary rules of justice (Cole, 2004). Guantanamo can be seen as a kind of 'non-space', a territory excluded from the US territory, where the usual rules of national and international law do not apply. The US government presented an argument that since al-Qaeda is an organization and not a state, the rules of the Geneva

Convention do not apply to al-Qaeda combatants. Guantanamo prisoners – 395 as of this writing, although about 775 have been held at the camp – have been in effect banned from the social order and set outside the law, reduced to what Agamben terms 'bare life'. Their inhumane treatment is a result of a legal 'black hole' they find themselves in, placed outside the legal system and stripped of its most basic protection and human rights (Cole, 2004).

The meaning of exception is, of course, manifold, and in the present security climate the exceptionalism can be felt on several levels: legal, cultural, political and, not least, social. Again, this is a topic too broad to be covered here. We shall therefore limit discussion to one more example of contemporary exceptionalism: the changing attitudes towards torture. The use of torture is by no means a novelty in the history of 'civilized' nations, although its uses have often been described by euphemisms, such as the 'special procedures' used by France in Algeria, 'moderate physical pressure' against Palestinians in the occupied territories, and 'depth interrogations' used by the British in Northern Ireland (Cohen, 2006). In 2005, Russia was for the first time found guilty of torture in Chechnya by the European Court of Human Rights, although the number of cases filed against it runs much higher.[5] The tragic face of torture was famously revealed by the Abu Ghraib photos, and its bureaucratic endorsement by the Bush administration became clear in August 2002 with the leak of an internal US Justice Department memo. The memo argued that when acting as commander-in-chief, the US president is not bound by national and international laws banning the use of torture (see Greenberg and Dratel, 2005). According to Cohen (2006), we have been witnessing a paradigm shift in the US, which put a high premium on the ability to get quick information from captured terrorists while giving less weight to the rights of subjects and the niceties of international law. As Cofer Black, director of the CIA's Counterterrorist Center, put it in Congressional testimony: 'after 9/11, the gloves come off' (Cole, 2004: xviii). In the context of asymmetric warfare, so-called 'human intelligence', rather than advanced weaponry, becomes of primary importance, consequently increasing the pressure for 'more efficient' interrogation techniques. The Bush administration has attempted to evade the Geneva Conventions and to narrow the legal definition of torture, by justifying the use of various coercive interrogation techniques euphemistically described as 'torture lite' (Cohen, 2006). The interesting point here is that implosion of the rule of law has been, as often before in history, orchestrated by some of the smartest lawyers and members of the legal establishment (Greenberg, 2006: 14). However, the paradigm shift with regard to torture has not been confined to the corridors of the Pentagon and the US Justice Department, but has been far more profound. '"Time to Think About

---

[5]http://news.bbc.co.uk/2/hi/europe/4295249.stm

Torture", said *Newsweek* (5th November 2001)' (Cohen, 2006). In the changing, post-9/11, US security climate, torture was no longer a 'taboo', too unthinkable and uncivilized to be discussed, a clear line which no democratic legal system should cross, no matter how serious the consequences. And although the public discourse in European countries tends to differ from the US, a recent report by the European Parliament brings to our attention the silent complicity of the European and other governments in the so-called 'export' of terror suspects for interrogation to jurisdictions which have lower human rights standards. The report concludes that at least 1,245 CIA rendition flights used European airspace or landed at European airports (*Guardian*, 2006).[6]

Although the notions of the 'state of exception' and 'exceptionalism' undoubtedly have much leverage in explaining these developments, some have questioned whether we are actually faced with events which can be described as exceptional. The use of torture has been explicitly or implicitly advocated by numerous members of the US and other administrations. Moreover, Brown (2005) argues that the conditions of Abu Ghraib and Guantanamo, although abnormal in their brutality, are also essentially contextualized in the American domestic vocabulary of punishment, particularly in the institution of the maximum security prison or the 'supermax'. Prison cells in these 'places of exception' bear remarkable visual and institutional similarities to 'normal' maximum security prisons across the United States. Abu Ghraib and Guantanamo thus reveal 'the normality of the abnormal' (ibid.: 973). In the supermax, designed to house 'the worst of the worst', the excessive pursuit of security has created extremely dehumanizing environments for inmates and guards. Moreover, the biographies of the Abu Ghraib actors overtly or indirectly converge with the US prison system, where several of them had been employed. In this perspective, the cases of Guantanamo and Abu Graib can be seen as examples of exportation of the US penal complex abroad. This perspective challenges the theory which sees Abu Ghraib as a problem of abnormal individuals – a 'few bad apples', as the Bush administration seemed to suggest. Rather, the scandals of Abu Ghraib and other abuses committed in the war on terror have to be seen as a question of 'rotten baskets', perpetuated by specific cultural and institutional conditions. Guantanamo has been described as a 'gulag of our times', yet it is important to keep in mind that for some decades the US has been moving towards a gulag condition on their domestic penal field as well (Christie, 2000). In this way, what appears to be exceptional needs to be contextualized in the progressive cultural change which has marked the (Anglo)American penality in the past decades (see for example Pratt, 2000; Garland, 2001a). Guantanamo Bay and Abu Ghraib may be the most powerful memories of the war on terror left to posterity, but

---

[6]http://www.guardian.co.uk/print/0,,329647213-110878,00.html

they can also be seen as examples which provide an insight into the 'abnormal' nature of the US penal system and make acutely visible the fundamental contradictions of imprisonment. Torture and punishment are 'grounded in the same fundamental practice: the infliction of pain' (Brown, 2005: 991).

The 'abnormalities' of Abu Ghraib and Guantanamo touch upon some of the most central criminological themes, forcing us to examine the very nature of prison as an institution. Dehumanizing effects of imprisonment, on inmates and guards alike, have been revealed in classic studies, such as Philip Zimbardo's and Stanley Milgram's famous experiments in the 1960s and 1970s, and Goffman's (1961) writing on total institutions, to name just a few. The statements made by some of those involved in the Abu Ghraib scandal, that they were 'just following orders' and 'protecting their country', as well as their apparent pride in the photos, which were being shared, reveal the deeper social, cultural and institutional conditions which support these acts. It is a telling example that prior to its disclosure, one of the abuse photos, of a group of naked prisoners piled on top of each other, was used as a screen saver on a computer in the US military intelligence office in Abu Ghraib (Cole, 2005: xvi). As a historical analogy, Morrison (2006) reports German soldiers during the Second World War proudly sharing photos of themselves in front of mass graves of civilians at the Eastern front. Rather than focusing on acts of violence as questions of individual and group abnormality, these perspectives turn our attention to 'the cultural conditions and structural contexts that culminate in acts of violence' (Brown, 2005: 979) – a valuable point for understanding both terrorist acts and the abuse committed in the name of their prevention.

The war on drugs

The current war on terror is by no means a historic novelty in terms of the blurred lines between crime control and warfare. The war on drugs was, and continues to be, a global 'war', relying heavily on various strategies for transnational police and customs co-operation and international military interventions, most notably the US military intervention in Colombia. The war on drugs continues, although the public focus seems to be shifting somewhat from the drug trade as a morally reprehensible activity in itself to the trade as a financial supply-line for terrorism. As in the war on terror, the US has been at the forefront of drug-related international policies, which has resulted in what Nadelmann (1993) terms Americanization of international law enforcement. 'The modern era of international law enforcement is one in which U.S. criminal justice priorities and U.S. models of criminalization and criminal investigation have been exported abroad' (ibid.: 469). Furthermore, Woodwiss (2003: 19) points out that parallel to Americanization of several criminal justice systems, there has also been 'an "Americanization" of the international community's response to drugs built around the framework established by the United Nations'.

In the pre-9/11 era, the war on drugs was 'the flag-ship of the transnational police enterprise and, hence, has assumed centrality in the preoccupations of global governance' (Sheptycki, 2000b: 18). The drug problem, and more generally, the threat of **transnational organized crime**, proved to be – even before the present securitization surge – one of the major vehicles of European integration and transnational police co-operation (Sheptycki, 2000b; Walker, 2003). 'Crimes associated with the illicit market in psychoactive substances have underwritten much of the public understanding of the need to foster the transnational police enterprise' (Sheptycki, 2000b: 202). The reasoning behind the war on drugs was the idea that one should prevent danger on the global level by forging a series of international treaties and initiatives, among others within the UN, the EU, Interpol, World Customs Organization and Schengen, as well as by co-operating with various NGOs and other non-state actors. In that respect, the global anti-drug efforts also present an example of development of global governance and of 'pooling of sovereignty', where the 'transnational system developed its own bureaucracy existing "above" that of the apparatuses of nation states' (ibid.: 216; see also discussion in Chapter 6).

The war on drugs also followed a similar pattern of fierce rhetorical campaigns in which drugs, like terrorism today, obtained the position of a 'suitable enemy' (Christie, 1986). It has had a profound impact on most Western penal systems and has been an important motor behind the growth in imprisonment, particularly in the US, as well as in other countries (Stern, 2006). Around 20 per cent of US prisoners (c. 450,000) are in prison for a drug offence. According to some estimates, about a quarter of the world's prison population is imprisoned because of some connection to illegal drugs (Stern, 2006: 137). However, the choice of punitive and aggressive law enforcement solutions has not only had devastating human consequences on the users, their families and communities, but has also been largely ineffective in limiting the demand and supply of the substances. The seemingly unstoppable supply of drugs is fundamentally related to the issues of global development and poverty. Afghanistan, one of the world's poorest countries, accounts for 90 per cent of the world's heroin production, regardless of the Western military presence there (UNODC, 2007). In the case of drugs, just as in the case of illegal migration and terrorism, it becomes obvious that the security problems of the West are essentially questions of development for the developing world (although the security aspects of these activities for citizens of developing countries should by no means be underestimated). There is therefore a fundamental interdependence between development and security issues, an aspect which tends to be downplayed and underestimated by the proponents of militarized solutions to these problems.

We can see that the new global (dis)order is marked not only by the internal/external security interdependence described earlier in this chapter, but also by the development/security interdependence (Human Security Report, 2005). Furthermore, this development/security nexus is of vital importance for understanding not only the relations between the global North and South, but also crime and security challenges on the level of individual nation states. Globalization and the neo-liberal ethos have according to numerous, particularly Marxist, accounts played a destructive role in the process of social disintegration and the growth of the illicit economy. Davis (1998), for example, describes the explosive growth of the drug economy in Los Angeles as a direct result of long structural (economic, cultural, educational, etc.) disinvestment from the inner city black and Latino neighbourhoods. As businesses internationalized and jobs were moving overseas, the drug lords grasped the chance 'to insert themselves into a leading circuit of international trade. Through "crack" they have discovered a vocation for the ghetto in L.A.'s new "world city" economy' (1998: 309). However, Davis himself and other analysts are cautious about simplistic descriptions of the drug economy as 'business as usual'. Rather, the investment in the drug economy has been seen as part of a profound social and cultural transformation. The new lifestyle has not only become a substitute for work, but also a new source of identity, excitement and belonging (Young, 2003; see discussions in the previous chapter).

The 1990s brought a renewed interest in one of the central criminological and sociological concepts, **anomie**, which had been for some time in a state of 'hibernation'. Anomie can be described as a condition of normlessness, which is conducive to deviance due to people's inability to achieve their social goals. The most famous criminological contribution to anomie came from Robert Merton and his 'strain theory'. Drawing on the work of Durkheim, Merton argued that anomie is a result of an imbalance between cultural goals and expectations, and individuals' opportunities to achieve them by legitimate means. Globalization is frequently seen as a breeding ground for 'global anomie' by privileging the winning mentality and encouraging new needs and desires through the proliferation of consumerism, at the same time as it has failed to deliver its promises for the vast majority of the world's population (Passas, 2000).

> As market society advances, the value of work and its ability to bind individuals into a productive community life is progressively demeaned in favour of the valorization of consumption for its own sake – and of getting what you want, or getting ahead of others, by whatever means will suffice. When that cultural shift is combined with the decimation of opportunities for good work, it produces a dual assault on one of the most crucial

mechanisms of social support, social control and communal engagement.
(Currie, 1997: 163)

The tension has been acutely felt in so-called transitional countries, such as the former Eastern bloc states, most notably Russia in the 1990s (Castells, 2000). Here, the rise of neo-liberalism has been connected not only to the widening discrepancies between people's desires and their means to achieve them, but also to the demise of a strong state system and the proliferation of illicit opportunities (Castells, 2000; Passas, 2000). 'The corrupted process of privatization has generated widespread rationalizations, such as, "it is OK to steal from the state" or "everyone is doing the same thing"' (Passas, 2000: 35). Neo-liberalism's victory has therefore been also a victory of a value system which puts a premium on consumption, individualism and the search for quick and easy ways towards success at the same time, as we shall see in the next section, as the opportunities of reaping profits from illicit activities proliferated.

Illicit flows and the global criminal economy

In the closing section of this chapter we shall continue to pursue the topic of the criminogenic effects of globalization by examining how economic globalization has fostered new opportunities for criminal activities. According to numerous academic and political observers, the globalization of illicit flows and activities is the mirror image of a dark side of the global mobility of capital, people and information (see also discussion in Chapter 2 on people smuggling and trafficking). The development was, again, influentially articulated in Manuel Castells's trilogy on the information age, particularly in volume III (2000). Castells applies his imagery of transnational networks to the field of organized crime by claiming that national and local organized crime groups have gone through a process of internationalization. Resembling business networks, these groups are now able to link up with criminal groups in other countries and establish international networks for the production, management, financing and distribution of their products and services. According to Castells (2000: 171), their strategy

> is to base their management and production functions in low-risk areas, where they have relative control of the institutional environment, while targeting as preferential markets those areas with the most affluent demand, so that higher prices can be charged.

These networks have the ability not only to escape prosecution on the national level, but also to infiltrate the law enforcement, judicial and political systems of several countries, as well as to penetrate the global financial systems. 'Money laundering, and its derivatives, have become a significant and troubling component of global financial flows and stock markets' (ibid.: 207). The size of this capital is difficult to estimate; nevertheless, there have been several estimates running as high as hundreds of billions, even trillions, of dollars (Castells, 2000; Galeotti, 2004).

International crime connections are by no means a historic novelty. Transnational illegal linkages have existed throughout history in more or less organized forms. Castells nevertheless bravely steps into an empirical and theoretical field which has been traditionally reserved for organized crime researchers and various 'Mafia experts'. His views have gained a considerable following, particularly among policy makers and law enforcement representatives. The language of global criminal networks conjures an image of a global economy 'hijacked by smugglers, traffickers and copycats', as Moses Naim, editor of the influential *Foreign Policy* magazine, puts it. 'Italian syndicates sell Latin American drugs in Europe, Russians buy stolen cars from the Japanese Yakuza, Albanians move Asian heroin for Turkish drug clans' (Galeotti, 2004: 1). This is a view of nation states and the world economy under imminent threat, and as such, it serves as an invitation 'to develop more intrusive, authoritarian, and muscular forms of law enforcement' (Abraham and van Schendel, 2005: 4). Critics have therefore pointed out that this notion of transnational organized crime, resembling a powerful multinational octopus, tends to be used to give legitimacy to the development of transnational policing systems (Hobbs and Dunnighan, 1998; Sheptycki, 2000a). It can be used externally, as a strong political appeal for increased funding of police organizations, as well as internally, within intelligence communities, to give credibility to specific types of police work by presenting them with images of worthy opponents. Fighting transnational organized crime gives prestige and it responds to the traditional, 'macho' perceptions of what is 'proper police work' (Gundhus, 2006).

The growing prominence of transnational organized crime corresponds with the increasing internationalization of policing particularly, as mentioned above, the international, US-sponsored, war on drugs (for an overview of the concept of TOC see Edwards and Gill, 2003). The US conceptualization of transnational organized crime, and its responses to the problem, have according to Woodwiss (2003) dominated international debates and the proposed solutions to the problem. In that respect, the present political and law enforcement focus reveals the global export of a distinctly US concept (see Chapter 8 for a discussion of criminal policy transfers).

> As well as being, in some senses, the 'home' of the concept and phenomenon of organised crime, the US has also, since the Second World War, been the pre-eminent source of the idea that criminal law enforcement must

> dominate approaches to organised crime control. Thus, the 'international-isation' of US perspectives on security is considered an important motor of policy change and learning. (Edwards and Gill, 2003: 3)

The critique of Castells's approach, and the proliferating discourse about transnational organized crime, has pointed out that it is too general and lacks nuance to local conditions and historic contexts (Johansen, 2001; Edwards and Gill, 2003). Critics have argued for the need to see beyond the transnational and omnipotent criminal conglomerates and acknowledge the relevance of 'glocal organized crime' and 'the importance of the local context as an environment within which criminal networks function' (Hobbs and Dunighan, 1998: 289). Castells's model thus overlooks the multiplicity of micro-practices and associations that, 'while often illegal in a formal sense, are not driven by a structural logic of organization and unified purpose' (Abraham and van Schendel, 2005: 4). These small-scale 'armpit smugglers' 'may together account for huge quantities of contraband, but they do not represent global syndicates of organized crime' (ibid.). Extrapolations from the overall estimates of illicit flows to the powers of transnational organized crime groups may be overstated and misleading.

The notion of transnational organized crime paints a simplistic, black and white picture, where the boundaries between licit and illicit activities appear to be clear cut. However, historically, the lines between illicit activities and state laws have been far from clear. Tilly's famous comment that the state was simply the most efficient and effective form of organized crime has a long historic resonance as the lines between state authorities and bandits have shifted back and forth. Also today, the spectrum between state-authorised activities, for example the arms trade, and illegal aspects of the business are often hard to discern. The world superpowers function as the main providers of arms even to states under international embargo (Castells, 2000). As such they form 'dirty economies' where licit and illicit activities overlap in various shades of grey (Ruggiero, 1997; Johansen, 2001). The subject of powerful transnational crime networks brings up an important issue in globalization studies: the question of state sovereignty. The penetration of states by illicit activities is popularly referred to as the problem of weak or *'failed states'*. Rather than seeing these countries as a developmental and humanitarian problem, they are increasingly discussed as a security issue due to their vulnerability to various organized crime networks. These networks are perceived to be so powerful that, according to anthropologist Carolyn Nordstrom (2000), they represent 'shadow sovereigns'. These shadow networks are not marginal to the world's economies and politics but have become central aspects of the world order. For example, heroin production represents about 50 per cent of the Afghan GNP and as a consequence the illicit authority of drug lords and war lords is effectively paralysing the establishment of state sovereignty in the country.

The problem of transnational organized crime, and its hidden financial empires, also mirrors more general concerns about the ungovernability of global corporations and financial institutions which are escaping the control of nation states. 'The enormous and perhaps even the incalculable wealth hidden in offshore banks is testimony to the de-centring of the state in the transnational age' (Sheptycki, 2000a: 5). The independence of (licit and illicit) global flows from state control has resulted in the weakening of the state. The problem indicates the fragility of the present world order and 'calls into question many received – criminological – wisdoms about the locus of effective, sovereign crime control' (Loader and Sparks, 2002: 98). Here, as we shall see in the next chapter, the popular 'withering away of the state' thesis makes numerous relevant points. Nevertheless, spaces where *illicit private authority* becomes the norm are not only a question of failed state sovereignty. The power of law can also be used to create spaces where illicit activities are welcomed, such as the money laundering havens of the Cayman Islands, Bermuda, Jersey, and similar sites (Abraham and van Schendel, 2005: 20). These spaces are protected by state sovereignty but are nevertheless a locus of activities which are by many considered to be unethical. These examples again reveal the dual and contradictory nature of the global order, in particular global policing and surveillance efforts. On the one hand, we saw in this chapter how the logic of surveillance and visibility is penetrating innumerable new domains, including financial flows, as exemplified by the controversies surrounding the informal hawala money systems. On the other hand, spaces like the Cayman Islands continue to avoid visibility and to function as a lifeline to various types of illicit and illegal activities across the world. We shall continue to examine the contradictory nature of state sovereignty in the next chapter.

Summary

This chapter explored a range of issues relating to the transnational nature of contemporary criminality and other security threats. It points to the increasing interconnectedness of external and internal forms of security, as transnational risks are able to penetrate national borders. Several forms of transnational risk were discussed: terrorism, international illegal trade in narcotics and the more general category of international organized crime. Globalization has been credited with increasing the scope of global criminal networks through the transnational linkage of organized crime networks. We examined the potential advantages and drawbacks of transnational organized crime discourse. It was also pointed out that international and national responses to these types of threat often rely on military and militarized forms of control, thus blurring the lines between crime control and warfare. In particular, the present 'war on terror' has intensified the tendency of risk societies to put priority on security rather than justice. In the fearful post-9/11 climate, the need for security has been a central justification behind a series of new control measures, which have curtailed civil liberties in the name of security, leading some to describe the development as a 'state of exception'. Furthermore, 9/11 stands as a landmark in the proliferation of surveillance practices and technologies in numerous contexts of everyday life. From the ubiquitous CCTV camera, biometric residence permits, passports and identity cards to increasing monitoring of Internet communication, to name just a few, it seems that 'Big Brother' is everywhere. However, surveillance today is not only, perhaps not even primarily, a question of state surveillance, but also a practice of monitoring and data collection for commercial purposes. Surveillant practices are ingrained in routine and mundane activities, such as shopping and driving. The popularity of blogging, webcams and online videos also reveals that we, as citizens, are increasingly taking part in the practices of (self) surveillance and visibility.

STUDY QUESTIONS

1   Discuss the various types of security interdependence mentioned in this chapter. Can you come up with additional examples?

2   Terrorism reveals the processes of social construction of crime. What are the reasons for the politically contested definitions of terrorism?

3   Security is used as a justification for numerous control measures, which curtail citizens' freedoms and civil liberties. Are security and freedom necessarily opposing values? Discuss some of the paradoxes of security.

4   What are the criminogenic effects of globalization and which criminological theories might prove useful in their explanation?

FURTHER READING

Since 9/11 terrorism has been the subject of innumerable books. For a recent criminological contribution see Mathieu Deflem's (2004) *Terrorism and Counter-terrorism*. Tore Bjørgo's (2005) edited volume *Root Causes of Terrorism* charts the territory of causes, rather than the more frequently addressed responses to terrorism. For an excellent account of the deteriorating state of civil liberties in the US in the aftermath of 9/11, see David Cole's (2005) highly acclaimed *Enemy Aliens*. The topic of surveillance offers a wealth of literature. David Lyon's work (2001, 2003a, 2003b) represents a major contribution to the field of contemporary surveillance studies. His edited volume (2006) *Theorizing Surveillance* offers excellent discussions on the panopticon. Kevin Haggerty and Richard Ericson's (2006) edited volume *The New Politics of Surveillance and Visibility* is also an updated recent contribution. Michel Foucault's (1977) *Discipline and Punish* is by all standards a criminological classic and a major reference point for students of surveillance and imprisonment. Statewatch organization, a relentless observer of surveillance trends and the state of civil liberties in Europe, operates an extremely informative and updated webpage: http://www.statewatch.org/. For anyone interested in the details of the US torture memos, Karen Greenberg et al.'s (2005) extensive *The Torture Papers* is an obligatory read. For a detailed discussion of the concept of anomie see Nikos Passas and Robert Agnew's (1997) *The Future of Anomie Theory*, while Mark Findlay's *The Globalization of Crime* (1999) contributes a well-informed discussion of crime in the context of global transition. Transnational organized crime is the subject of a growing number of volumes, such as Adam Edwards and Peter Gill's (2003) *Transnational Organized Crime* and Dina Siegel et al.'s (2003) *Global Organized Crime*. You can also follow the currents of organized crime debates in journals like *Global Crime* and *Trends in Organized Crime*.

6

Beyond the State: Globalization and State Sovereignty

Chapter Contents

Globalization and state sovereignty	**131**
The state and the crime problem	133
The new regulatory state	134
Crime control as commodity	**136**
The private security market and private policing	138
Normative issues in the privatization of social control	140
Critique of the 'withering of the state' thesis	**143**
Transnational policing	**145**
Summary	148
Study questions	149
Further reading	149

OVERVIEW

Chapter 6 examines the following issues:

- Theoretical accounts of the changing role of the nation state due to globalization and the impact of neo-liberalism.
- The 'withering of the state' thesis as it pertains to the field of crime control.
- Pluralization of security governance and the various theoretical accounts of this development.
- The growing privatization and commodification of crime control and security.

KEY TERMS

commodification	neo-liberalism	responsibilization strategy
consumerism	(illicit) private authority	restorative justice
global governance	regulatory state	state sovereignty
governmentality		

> More than 1,000 illegal immigrants from Afghanistan, Iran, Iraq, Indonesia and other nations are detained in the blistering desert of Australia's Outback. Across the ocean, South African prisoners sleep in newly built cells. Thousands of miles away in Yorkshire, England, 16-year-old violent offenders peer out of small cell windows overlooking the Cheswald River. All have one thing in common: They are watched over by guards of a U.S. company. Wackenhut Corrections Corp., a Palm Springs, Fla., company, operates 55 prisons, immigration detention centers, juvenile facilities and psychiatric hospitals, with a significant chunk of its business coming from overseas. In the United States, the company operates 36 facilities, including detention centers for the Immigration and Naturalization Service ... Outside the United States, the company runs 19 facilities, including a maximum-security prison in South Africa and five immigration detention facilities in Australia designed to accommodate the influx of illegal immigrants. (Lemke, 2002)[1]

Throughout most of its history, criminology has 'assumed the Hobbesian conception of political community: of sovereign states securing within their own borders the conditions of domestic peace by monopolising the means of internal violence' (Hogg, 2002: 212). Issues of law, justice, community and safety have

---

[1]Insight on the News at: http://www.findarticles.com/p/articles/mi_m1571/is_14_18/ai_84971439

been implicitly built on the notion of a bounded territory and state sovereignty. This, however, is gradually beginning to change. The global flows, networks and mobilities discussed in this book disrupt this seemingly organized and state-centred system. They bring into question the centrality of the nation state as the main provider of security and as the main agent of punishment and social control. The above case of the Wackenhut Corrections Corporation is illustrative for two reasons. On the one hand, it shows how the running of institutions of punishment and social control, once appearing to be the sole prerogative of state power, is being taken over by private actors. On the other hand, it marks the multinational nature of these actors and their activities.

This chapter examines the changing role of the nation state in a globalizing world and the transformations in the nature of *state sovereignty*. We shall address the emerging dynamics, and the blurring lines, between the state and private actors when it comes to punishment, social control and the provision of security. New levels and forms of governance will be discussed, such as private, local, inter- and supra-national authorities. We shall see how state power and sovereignity are being relinquished in several ways: 'outwards' to the commercial sector and the private security industry; 'downwards' to citizens, private organizations and municipalities; and 'upwards' to the emerging new levels of international co-operation and global governance (Loader and Walker, 2001: 10). And finally, a question will be asked: do these developments in fact signify a diminution of state authority and a reduction in the coercive capacities of states?

Globalization and state sovereignty

Historians usually place the emergence of the modern nation state in Western Europe in the 18th and 19th centuries, although its origins can be traced further back to the 16th century (Held, 1995). In that respect, the primacy of the state as the omnipresent regulator of human life is a relatively recent development in human history. Sociologist Max Weber (1948) famously defined as one of the central traits of the nation state that it exerts monopoly of legal control of the right to use violence over its territory. The state, he argued,

> is a human community that (successfully) claims *monopoly of the legitimate use of physical force* within a given territory. Note that 'territory' is one of the characteristics of the state. Specifically, at the present time, the right to use physical force is ascribed to other institutions or individuals only to the extent which the state permits it. The state is considered the sole source of the 'right' to use violence. (Weber, 1948: 78)

This monopoly of violence, although never absolute, is embodied primarily in the state institutions of the army and the police. In the past two centuries, the regulatory powers of states expanded through an extensive net of bureaucratic and fiscal institutions, welfare arrangements, education, media, health, diplomacy, and so on. Increasingly, states came to exercise not only a monopoly of physical and judicial power, but also a 'power over life' of its populace, neatly administrating and registering life from birth certificates to death certificates.

We do not have the space here to examine these historic developments in detail, even though they have merited the attention of several contemporary students of social control (see for example Burchell et al., 1991). What is important at this point is that the progress of global transformations has, according to many social commentators, contributed to a profound shift in the nature and role of the state, sometimes even to an imminent decline of the nation state. Particularly the first wave of globalization analysts saw the proliferation of transnational connections, the rising power of multinational corporations, and the growth of new international organizations as a sign of the 'withering of the nation state' (Ohmae, 1990; Reich, 1991). Under the influence of neo-liberal policies, a growing number of areas came to be 'deregulated' and privatised and/or subjected to marketized ordering mechanisms. The provision of health, education and other services, including punishment and security, gradually ceased to be primarily the domain of the nation state, if indeed, they ever were. The shift from the state to market solutions had important practical consequences for the provision of these services, particularly to disadvantaged groups and individuals. Furthermore, the shift also created new notions of the state and its responsibilities. If the (often idealised) welfare state aspired to universality in its relations to its citizens, the *neo-liberal* state, on the other hand, is inspired by *laissez-faire* ideologies and accepts a far greater degree of social fragmentation.

Following the rather pessimistic first wave, the second wave of globalization theorists supported a more sceptical view of the 'withering away' thesis, pointing out the persisting importance of the national and the nation state in many areas, including the economy (Hirst and Thompson, 1999). The first wave of globalization theorists was criticizeed for ignoring the persistence of the nation state and the crucial role of government in influencing the structure and dynamics of the new economy (Castells, 1996). Holton (2005: 5) divides the recent debates about the fate of the nation state into 'three broad waves of analysis, namely *hyper-globalism*, *scepticism*, and a third option, which might be called *post-scepticism*'. The latter is often referred to as the 'third way', emphasising the importance of both market liberalism and state involvement, promoted particularly by the later writing of Giddens (1998), and associated with the politics of the British prime minister Tony Blair. In recent years, the 'third way' seems to have gained almost as many critics as globalization itself, indicating a profound shift in the discussions away from the 'withering away of the state' thesis.

Regardless of the terms involved, the intensely debated transformations of the state can be seen from several perspectives. There seems to be little doubt that the state is being fundamentally transformed in the process. We saw in the previous chapter how the powers of the global criminal economy and of transnational organized crime are undermining the ability of some states to exert control over their territory and to act as guarantors of a minimum of peace and security for their citizens. However, the weakening of the state is not only a defining feature of the so-called weak or failed states, but has been to a varying extent a general trait of the state in the globalizing world order. This development became painfully obvious in the case of New Orleans and the disastrous Hurricane Katrina, when one of the seemingly most powerful states in the world exposed the 'Third World' conditions in its midst. Nevertheless, we should be careful of generalizations as the nature of nation states varies greatly, from the relatively strong Scandinavian welfare models to numerous weak states in the developing world which are torn apart by ethnic conflict, corruption and organized crime. In fact, in many developing countries the Weberian model of state organization cannot simply be assumed to begin with (Goldsmith, 2003). Furthermore, we shall see throughout this chapter that when it comes to issues of punishment and crime control, developments defy clear categorizations as weak and strong forms of state sovereignty. While nation states may be escaping responsibility and blaming global market forces for the social problems of their populace in some areas, for example monetary policy, social security or health care, this may not necessarily be the case when it comes to penal policy.

The state and the crime problem

The above discussion of the changing nature of state sovereignty has had a strong resonance within the field of crime control studies. If one of the defining traits of the modern nation state has been its gradual monopoly of power, this monopoly was particularly evident in its ability to preserve law and order on national territory and to provide security for its citizens. Well functioning penal institutions and an effective police force represented a powerful symbolic, if not a realistic, image of state sovereignty and a justification for its existence. This mythical representation of state authority has in the past decades undergone profound transformations in many contexts across the world. In his account of Anglo-American penal developments, Garland (2001a) points to the eroding trust in the ability of the state to 'solve the crime problem'.

> In crime control, as in other spheres, the limitations of the state's capacity to govern social life in all its details have become ever more apparent, particularly in the late modern era. So, having arrogated to itself control functions and responsibilities that once belonged to institutions of civil society, the late modern state is now faced with its own inability to deliver the expected levels of control over crime and criminal conduct. (Garland, 2001a: 110)

Challenges to the myth of state sovereignty come from several directions. The growth of penal populism and a return to a more emotional tone of penal politics was partly nurtured by public disillusionment and a profound sense of distrust in the modern institutions of government and in traditional party politics (Pratt, 2007; see also discussions in Chapter 4). The once unquestioned belief in the ability of penal experts to manage the crime problem was increasingly questioned, producing a perpetual sense of crisis and introducing new defensive rationalities (Garland, 2001a; Pratt, 2007). In addition, the belief in the state was being challenged by new modes of neo-liberal governance, which foster competition and market thinking.

Consequently, several researchers have pointed out the need to move beyond the state-centred thinking about crime and justice – from methodological, theoretical and normative standpoints. Various **restorative justice** approaches and initiatives powerfully advocated the return of conflicts to local communities and the civil society (Christie, 2004). On the other hand, as we shall see in Chapter 8, the need to broaden criminological perspectives beyond the nation state order has also been anchored in more general concerns and normative arguments about the need to take into account questions of international justice, state crime and genocide (Green and Ward, 2004; Morrison, 2006).

The new regulatory state

Lately, one of the leading assaults on the theoretical primacy of the state has come from the Foucauldian **governmentality** theorists. Taking up Foucault's encouragement to 'cut off the king's head' in political thinking and social sciences, this growing body of literature aims to think alternatively about the diverse ways in which neo-liberal societies govern the conduct of their citizens (see for example Rose, 1999). By focusing on 'technologies of government', and the new rationalities and models of the persons subjected to government, such approaches reframed the traditionally dominant role accorded to the state in studies of social control (Burchell et al., 1991; Rose, 1999). It was argued that rather than being directly involved in regulating social behaviour, neo-liberal societies are being 'governed at a distance' – indirectly drawing upon a series of regulatory techniques, intervening upon persons, activities and events far removed in space and time (Rose, 1999). Unlike the old Keynesian state, this new *regulatory state* (Braithwaite, 2000) no longer directly orchestrates the activities of social control nor is it the only actor involved in regulating social life.

If traditionally the issues of security and justice were the main prerogative of the state, the neo-liberal styles of governance, on the other hand, encourage individuals, institutions and local communities to take active responsibility for managing their crime problems, in line with other risks and uncertainties. In one such example, Oslo police sent out 15,000 SMS messages to citizens, aged between 20 and 35, instructing them to take precautions against pickpocketing and violence. Although in itself an unusual example, the SMS messages openly show how even in one of the strongest welfare states in the world the police actively seek to enrol citizens in the task of governing security (see also Johnston and Shearing, 2003). This distribution of responsibility responds to what has elsewhere been described as *responsibilization strategy* within contemporary social control (Garland, 2001a). It involves a way of thinking in which governments actively enlist participation by private citizens, non-state actors and agencies and thus share the burden of controlling unwanted social phenomena. The governance of crime is thus becoming an increasingly complex and untransparent matter, combining a number of actors on various levels and with varying objectives. It is a task not simply for the state and governmental institutions but also for private actors, ready to step in when states become unwilling or unable to respond to the crime challenge.

We have already touched upon several examples of the responsibilization approach throughout this book. Commercial airlines and other commercial agents are effectively co-opted into the task of 'policing at a distance' the borders of the Western fortress continents (Bigo and Guild, 2004). Through various technologically supported strategies, such as airline liaison officers and the obligation of airline carriers to communicate passenger data to border authorities, contemporary governance is able to constantly expand the range of actors who participate in global risk communication networks. Another example, discussed in Chapter 3, is the public–private partnerships, which have supported the massive investment in CCTV surveillance, particularly in the UK, where local authorities and commercial operators often share the financial burden. Furthermore the growth in mass private property means that private security companies play a vital role in providing security and shape the nature of public life in cities across the world. Similarly, we saw in Chapter 5 how governments seek to enrol citizens in their security and surveillance strategies against terrorism. Neo-liberal forms of government encourage the public, local communities, neighbourhood watch groups, businesses and other institutions to become active agents in providing their own security, rather than relying on the state to do so.

The following vignette from Toronto's International Airport offers an insight into the developments (Rigakos, 2002: 37):

> Passengers move along various queues for airline tickets, baggage checks, and car rentals. Perhaps less noticeable are two of Canada's federal police talking to a pair of constables from the Peel Regional Police Service. After the discussion ends, the RCMP officers begin to patrol, nodding hello to two security officers from Excalibur Security making similar rounds. Farther along, they watch two armed Brinks guards carry money satchels from a nearby currency exchange kiosk. They wind up by Commissionaires issuing parking tickets and Group 4 Securitas security guards checking the luggage of passengers ...

In order to bring attention to the dispersal and plurality of security providers some commentators talk of plural policing (Jones and Newburn, 1998, 2006). The 'plurality' here refers not only to the commercial actors, but also to the emergence of local and municipal policing bodies, such as neighbourhood wardens in the UK, local municipal police organizations in France and police auxiliaries and 'city guards' in the Netherlands (Jones and Newburn, 2006: 4). Similarly, Johnston and Shearing (2003: 147) speak in terms of nodal governance – a network of security providers where 'no set of nodes is given conceptual priority' (see also Wood and Shearing, 2007a).

Crime control as commodity

Privatization of social control has been one of the most visible signs of (and an important driving force behind) the transformations of state sovereignty discussed above. Similarly to other public services, the rise of the neo-liberal state coincided with the introduction of market solutions and market rationalities in the field of punishment and social control in general. Today, the numbers of private security personnel outnumber state police forces in many developed countries, although the exact numbers are notoriously difficult to establish. Security, punishment and social control are no longer perceived primarily as public goods, but have become commodities which can be purchased like any other commodities; depending, of course, on the purchasing power of the customer (Jones and Newburn, 1998). One of the most controversial forms of privatization has been the privatization of prisons and other penal institutions, such as youth correctional facilities and training centres, as well as immigration detention facilities. Private prisons have become an integral part of the penal system in several English-speaking countries, such as the US, UK, Australia and South Africa (Harding, 1997; Christie, 2000; Stern, 2006). In Chapter 4 we saw that private companies are often responsible for the management of unwanted, globally mobile, populations, such as illegal immigrants and asylum seekers. However, it is the privatization of prison facilities which has received most of the attention and has been at the centre of the politically and emotionally charged debates about privatization of punishment. One of the largest players in the game, Corrections Corporation of America, is the fifth-largest corrections system in the US, behind only the federal government and three federal states. Managing more than 62,000 inmates in 63 facilities[2], the inmates of this company alone far outnumber the combined prison populations of Canada, Ireland, New Zealand and Austria.

Nevertheless, privatization of prisons in its full sense has been adopted only by a minority of penal systems, while many others have opted for semi-private solutions – contracting out parts of the services. As Christie (2000: 98) observes: 'Prison means money. Big money. Big in building, big in providing equipment. And big in running.' For these reasons, prisons can be an important source of income in terms of supplying jobs and business opportunities for many local communities. Consequently, the privatization of prisons, and a more general perception of prisons in business terms, can influence penal policy. Not only direct lobbying by the prison industry and local communities, but also the presence of commercial companies at conferences and other professional events can have an impact. 'The public sector people begin to talk of prisons as "a business". Their aim becomes to "deliver a world-class product at lowest cost"' (Stern, 2006: 118). A glimpse into this commercial worldview and self-image is readily available on the web-pages of the private companies involved. The up-to-date price of their stocks figures, prominently displayed on the web-pages of Group 4 Securicor, symbolically indicates their loyalty to their shareholders, customers and prospective investors, rather than to the nation state.[3]

Here lies potentially the deepest impact of the commercialization of prisons. Private prisons have fulfilled neither the rosy pictures presented by their proponents, nor the pessimistic scenarios of their critics, although they have by no means been scandal-free (Stern, 2006). Some have argued that the public sector has improved by competing with private prisons and by increased transparency and performance measurement. Nevertheless, the deepest impact of privatization of prisons may be the introduction and promotion of short-term,

---

[2]Source: http://www.correctionscorp.com/aboutcca.html
[3]www.g4s.com/home/about.htm

cost-benefits thinking within the public sector. The language of economics, efficiency and technological solutions is thus favoured at the expense of more normative, long-term penal policy debates. The impact of neo-liberal policies lies therefore not only, perhaps not even primarily, on the practical level. Private prisons, after all, account for a minor share of the overall prison population in their respective countries. Rather, as the governmentality theorists point out, the impact of neo-liberalism is more indirect, having to do with changing governmental rationalities, value systems and the terms of penal policy debates. Public prisons and penal discourse in general begin to appropriate economic vocabulary and the private sector's definitions of quality – often referred to as the 'new public management'.

The private security market and private policing

Prisons, however, represent a small part of the burgeoning crime control industry. The commodification of social control is a far more extensive phenomenon, which needs to be contextualized not only through the language of diminishing state sovereignty, but also within the context of the risk society and the fear of crime, discussed above in Chapters 1 and 5. The increased disembedding of social life, and the heightened sense of insecurity in late modernity, can be seen as contributing to the rising demands for commercial security. The pervasive global inequalities have given further nourishment to this development. Walking in the streets of Moscow, one is struck not only by the conspicuously expensive cars of the newly rich, but also by the numbers of private security personnel following them. We saw, in Chapter 3, how gated communities try to protect their prosperity by investing in technological security systems and private police personnel, and how many a city centre today is put under the surveillance of CCTV cameras. This vast technological paraphernalia – comprising alarms systems, surveillance equipment, electronic admission systems, gates, bars, locks, etc. – can be seen as an example of individuals and companies being 'responsibilized' and actively managing their risks and insecurities. Security is, therefore, no longer a public good, but becomes a commodity, reflecting the hegemony of consumerism in contemporary culture and society. As a consumer product, security ceases to be only a material and a utilitarian act, and also becomes an emotionally-laden activity (Loader, 1999). It has to do with fear and anxiety, social status, advertising and the search for novelty, thus forming 'a potent, potentially self-perpetuating mix; one which the crime control industry has a vested interest in cultivating and sustaining' (ibid.: 382). Duclos (2005) describes the development as the 'capitalism of fear'.

The development towards the ***commodification*** of security becomes particularly evident in the case of private policing or parapolicing. Many world cities today are patrolled not only (perhaps not even first and foremost) by the public police force, but by the private security industry. They routinely patrol facilities such as shopping malls, transport terminals, airports, office buildings and leisure facilities, which are important arenas of public social life (Wakefield, 2003). One should keep in mind though that the extent and the modes of these activities vary greatly from country to country (Jones and Newburn, 2006). And although a majority of private security providers are relatively small national and local actors, large multinationals clearly have a strong presence. Group 4 Securicor, for example, operates in over 100 countries across the world, employing more than 400,000 people. It is, in other words, a 'proper' multinational conglomerate.[4] Another market leader, the Securitas Group, employs more than 200,000 people, operates in over 30 countries and accounts for about $6 billion in annual sales.[5] Nevertheless, as we saw in the case of private prisons, their impact has been just as much in changing mentalities as in their actual size. The same could be also said of private policing. Now, not only private police think of their activities as consumer products; the public sector too increasingly perceives itself as a deliverer of services which have to satisfy its customers. The police are aiming to become more 'business-like', adopting managerialism and market definitions of efficiency, quality and financial accountability (Loader, 1999).

There is therefore a blurring of the public–private distinction, and as a consequence new, hybrid rationalities and ways of dealing with problems emerge. The public sector increasingly resembles the business world, while the private security sector emulates the public police (Rigakos, 2002). Contractual relations and market vocabulary are permeating penal systems and diluting their previously distinct public character. Others, on the other hand, have pointed out the differences between the public and the private modes of control. While the activities of public police have traditionally focused on reactive law enforcement, the focus of private control is not primarily on coercion and the use of force (although this clearly is a possible option as well), but first and foremost on proactive intervention and problem-solving (Johnston and Shearing, 2003). One of the earliest explorations of this mentality came in Shearing and Stenning's (1985) groundbreaking case-study of Disney World. Here, the authors describe a style of governance which is consensual rather than openly coercive but nevertheless effectively ensures human behaviour in line with Disney's idea of order. They point to the fundamentally different ways in which social control is conducted by the criminal justice system, and the more amoral and instrumental mode of operation favoured by the private security systems.

---

[4]www.g4s.com/home/about.htm.
[5]http://www.securitasinc.com/

Normative issues in the privatization of social control

The next issue we need to address is that of the normative consequences of the developments outlined above. Here, the discussions to some extent chime with the debates about privatization in other arenas of social life, while the rise of the crime control industry brings up a distinct set of issues and dilemmas. Privatization of punishment stands at the symbolic centre of the public–private debates and persistently pushes the limits of which areas it is possible to privatize. What appeared to be unthinkable only a decade ago is perceived as normal today. Among the more optimistic criminological voices, Johnston and Shearing (2003: 12) question whether the increased involvement of non-state agencies in the provision of security is by definition a 'bad thing'. In their view, private security solutions give priority to non-punitive modes of thinking – problem solving rather than punishing. The focus is on crime prevention, changes in environmental design and other physical features of the environment, rather than on retrospective prosecution and punitive sanctions. In this respect, private policing can represent an alternative to criminal law and a move away from the punitive, state-centred forms of conflict resolution – an approach which can particularly come to the advantage of poor communities by strengthening their 'local capacity governance' (Johnston and Shearing, 2003).

However, the privatization of social control also carries a more pessimistic promise, which is inherent in any process of social fragmentation and privatization of state services. Phenomena such as gated communities and mass private property show a far less democratic side of the new forms of governance, giving them 'a distinctly "feudal" resonance' (ibid.: 149) and connotations of 'private justice' (Rigakos, 2002). Christie (2000) points to two major problems with private policing: their class bias and their potential for abuse in situations of severe political conflicts. Privatization of social control represents a move away from the view that the 'provision of a secure environment is necessarily a joint accomplishment the benefits of which cannot easily be restricted to a determinate group of users who have paid the appropriate charge' (Loader and Walker, 2001: 18). The notion of punishment and security as market-regulated commodities indicates a withdrawal from the common political sphere, echoing one of the major political dilemmas of our times: *consumerism* versus citizenship (Klein, 2000). As Zedner (2000: 209) points out: 'Commodification of basic social goods like security thus has the effect of reducing citizenship to a brand of consumerism.'

We can see that this view is far more sceptical of the potential that the fragmentation of security governance may have for disadvantaged communities. The problem becomes acute in weak states, where state neglect of the security needs of citizens has led to conditions of extreme violence and insecurity. Security is, like other goods in the global order, an unequally divided commodity. According to data provided by the World Health Organization (2002), only 10 per cent of all violence-related deaths occurred in high-income countries. In the African and Latin America regions average homicide rates are over twice as high as in the rest of the world, although there are large national, ethnic and age variations (ibid.). Here, the security vacuum has not been filled only by market security forces, but also by other non-state actors such as paramilitary and organized crime groups and ethnic militias. We can see that not only legal *private authority* (such as private security companies, gated communities, etc.), but also *illicit private authority*, can fill the gaps in state sovereignty. In these contexts, 'the ideal of the protective state' seems to survive even the worst histories of state repression and abuse, largely due to the public awareness of the limitations of the alternatives (Goldsmith, 2003: 9). However, the failure to provide security for citizens is not only a trait of the so-called failed states (see discussion in Chapter 5), but is present to a greater or lesser extent in numerous countries in the global North and South. A crucial criminological question in this context is how to provide security to the disadvantaged communities which suffer from a 'security deficit' and which lack the capacity to purchase security as a commodity (Wood and Shearing, 2007a). Here, the growing body of work on local capacity governance and restorative justice has a lot to offer as it seeks to establish 'mechanisms that centre on the knowledge and capacity of weak actors in building new ideas for security governance' (ibid.: 155; see also Braithwaite, 2004; Christie, 2004).

Some observers have questioned whether the growth of private policing represents an alternative to the use of criminal law or simply an expansion of the existing social control apparatuses. Høygård (2002), for example, shows how in Oslo graffiti moved from an almost non-existent category in the official crime statistics to a (financially) heavily penalized activity, chiefly through the aggressive enforcement strategy of the city's public transport authorities and their security personnel. Similarly, private prisons increase the state's capacity for incarceration, thus enabling the implementation of punitive penal policies. The private security industry does not come as a replacement of the existing penal sector, but represents its overall expansion – a development which it has a financial interest in maintaining. Critics of privatization have raised the question of whether the financial interests of the security industry represent an effective block against the attempts to implement less punitive penal policies and thereby reduce the size of the market. However, it is important to keep in mind that state ownership is far from being a guarantee of accountability, equality and decency. Competing with the private sector has arguably made public prisons more focused on maintaining their standards, and public police more responsive to public demands. Furthermore, the notion of the field of 'justice as a marketplace' is by no means a historic novelty (Zedner, 2006). Private security arrangements were extensive in pre-modern societies. The main difference today is, according to Zedner (2006: 84), that 'whereas pre-industrial markets were small and localized, today's markets are global and, at the top end, dominated by multinational conglomerates'.

The increasing scale and the global reach of private security providers are important new elements in the picture of contemporary global security. The normative issues connected with the privatised provision of security become even more acute in the case of the privatization of war. Not only are the lines between crime control and warfare increasingly difficult to distinguish (as we saw in Chapter 5), but we are also witnessing a certain hybridity of the actors involved in the field. For example, take a look at Blackwater. The company has been responsible among other things for providing security for prominent American government officials and diplomats during their stays in Iraq. On the company's web-pages we can read:

> We have established a global presence and provide training and opera-
> tional solutions for the 21st century in support of security and peace, and
> freedom and democracy everywhere ... We continually prove to be faster,
> better, cheaper, and more efficient and effective than conventionally man-
> aged forces. Our customers include local, state, and federal law enforce-
> ment agencies, the Department of Defense, Department of Homeland
> Security, and most other federal agencies, multi-national corporations,
> non-governmental organizations, and friendly nations from around the
> world.

Blackwater stepped in with helicopters and personnel to protect their clients from the looting which emerged in the aftermath of Hurricane Katrina in New Orleans, when the state could no longer manage the task (Witte, 2005). The company has won not only profitable contracts in Iraq, but also contracts to combat opium cultivation in Afghanistan, showing how the lines between warfare, crime control and even humanitarian aid are getting increasingly blurred.

Today, private companies represent the second largest military force in Iraq, after the US Army. According to some estimates, there are currently 48,000 employees of private security firms in Iraq.[6] Although the situation in Iraq may appear exceptional – and it clearly is with regard to the number of private military personnel involved – the use of such forces is not unusual. The United Nations have in recent years regularly employed private companies to secure their humanitarian missions and personnel. What are popularly referred to as 'mercenaries' or 'soldiers of fortune' have a long history, sowing considerable doubt about the assumption that a monopoly of violence is in

---

[6]http://www.guardian.co.uk/print/0,,329614907-103550,00.html

fact a hallmark of state sovereignty (Thomson, 1994). However, there is no doubt that the 'outsourcing' and 'privatization' of war have reached new heights since the 1990s (Singer, 2003). We do not have the space to examine in detail the dynamics of the private military field. Nevertheless, the topic exposes with great urgency some of the normative issues related to the privatization of crime control: the problems of accountability, transparency, legitimacy and the contested role of the state.

Critique of the 'withering of the state' thesis

While the reports from the battlefields of Iraq may seem the paradigmatic example of the demise of the state monopoly on the use of force, some observers have been far more sceptical of the 'withering of the state' thesis. As we saw in the previous chapter, we have been witnessing a remarkable expansion and growth in state surveillance capabilities in the aftermath of the September 11th attacks. And as we saw in Chapter 4, far from outgrowing the nation state, globalization has in some contexts gone hand in hand with the resurgence of the national as a locus of identity making and cultural belonging. One of the most visible signs of this development in the crime control field has been the expansive growth of prison populations across the world (Christie, 2000; Stern, 2006). In the past five years, prison populations have grown in about two-thirds of all countries. In many cases, they have doubled or tripled in the past two decades (Stern, 2006: 99). Only a small part of the world's 9.1 million-strong prison population is in fact detained in private prisons, although the percentage may be higher for immigration detention facilities. We can see that in spite of losing its monopoly on the use of force, the nation state still crucially relies on it to enforce its laws and regulations, often with renewed urgency.

Critics of the 'withering of the state' thesis therefore point out that we need to move beyond simplistic perceptions of the state as a victim of a 'hostile take-over' by private service providers, non-state agencies and local communities. It may in fact seem that even though the modern nation state may be losing its power, it is essentially not losing its *influence* (Castells, 2004: 303). Furthermore, while the accounts of the privatization of social control may fit well with Anglo-American developments they may not cover equally well the developments in non-English-speaking countries (Shearing, 2004; Jones and Newburn, 2006). The complexity of global transformations once again becomes evident. Even in the UK, which often appears to be a pioneer in market solutions, far from being dead, 'ambitious interventionist government is alive and well' (Crawford, 2006: 455). Crawford argues that in recent years we have 'witnessed the expansion of state control into institutions previously shielded from the force of governmental control', as well as a proliferation of new techniques for controlling troublesome behaviour. Rather then 'withering away', the British state seems to be expanding its net and repertoire of social controls and sponsors social engineering projects similar to those that lay at the heart of the 'old style' welfare state. Instead of the 'hands off' government envisaged by the neo-liberal ideologists, there is increasing evidence that 'hands on' governance still seems to have much purchase on contemporary strategies of social control (Crawford, 2006).

The state in the new global order is therefore not simply accepting its diminished role but is instead, with varying degrees of success, attempting to reassert its authority, often by appearing to do something about the problem of crime. Some observers have suggested that due to the inability to influence global economy, the field of crime control seems to sustain the illusion that action on the national level is and can be efficient (Bauman, 1998, 2004; Christie, 2004). In Bauman's (1998: 120) account the nation state, emptied of most of its tasks by global market forces, is left almost solely with its task of providing safety and functions merely as an 'over-sized police precinct'. On a similar note, Garland (2001a) describes a twofold process where the welfare state partly gives up a number of its social responsibilities, while at the same time trying to show its power by 'acting out' on issues of crime control. These shifts were particularly visible under the 1980s Reagan and Thatcher governments in the US and UK, respectively. As Garland (2001a: 98) observes:

> The often contradictory combination of what came to be known as 'neo-liberalism' (the re-assertion of market disciplines) and 'neo-conservatism' (the re-assertion of moral disciplines), the commitment to 'rolling back the state' while simultaneously building a state apparatus that is stronger and more authoritarian than before – these were the contradictory positions that lay at the heart of the Thatcher and Reagan regimes.

We can see that the 'minimal state' of neo-liberalism is also 'a *penal* state in ways that are often more intense and more politically central than was the case for its predecessor "state regimes" of the post-war period' (Loader and Sparks, 2002: 95). And although we have seen a prolific growth of private security forces, this development has in several contexts been accompanied by an expansion in state police forces as well. Looking at the case of London, the Metropolitan Police Commissioner stated recently that the Metropolitan Police force 'is bigger than the Royal Navy; we are the largest single employer in London; in another world, we would be a FTSE 100 company' (cited in Crawford, 2006: 463). Furthermore, in many national contexts, the existence and efficiency of private security markets depend on the (formal and informal) support and assistance of the state apparatus. The sovereign state, with its overwhelming potential for (although no longer monopoly of) the use of force, still plays a crucial role in the maintenance of social order.

Transnational policing

The disconnection between policing and the nation state seems to be relevant not only when it comes to the question of private policing, but also in issues of internationalization and transnationalization of policing. Police practices increasingly transcend national boundaries, partly in pursuit of the illicit flows they are trying to control, and partly developing their own, independent dynamics. And even though the events of September 11th clearly represent a historic shift in terms of intensification of transnational policing and surveillance, it is important to keep in mind the historic and organizational antecedents of these developments. In his historic account, Deflem (2002) shows how international police co-operation has a rich and complex history, rooted in combating such historic 'evils' as anarchism, Bolshevism, white slavery and nationalist movements. Drawing strongly on Max Weber's account of bureaucracy, Deflem argues that the development has been enabled by a process in which international police agencies gradually gained a degree of bureaucratic independence from the state. Policing practices which transcend national boundaries, therefore, constitute not only an extension of state powers, but also gradually develop a certain degree of autonomy from the state.

Also here the question arises whether this form of policing can be seen as an argument for or against the 'withering of the state' thesis. International and transnational police co-operation may to some point represent an extension of states' powers to effectively police their own territories. However, the development also clearly represents a challenge to the state–policing nexus (Walker, 2003). Some scholars have argued that these connections are qualitatively transforming the nature of policing practices, making them not only *inter*-national (i.e. still having the state as a main reference point), but also *trans*-national (i.e. transcending the state system) (Sheptycki, 2000a). When it comes to the former, Interpol can be seen, according to Walker (2003: 117) as 'the paradigm case of an *inter*national police organization' – lacking in 'legal, symbolic and material resources to be anything other than parasitic on national police authorities'. International policing has been, throughout its history, intrinsically, and perhaps paradoxically, closely bound up with the specific concerns of participating nation states (Deflem, 2002). Historically, the 'war on drugs' has been one such concern, fuelling particularly internationalization of US law enforcement (Nadelman, 1993; see discussions in the previous chapter). According to Walker (2003: 122),

> We see the development of a strong US capacity in international policing shadowing their more interventionist foreign policy generally in both Cold War and post-Cold War eras. In a globalizing world, the USA increasingly

responded to the interconnectedness of its economic and political stability with external forces in a proactive manner, and policing was necessarily part of that policy thrust.

Nevertheless, there seems also to be growing evidence of the relative autonomy of the transnational policing networks from the individual nation states. The development has been pronounced in the context of the European Union and its emerging structures of 'freedom, security and justice'. The Tampare Summit in 1999, the gradual expansion of Europol and the current mobilizations against terrorism have moved the issues of European police co-operation from the relative periphery to be one of the main motors of European co-operation and integration. As Walker (2003: 121) aptly puts it, internal security has changed from a 'poor cousin of European integration' to a mature member of the family, in some regards 'vying for the mantle of head of the family'. The creation of a common European arrest warrant, the newly established network of judicial authorities – Eurojust, the creation of a common European border control agency (Frontex) and the Police Chiefs Operational Task Force – are only some of the newly institutionalized forms of this development. There are, however, also parallel, less institutionalized, more ad hoc developments, which are accelerating the pace of European trans-border policing, giving the EU security field increasingly the semblance of a state-like function (Mathiesen, 2003).

The field of transnational policing, and European policing in particular, has been open to problems of accountability, due to the lack of transparency and the plurality of networks and actors involved (see special issue of *Policing & Society*, 2002). The development is potentially creating a 'democratic deficit' (Loader, 2002), chiming with the dilemmas faced by the introduction of private security networks. The signing of the Schengen Agreement in 1985 and the introduction of the Schengen Information System (discussed in Chapter 2) were among the earlier developments which highlighted the problems of accountability. As Mathiesen (2006: 128) points out, national media and parliaments – the traditional guarantors of accountability – no longer have the capacity nor the time to dig deeply into these issues, so must accept the premises of the executive branch and police agencies. The various European systems are becoming 'interlocked' and 'de-coupled' from the nation states, not only through formal agreements, but also through informal agreements, thus gathering an internal sociological momentum (ibid.). The issues of autonomy of transnational policing networks also have to be situated within the sociological context of the development of specific transnational police subcultures – a professional 'fraternity', which sees its tasks as a sheared mission (Sheptycki, 2002a).

The case of Schengen also brings to our attention the 'centrality of technology to the reconfiguration of what one can call the space of government' (Barry, 2002: 2). The exchange of information is a vital part of the global anti-terrorism efforts, the *computer system*

Schengen Information System and the more extensive Sirene System, police and customs co-operation, Europol's activities, the ECHELON system, and so on (Mathiesen, 2006). The so-called information revolution has fundamentally changed the scope of contemporary policing by reducing the constraints of time and space and enabling action at a distance. If geography and territorial boundaries before represented the main frame for defining the space of government, now, on the other hand, government operates 'in relation to zones formed through the circulation of technical practices and devices' (Barry, 2002: 3). This centrality of global technological networks is articulated in Arjun Appadurai's (1996) concept of technoscapes – technological zones of circulation where technical devices, practices and artefacts are closely connected and compatible. Loader (2004: 67) points out that when it comes to the field of European policing, this is 'an almost entirely *informationalised* activity – a practice oriented not on-the-ground delivery of visible police functions...but towards supporting such practices through the generation, storage and dissemination of information'.

The technologically mediated aspect of policing was described in Ericson and Haggerty's (1997) *Policing the Risk Society*, where the authors suggest a more general transformation of policing towards knowledge work and risk communication with other state and non-state agencies.

> [T]he role of the police as risk communicators in the service of external institutions changes the way in which the police provide security to individuals, organizations, and institutions. In risk society the traditional police focus on deviance, control and order is displaced in favour of focus on risk, surveillance, and security. (1997: 18)

And even though images of police as 'intelligence workers' often present a far too efficient, strategic and comprehensive picture of contemporary policing (Sheptycki, 2004), one should keep in mind the qualitative changes which are in fact taking place. The often repeated argument about the inefficiency of European cross-border information sharing overlooks and underestimates 'the import of the activities that *are actually taking place* on a specifically European level' (Loader, 2004: 67). New technologies thus seem both to transform the traditional territorial scope of policing and to represent an important challenge in terms of their control. We shall examine this issue further, in Chapter 7, with regard to the regulation of the Internet.

Transnational policing is in significant ways also embedded in the changing character of the international legal system and discourse. Criminal law, together with other forms of legal regulation, is being progressively internationalized. States have accepted treaty regimes whereby international authorities exercise regulatory power that interferes with their sovereignty. Parallel to the increasing awareness of various forms of transnational threats (such as terrorism, trafficking and money laundering), there has also been an internationalization and harmonization of legal responses to these threats. New international legal norms and regimes are produced and managed by international institutions such as the EU and the UN, as well as by more or less formalised international networks, such as for example the EU networks for the co-operation of prosecutors, judges, and various levels in police organizations. The limits of state sovereignty are therefore further challenged by international law and the emerging forms of **global governance**, where state sovereignty becomes multiple, overlapping and shared (Held, 1995). And parallel with the trend towards pluralization of policing and security providers, there has been a similar trend towards global legal pluralism, which indicates the fragmented and polycentric nature of the contemporary legal landscape.

The topic of global governance and internationalization of law will be addressed further in the last chapter. At this point we can conclude our discussion by pointing to the complex and contradictory nature of these developments. The issue of declining state sovereignty, and the consequent rise of competing (private, inter- and transnational) forms of governance, represent a conceptual, normative and political challenge to critical criminology. Since the 1970s, critical criminology has seen the state primarily as a problem; now, on the other hand, a tempting solution for some seems to be to call for strengthening of the state in order to reverse the effects of neo-liberalism and the spread of power to (potentially ungovernable and politically unaccountable) transnational forces and actors. However, are we simply to join the sceptical voices of the globalization critics and try to reverse the times, or are we to seize the opportunities for new forms of political and social action provided by the emerging of global forums? We shall explore the issue further in Chapter 8. Before that, we are going to look at yet another potential challenge to the state and its control apparatus: the Internet.

Summary

The declining powers of the nation state have been one of the most politically discussed and lamented aspects of globalization. 'Globalization involves a "massive shake-out" of societies, economies and the institutions of governance' (Held and McGrew, 2003: 122). The increasing power of global corporations, international monetary institutions and global forms of identity making and belonging has led several analysts to predict the imminent decline of the nation state. Privatization of state functions and assets is one of the prime (symbolic) examples of the 'abdication of the state'. Developments in the field of crime control and security are no exception, and this chapter explored the massive growth of the private security industry in the past three decades. Not only policing tasks, but also the running of prisons and other criminal justice services are increasingly left to private contractors. The development is most influentially theorized within the so-called governmentality approach, which sees the new role of the state as regulatory: steering rather than rowing, when it comes to the provision of security. This type of governance demands of citizens and businesses that they take active responsibility for their own safety (the responsibilization thesis). Security thus often becomes a question of individuals' purchasing power – a commodity rather than a public good.

However, the role of the state has not only been diminishing when it comes to matters of criminal justice and crime control. The past decades have seen an unprecedented growth in prison populations in numerous countries across the world, particularly in the Anglo-American context. The US prison population has risen at a tragically breathtaking pace since the 1970s to the current unprecedented level of 723 per 100,000 inhabitants, making the country, together with the Russian federation, the greatest incarcerator in the world. Similarly, the UK prison population has almost doubled in the past 15 years, while the Dutch has nearly tripled. This development marks a transformation from the more inclusive welfare-oriented nation state to the contemporary security state.

STUDY QUESTIONS

1   How does globalization affect state sovereignty? Can you think of examples indicating the demise of the (welfare) state in your country?

2   What ethical dilemmas are inherent in the privatization of crime control? Which state services should in your view remain public?

3   What is the responsibilization strategy? How are you being responsibilized in your daily life when it comes to issues of crime?

4   How is transnationalization of policing transforming state sovereignty?

FURTHER READING

David Garland's (2001a) *The Culture of Control* provides an influential Anglo-American criminological account of the demise of the modern welfare state. With regard to the privatization of crime control, Nil Christie's (2000) *Crime Control as Industry* is an early classic, now in its third edition. Commodification of security is the topic of Alison Wakefield's (2003) *Selling*

Security and George Rigakos's (2002) *The New Parapolice*. The field of pluralization of policing has lately received a considerable amount of criminological attention. Les Johnston and Clifford Shearing's (2003) *Governing Security* offers a valuable overview of the debate, as well as suggesting alternative modes of security governance. Trevor Jones and Tim Newburn's (2006) *Plural Policing* is the most recent and updated contribution in the field. The issue of privatization of war and the private military industry is discussed, among other topics, in Peter W. Singer's (2003) *Corporate Warriors*. The field of transnational policing is the theme of James Sheptycki's (2000a) edited volume *Issues in Transnational Policing* and *In Search of Transnational Policing* (2002b), as well as Peter Andreas and Ethan Nadelmann's (2006) very recent contribution *Policing the Globe*. Looking at the transnationalization of police work from a different perspective, Donatella della Porta et al.'s (2006) *The Policing of Transnational Protest* examines the policing of anti-globalization protests.

7

Controlling Cyberspace?

Chapter Contents

Technology and social change   153

Identity in a disembodied and disembedded world   156

Cybercrime – old wine in new bottles?   158

Governing cyberspace   161

Virtual and virtualized communities   165

  Summary   169

  Study questions   170

  Further reading   170

OVERVIEW

Chapter 7 examines the following issues:

- The nature of cyberspace, as a social space and as a motor of globalization and globalism.

- The notion of a viewer or synoptic society and how it creates new parameters of surveillance and new discursive arenas for crime and punishment.

- The issue of cybercrime: its nature and the challenges it represents for contemporary governance, and for criminological theory.

KEY TERMS

biometrics	dataveillance	synoptic (viewer) societies
commercialization	digital divide	technological determinism
crime mapping	social construction of crime	virtual communities
cybercrime		

In December 2006 the Internet and the camera-equipped mobile phone gained a central place in Iraqi history thanks to the notorious video of Saddam Hussein's execution. As TV debated the morality of showing explicit images of what it trumpeted as the 'Death of a Dictator', the video of Saddam Hussein's execution was already circulating on the Net, endlessly reproducing itself as it was linked from site to site.[1] The disturbing images spread across the world in a matter of hours and made the front page in newspapers across the world the day after. Millions of people clicked in on YouTube to see the last minutes of a dictator's life. Death is no longer a private affair, nor is punishment the detached, rationalized administration of pain. The harrowing public displays of penal executions, which once seemed to belong to the bygone past of uncivilized medieval penality, are now only a click away. A question can be asked, of course, what the consequences are, if any. An execution is still an execution, in all its inhumanity, regardless of whether we participate in it as spectators. Or is it the same, and are *we* still the same?

Our daily lives are mediated by a growing number of technologies, also when it comes to questions of crime and deviance and the administration of justice. In the previous chapters we discussed CCTV cameras and other technological

---

[1] http://www.guardian.co.uk/print/0,,329673678-103681,00.html

paraphernalia used in contemporary crime control. In this chapter, our attention will turn to the Internet. The Net can be seen as the prime example and a symbol of global connectivity, as the iconic global fluid. Increasingly, our professional and leisure activities are shaped by this connectivity. The Internet has become a site for sharing the most private and personal aspects of people's lives – often without the consent of the subjects involved. Celebrities and politicians find their secrets and intimate details of their lives revealed to the public, while blogging has become a global pastime. Newspapers are daily filled with more and less serious types of threats presented by the Internet, from identity theft to cyberterrorism, cyberstalking, 'grooming' and paedophilia. The challenges of global governance are perhaps best exemplified by the extraterritorial and seemingly unregulated nature of cyberspace. In this chapter we shall examine some of the changes and challenges these developments represent for our understanding of crime and crime control, and more generally, their impact on the nature of our sociality and our perceptions of ourselves and others.

Technology and social change

Technologies have long been seen as important agents of social change. From the invention of print, and railways, to automobiles and television, not to mention the lethal technologies of war, technological change has had a dramatic impact on social behaviour. In recent decades, the rise of information and communication technologies has significantly shaped the ways we lead our lives, design our institutions and produce our knowledge. We are witnessing a rapid growth of these technologies in virtually all areas of our daily lives. They are ingrained in such mundane tasks as communicating with our spouses and children, paying bills, gaining access to places of work and leisure or booking hotel rooms and cinema tickets. Academic work, although largely remaining print and speech based, is also incorporating new innovations such as email, presentation of courses, persons and books on the Internet, electronic publishing, distance learning, and of course there are few academic texts today which are written without the help of computers. The Internet can be seen as the backbone of these transformations and its impact is hard to ignore (Castells, 1996, 2001). Only the sheer speed of its proliferation is astonishing. The Internet took three years to reach its first 50 million users, while it took television 15 years and radio 37 years to achieve the same (Naughton cited in Jewkes, 2007: 4).

However, the social impact of these transformations is far from clear. The 1990s saw the Internet as a transformer and bearer of radical change, described in numerous prophetic bestsellers about the 'third wave', the coming of the virtual society and the information revolution. The Net was seen as the prime bearer of global transformations, a borderless frontier, leading to the 'death of distance' and eroding the scope of the nation state. In Castells's influential opus, the Internet is seen as the prime example of the 'space of flows', as the inherently global technology which defines the essence of the emerging network society. The Internet is 'the technological basis for the organizational form of the Information Age: the network' (Castells, 2001: 1). Paraphrasing Marshall McLuhan's famous 'the medium is the message', Castells boldly claims that in the information age 'the network is the message'.

> Core economic, social, political and cultural activities throughout the planet are being structured by and around the Internet, and other computer networks. In fact, exclusion from these networks is one of the most damaging forms of exclusion in our economy and in our culture. (2001: 3)

The social effects of technologies are a hotly debated issue within the social sciences. The early writing about the Internet has consequently been accused of **technological determinism** and critical voices tried to moderate the euphoria by pointing out that the effects of technological change may be far less dramatic and predictable. It was claimed that rather than society being shaped by technology, technological developments and uses are shaped by a series of socio-economic factors. This so-called 'social shaping of technology' approach pointed out that technological change has to be understood within the larger framework of social change (see for example Woolgar, 2002). Technology operates in a social context and it can have unforeseen and unintended consequences, as well as different meanings to people in different social and organizational positions. The social shaping approach points out that the Internet is not only a global, 'free floating' medium, but is used in local spaces and shaped by local contexts and constraints. Moreover, as we saw in the previous chapter, the nation state still seems to be a major force in shaping globalization just as much as technology does. The Internet has after all its origins in Arpanet, a computer network set up by the US Defense Department in order to build its military might in the Cold War race (Castells, 2001). The uses of the Internet are shaped by a series of socio-economic factors such as consumerism and market thinking, which also shape many other aspects of our existence. Relationships of power, gender, race and global economic inequality are permeating cyberlife, and are inscribed in cyber-relations, as they are in terrestrial life (Jewkes and Sharp, 2003; Cunneen and Stubbs, 2004). Rather than being a universal medium, the Internet reflects the deeply stratified and divided global condition. Internet access is unequally distributed, creating a **digital divide** along class, racial and ethnic lines within countries, as well as between the global North and the global South (Castells, 2001). Cyber-connectivity is therefore a sign of privilege on the global level.

Traces of technological determinism are still common features of popular and media representations of the Internet which tend to overstate the power of the Internet and underplay the importance of other social forces and of the individual actor. 'Where the human element *is* central to a story, it tends to be dominated by positivist notions of vulnerable offenders' (Jewkes, 2007: 5). Children in particular are seen as easily falling prey to various cyber-dangers. Think of the recurring debates about the negative effects of video games on juvenile violent crime. 'Killed by the Internet' stories, as Jewkes (2007) points out, appear at regular intervals in the media, leading to calls for greater government and self-regulation of this apparently dangerous medium. The Internet has, perhaps more than other technologies, had its fair share of critics and enthusiasts. Critics have pointed out the need to move beyond simplistic cause and effect thinking about technology. The increasing embeddedness of information and communication technologies in forms of everyday life makes it difficult to see these technologies as isolated in their social effects (Rasmussen, 2000). 'No longer do they belong to the "sub-stratum" which merely *effect* cultural processes. As with television, they are *themselves* cultural products' (ibid.: 5, italics original). Therefore, in order to examine the implications of technological change we need to inscribe it into the real life contexts in which it emerges. Castells (2001: 5) sees the Internet as particularly malleable technology, 'susceptible of being deeply modified by its social practice, and leading to a whole range of potential social outcomes – to be discovered by experience, not proclaimed beforehand'.

These conflicting views reveal a more fundamental duality in the nature of the Internet – its potential to pervert and to democratize (Jewkes, 2003, 2007). The video footage of Saddam's execution discussed above clearly belongs to the first category, while, on the other hand, human rights groups arm individuals in conflict zones with video cameras so they can record and expose human rights abuses (Naim, 2007). The so-called YouTube effect has lately been acknowledged by political analysts, politicians and political activists alike. Video clips, often produced by individuals on their own, are viewed by people across the world. According to some estimates, 'YouTube receives 20 million visitors a month, who watch 100 million clips a day. There are 65,000 new videos posted every day' (ibid.). Here, everyone may get their 15 minutes of fame, as Andy Warhol once famously professed. In Chapter 5 we suggested that the development adds a new twist to the classic theme of panopticism and the surveillance society. We are living, as Mathiesen (1997) points out, not only in panoptic societies, where the few, with a great force, discipline and watch the many. We are also living in *viewer* or *synoptic societies,* where the new media allow the many to watch the few. Writing primarily about television, Mathiesen (1997) sees the development as a further step in the intensification of social control and the disciplining of our consciousness. Others, however, have noted its potential for political and cultural participation, as exemplified by YouTube's motto 'Broadcast Yourself'. In 2006, *Time* magazine chose its person of the year to be 'you' – the individual citizen, the contributor to YouTube and to the global encyclopedia Wikipedia, and the member of the online metropolis MySpace.

This (global) connectivity introduces a new dynamics to several aspects of contemporary crime and social control. Crime and deviance gain new forms and arenas. Teenagers can post video clips of their joy-riding bravado on the Net and, more tragically, mobile footage of violence and abuse. The Internet offers prostitution guides to potential sex tourists and local customers in almost any corner of the world. Moreover, discourses about crime and deviance take place in new environments, the nature and the effects of which are still quite unexplored. Online forums thus often reveal the uncensored face of vengeance and penal populism (Valier, 2004). Cyberspace challenges traditional notions of penal power and sovereignty which have been tied to territoriality and the nation state. In what follows, we shall explore further some of these challenges as well as the ability of new information and communication technologies to redefine our perceptions of time, space and identity.

Identity in a disembodied and disembedded world

'Are you the real you?' was a headline recently facing me in my morning newspaper. The headline referred to the growing concerns about the dangers of identity theft and identity fraud. The anonymity of the Internet, and the proliferation of information and communication technologies in everyday life, have increased the possibilities of identity-related offences (Finch, 2007; Smith, 2007). However, we should pause for a minute and examine first the concept of identity theft. The idea of identity loss and identity theft would sound almost absurd to an outsider. The assumption behind the notion of identity theft is that identity is something detached from oneself, having an objective and thing-like quality, like money, for example (Aas, 2006). This is to some extent the case in cyber and other computer-mediated environments. We access our computers with the help of passwords. We pay our bills in online banks, bookstores and other shops with the help of cryptic letters and numbers which identify us as the rightful owners of bank accounts. The password has become the ubiquitous bearer of identity in contemporary culture. When before, we had to meet in banks in person and sign the various documents, now the cryptic letters and words are all that is needed for computers to recognize us. Nevertheless, it may be useful to remember that, historically, pen and paper signatures, just like passwords, became accepted as a guarantee of legitimate identity due to modernization and the fact that people and organizations became more mobile (Lyon 2001). Passwords used in contemporary technological environments are merely a continuation of this trend towards abstract relationships in modernity and late modernity. We discussed this trend in Chapter 1 in terms of disembedding of social systems and time–space compression. Disembedded identities are 'lifted out' of social relations and local contexts of interaction and restructured across indefinite spans of time and space (Giddens, 1990: 21).

The disembedding of identity is not a trait specific to online communication, but is rather a general trait of several aspects of contemporary life. Living in an increasingly global world means doing things and identifying oneself at a distance (Aas, 2005b). We live our lives at a distance and increasingly communicate at man/machine interfaces. The dilemmas of anonymity and living in a world of strangers have been discussed at several points in this book (see Chapter 3). As a consequence, the trend towards surveillance and securitization of everyday life is increasingly extending to questions of identification and identity verification. Establishing stable identities of their subjects has always been one of the central tasks of modern nation states (Torpey, 2000; Lyon, 2001). However, in the present world of global flows and disembedded social relations the task of giving stable identities to mobile and versatile populations becomes extremely difficult, if not impossible. We saw in Chapter 2 how in the aftermath of the 9/11 attacks, authorities in numerous countries introduced **biometrics** to identify their foreign visitors and foreign residents (think for example of the US VISIT programme). Biometrics is also increasingly used to identify regular citizens in several countries through biometric ID cards (Lyon, 2005) as well as for commercial purposes, for example, as systems for regulating access to buildings such as courts and training centres, access to ATMs and computer files. The New South Wales police are following the example of the Los Angeles Police Department and are set to introduce portable fingerprint scanners by the end of 2006, thus enabling on-the-spot identity checks (*Computerworld*, 2005). The futuristic scenarios depicted in science fiction movies such as *Minority Report* suddenly seem less remote than before (Aas, 2006). Not surprisingly, biometrics is increasingly being considered as a solution for minimizing the risks of identity-related cybercrime (Smith, 2007).

Cyber-environments take the trend towards anonymity and disembedding of social relations to a new level. Some commentators, particularly in the early stages of the Internet, argued that the life on the screen encourages an understanding of the self as multiple, fluid and distinctly postmodern (Turkle, 1995). The liquid modernity described by Bauman (2000) gains in many ways its prime expression in cyberspace. 'Life on the screen' means that physical reality may be just one of the 'windows' one has opened at a particular point in life (Turkle, 1995). Life on line has been seen as different from the 'real' world, offering experiences unavailable anywhere else and providing 'a locus for creative authorship of the self' (Jewkes and Sharp, 2003: 3). This anonymity of cyber-environments can be by some experienced as liberating, as enabling social interaction without the prejudicial effects of corporeal presence. Identity is 'free-floating' and disembodied, free from real life constraints. This 'disentanglement from the body allows the self to break free from the usual constraints of corporeality which, in the physical world, may prevent individuals from displaying aspects of their identities that would be discredited or disapproved of by others' (Jewkes, 2003: 8). By putting on their 'electronic cloaks', people may experiment freely with their sexuality and become accustomed to new ways of thinking about relationships and identity (DiMarco, 2003).

> With no fear of exposing themselves to stigma, ridicule or physical harm, Internet users can negotiate new sexual identities, engage in secret sexual deviancy and acquire numerous sexual partners, while all the time protected by the 'electronic cloak' that is virtual reality. (ibid.: 53)

In this anonymous world, the conventional distinctions between public and private, licit and illicit, real and unreal, become obscured.

Other, increasingly numerous, voices stress the dangers of this type of social interaction. The anonymity of cyberlife offers not only numerous possibilities of role playing and identity experimentation. Traditionally, anonymity has also been seen as fostering deviance and criminality, due to social distance and the lack of informal social controls. Moreover, deviant individuals and groups, such as paedophiles, neo-nazis and other radical and racist groups, now find encouragement and belonging in online forums and communities. Cyber-chattels create new markets for buying brides and babies, thus recreating old historic perceptions of women and children as property, which can be traded (Letherby and Marchbank, 2003). Innumerable Internet marriage marketing sites offer First World men essentialized and racialized representations of Third World women as commodities. Women can be chosen according to ethnicity, age, social background and personal characteristics. They are treated according to marketing tactics employed for other types of 'products' (ibid.). These virtually mediated male fantasies often end in a tragically violent reality. Cunneen and Stubbs (2004) show, for example, that Filipino women are almost six times over-represented as victims of homicide in Australia; homicides largely committed by their Australian spouses and partners. On numerous marriage sites Filipino women, and Asian women in general, are presented as submissive and exotic male fantasies; representations which they are in no position to contest. As such, the Internet serves to reinforce unequal and oppressive social, cultural and gender relations.

Cybercrime – old wine in new bottles?

Looking at these examples, one is tempted to conclude that the Internet represents yet another arena or a tool for committing traditional acts of crime and deviance, for example hate crime, stalking, theft and violence. This indeed has been a proposition made by, for example, Grabosky (2001) who argues that virtual criminality is basically the same as terrestrial crime, only committed through a new medium – a case of 'old wine in new bottles'. 'While the technology of implementation, and particularly its efficiency, may be without precedent, the crime is fundamentally familiar' (ibid.: 243). Other commentators are more willing to acknowledge the novelty of cyberspace, not only in moving the boundaries of what is considered deviant (cyber-deviance), but also regarding novel forms and parameters of legally sanctioned deviant behaviour (*cybercrime*). Although the effects of, for example, theft may be the same, regardless of how it is committed, the global reach of information and communication technologies represents (quantitatively) a fundamentally new dimension. The technology 'acts as a "force multiplier" enabling individuals with minimal resources to generate potentially huge negative effects (mass distribution of email "scams" and viruses being two examples)' (Yar, 2006: 11–12). Unlike real world crimes, cybercrimes can be automated (Brenner, 2007). Bank robbers no longer have to meticulously plan the theft of millions of dollars. New technological capabilities at their disposal now mean that one person can effectively commit millions of robberies of $1 each (Wall, 2007). Furthermore, while some cybercrimes, such as theft and pornography, can also be committed in the terrestrial world, others, such as hacking, owe their existence to the specific nature of digital technologies and cyber-environments. Academic discussion on cybercrime therefore relates to both types of behaviour.

Cybercrime is an elusive phenomenon and can cover a number of acts and activities. Wall (2001: 2) points out that the term has no specific referent in law and is a concept mainly invented by the media. Yar (2006: 9) suggests that instead of trying to grasp cybercrime as a single phenomenon, it might be more productive to view the term 'as signifying a range of illicit activities whose "common denominator" is the central role played by networks of information and communication technology in their commission'. Most commentators acknowledge the fundamental shift represented by the transnational nature of crime in digital environments. Consider the following report about the elusive nature of child pornography:

> According to investigators in Austria, some 2,360 suspects from 77 countries downloaded horrific images of young children being sexually abused and raped. They were believed to have been shot in Eastern Europe and uploaded to the web in Britain, posted on a Russian website hosted by an Austrian company. Investigators say that in a 24-hour period they recorded more than 8,000 hits on the site from computer addresses in countries from America to Algeria and Macedonia to Mexico. Some of the material

was free but the Russian site was charging $89 (68 euros, £45) for access to a 'members only' section.[2]

The spatially distributed nature of cyberspace and cybercrime represents a series of challenges for criminal justice agencies trying to control the phenomenon. Different legislative systems and traditions are an obstacle to effective control and prosecution. What is prohibited in one jurisdiction may be legal in another. For example, Jewkes and Andrews (2007) report that Russia has become a major source of child pornography due to a legislative vacuum, despite the fact that the majority of the offensive material has its origin in other jurisdictions. Moreover, the deterritorialized nature of the phenomenon demands a new conceptual and practical framework from law enforcement and legal authorities (see discussion in the next section).

The deterritorialized nature of cyberspace and cybercrime is also a considerable theoretical challenge for criminological scholars trying to grasp these phenomena. Cybercrime and cyber-deviance in general represent a challenge to traditional – corporeal and spatially bound – criminological concepts (Yar, 2006). One thinks of traditional subcultural theories, as well as to some extent control theories, which are implicitly built on the assumption of face-to-face social interaction. In cyber-environments, on the other hand, the parameters of social interaction, communication and identity making are defined by technologies which function at a distance. The controlled–controller and victim–offender encounters are mediated by technological interfaces. Furthermore, Yar (2006) suggests that cybercrime challenges the traditional criminological relationship between offending and social marginality and exclusion. As we saw earlier, access to the Internet can in itself be seen as a sign of relative social privilege, even in developed countries. Cyber-deviants and offenders therefore disturb the classical image of offenders as belonging to the poorest and least educated strata of the population. Conversely, the skills and resources required to commission offences in cyberspace are concentrated among the relatively privileged, those enjoying higher levels of employment, income, and education (ibid.: 19).

A further dilemma in the understanding of cybercrime and deviance is the intricate and ethically often unclear relationship between mediated representations and 'real world' offences. What are, for example, the dangers of 'simply looking' at pornographic images of child abuse (Jewkes and Andrews, 2007)? Is the offensive material less offensive if the images are digitally manipulated 'pseudo-photographs' (Yar, 2006)? How do the traditional notions of legal responsibility adjust to these new environments? In the case of child pornography, criminal responsibility is increasingly attributed to spatially distant

---

[2] http://newsvote.bbc.co.uk/mpapps/pagetools/print/news.bbc.co.uk/2/hi/europe/6341737.stm

individuals who through their consumption of images create a market for 'real world' abuse. The phenomenon thereby highlights that the participants in a viewer society are not simply passive individuals connected by technological networks, but should be treated as responsible agents in a globally shared social space. This is not a dilemma specific to cyberspace. Living in globally connected environments means that individual, seemingly insignificant, choices can have grave ethical and social consequences on a global level, as pointed out by the environmental and ethical trade movements (see also discussion about global criminology in Chapter 8).

Governing cyberspace

The historic development of the Internet reveals a synergic effect of two unlikely influences: big science and military research, and the grassroots 'culture of freedom', represented by the early hacker culture (Castells, 2001). This duality of freedom and control is still a defining feature of cyber-environments, and shapes the present debates about the governance of cyberspace. From a functional point of view, the Internet can be described as a global infrastructure for data interchange, based upon a network of networks and a common set of protocols, address space of names and numbers. Its origins lie in the Arpanet research project, funded by the US Department of Defense, which opened up in the 1980s and became Internet (for a historic overview see Castells, 2001). The original design of the Arpanet was based on a decentralized and open architecture which presupposed no concept of central ownership and control. Under these conditions, the Net was able to grow rapidly as anyone could add to the architecture by adding a new service. Due to this architecture of openness, and the sheer volume of nodes and cyber-interaction, surveillance of the Internet requires a massive effort. The image of the Internet as 'ungovernable' has therefore a strong historic resonance.

The early perception that the Internet cannot be governed went hand in hand with the view that it *should not* be governed, that governmental intervention was in many ways contrary to its spirit of freedom. For many early cyber-citizens, or netizens, the Net represented a realm free of governmental intervention and real life inequalities. The so-called cyber-libertarians forcefully defended a 'hands off' approach to Internet governance. This notion of the Internet as an open, boundless frontier had a certain affinity with neo-liberal thinking which similarly promoted the virtues of minimal state intervention (see discussion of the state in Chapter 6). The view is well expressed in John Perry Barlow's manifesto, 'A Declaration of the Independence of Cyberspace'. Here, Barlow, a well-known Net personality declares:

> I declare the global social space we are building to be naturally indepen-
> dent of the tyrannies you seek to impose on us …Cyberspace does not lie
> within your borders …. You claim there are problems among us that you
> need to solve. You use this claim as an excuse to invade our precincts.
> Many of these problems don't exist. Where there are real conflicts, where
> there are wrongs, we will identify them and address them by our means.
> We are forming our own Social Contract…We are creating a world that all
> may enter without privilege or prejudice accorded by race, economic
> power, military force, or station of birth. We are creating a world where
> anyone, anywhere may express his or her beliefs, no matter how singular,
> without fear of being coerced into silence or conformity. Your legal con-
> cepts of property, expression, identity, movement, and context do not
> apply to us. They are all based on matter, and there is no matter here.[3]

The manifesto clearly reveals a perception of cyberspace as a realm which is radically different from 'real life' and antithetic to government intervention – a position which has had a lot of purchase among online participants and researchers alike.

However, the view of cyberspace as a realm of freedom has in past years been challenged on several points. Numerous, highly publicized, cybercrimes and dangers have revealed the Internet to be not only a space of freedom, but also of vulnerability, which calls for greater government intervention. The advocates of cyber-regulation – concerned citizens, media, politicians, as well as the business sector – have pointed out that governments can have a potentially positive role when it comes to dealing with issues such as pornography, spam, protecting intellectual property and privacy rights. A series of socio-economic developments has furthermore challenged the prevailing image of the Internet as a decentralized, boundless system, antithetic to state intervention, or any kind of regulation. Human rights organizations have criticized search giants, such as Google, Microsoft and Yahoo!, for colluding with governments in countries such as China, Iran and Vietnam that censor websites and prosecute and jail bloggers. A more fundamental assault on the liberty of the Internet has come from the trend towards *commercialization*, visible in numerous domains of 'terrestrial' life discussed elsewhere in this book. Lawrence Lessig's (1999) influential *Code and Other Laws of Cyberspace* pointed out that the environment of the Internet is changing under the influence of commercial interests and that its architecture is increasingly introducing barriers. Commercial service providers are erecting tollgates, names and numbers have become valuable merchandise and, not least, the growing amounts of spam reveal the commercial exploitation of cyberspace.

This intertwining of commercial and governmental interests has fundamentally transformed the early views that the Internet cannot, and should not, be

---

[3]Source: http://homes.eff.org/ ~ barlow/Declaration-Final.html

governed. Today, a variety of governmental and commercial technologies of control is curtailing the anonymity and privacy of cyber-citizens (Castells, 2001; Lyon, 2003a). According to Castells (2001: 171), these technologies can be divided into technologies of identification (such as passwords, 'cookies' and authentication procedures), surveillance and investigation. Rather than being extraordinary procedures, these surveillance practices are increasingly becoming routine aspects of online communication. One only has to think of how a routine purchase in an online shop usually results in a series of 'personalized' recommendations and commercial email offers. Data gathering is a vital aspect of the growing e-commerce, work-related surveillance and even politics. In the 2000 US elections, Castells (2001: 176) reports, a US company created a database which, using data from different sources, provided political profiling of as many as 150 million citizens, selling it to the highest bidder.

One of the vital reasons behind the increasing surveillance and governmental intervention in cyberlife has been the perception of the growing threat of cyber-crime. A series of more or less intense moral panics have created an image of the Internet as infested with dangerous individuals, which prey not only on people's bank accounts, but also on public morality and the wellbeing of children. In the case of cyberspace, we can again see a tendency towards 'governing through crime', discussed in previous chapters. The figure of the hacker has undergone a transformation from a 'brave new pioneer of the computer revolution' to a criminal, in extreme cases, even a 'folk devil' (Yar, 2006). The debates about cyber-crime reveal several aspects of contemporary technology fears, as well as the contested nature of the *social construction of crime* (see also discussion of terrorism in Chapter 5). Similarly, the recent moral crusades against cyberstalking (Wykes, 2007) and Internet piracy (Yar, 2007) expose the contested nature of criminality. In the case of music piracy, Yar (2007: 95–6) argues that

> we see the ways in which organized economic interests (the recording industry and its allies) have attempted to create a new moral consensus about music downloading as a form of harmful criminal activity, and those (predominantly young) people who engage in it as 'parasites' and 'thieves'.

The case of Internet piracy reveals the social dynamics of labelling, and the ability of powerful social actors to define certain behaviours as criminal, as well as resistance strategies employed on the part of those labelled deviant (Yar, 2007).

Debates about cybercrime can also be seen as an interesting example of risk thinking and the precautionary logic discussed in Chapter 5. '[M]uch of the debate about Internet regulation and censorship appears to be based on speculative notions of the anti-social and harmful impacts it may have at some point in the future' (Jewkes, 2007: 5). In some jurisdictions, 'grooming' – the seduction of children over the Internet with intent to obtain sex – has become an offence, or is under legislative consideration. The intention is to intervene before the offence is committed in the 'real world' and no physical victimization needs to take place in order to secure a conviction. Consequently, several legislative and institutional initiatives have in recent years enabled intensification of government surveillance of cyber-communication. Carnivore, the FBI's controversial search engine, is reportedly capable of 'sniffing' several million emails per second, and as mentioned earlier, the new European legislation requires Internet service providers to keep records of emails and Internet connections for up to two years.

However, while some observers see the above developments as signs of the imminent 'end of privacy' and the rise of surveillance society (Castells, 2001), others have pointed out the inadequacy and, ultimately, the futility of governmental intervention in cyberspace. The Internet has, since its inception, challenged traditional notions of policing and state sovereignty which have been tied to territoriality. As we saw in the previous chapters, challenges to the policing–territorial nation state nexus are increasingly coming from several directions, not the least transnational organized crime. Nevertheless, the challenges of policing a global space are magnified in cyberspace, where social interaction is freed from the constraints of physical space. As indicated by the case of child pornography presented above, offenders and victims may be situated in different countries across the globe. Unlike most terrestrial crimes, cybercrime does not require physical proximity between victim(s) and offender. The lack of 'physical' evidence and the lack of spatial connections make these types of offences extremely challenging to investigate (Brenner, 2007). Assumptions about 'where' crime is committed are an important part of criminological and policing vocabularies (Yar, 2006). Numerous approaches, such as 'routine activity', criminogenic zones, community policing and the like, draw their strength from establishing connections between policing and territories. Policing of the Internet, on the other hand, marks a move from the policing of territory to the 'policing of suspect populations' (Sheptycki, 2002a), and a move from surveillance to *'dataveillance'* (Clarke, 2003). Now, the capability of systematic monitoring of data flows gains primacy over knowing the local 'beat' and the local community. The information technologies are in several ways changing the deeply embedded assumptions of police practice (Ericson and Haggerty, 1997).

The problem of cybercrime demands international solutions to what are inherently global problems. These international solutions are gradually taking shape, as exemplified by the Council of Europe's Convention on Cybercrime (Brenner, 2007). The convention is the first international treaty on crimes committed via the Internet. Its objective is to ensure that domestic laws criminalize several categories of cybercrime and establish the procedural tools necessary to investigate such crimes under their own national laws. Over 40 countries have already signed the convention (ibid.). However, policing the potentially ungovernable cyberspace not only demands (inter)governmental intervention, but also needs to mobilize a series of responsibilization strategies such as self-policing on the part of the users and co-operation from the 'architects' of the system (Brenner, 2007). The notion of plural policing (discussed in Chapter 6) and the diffusion of police and regulatory tasks is therefore one of the trademarks of cyber-governance (Jewkes, 2003), and private regulation is also an extremely active force. The challenges posed by the extraterritorial nature of cyberspace thus illustrate several aspects of the changing parameters of contemporary penal governance, which is increasingly marked by its at-a-distance and fragmented nature.

Virtual and virtualized communities

The previous discussion indicates that traditional notions and constellations of space, control and community gain new dimensions in cyberspace. In what follows we shall briefly examine how cyberspace provides new notions of community and can offer new possibilies of communal engagement, and then, how virtual forms of interaction are also changing real life perceptions of crime and communities. The Internet, and information and communication technologies in general, have been credited with creation of so-called *virtual communities* (for a discussion on the meaning of the virtual see Shields, 2003; Aas, 2007). In cyberspace, community has become a non-geographical concept; it is created among individuals who are not concretely present for each other. Not only the Internet, but also mobile phones and television, and other forms of global connectivity mentioned in this book, have stretched social relations to unprecedented levels. Today, there is talk of the virtual office, virtual university, virtual relationships, virtual tours, and even virtual warfare. It is not uncommon, in academic discussions too, for a phenomenon's importance (and hence 'reality'?) to be illustrated by the number of 'hits' it gets on the Internet. Nor is it uncommon to 'google' a person or a phenomenon to gain an impression of their nature. Moreover, virtualization is a vital part of the global capitalist economy (Castells, 2001). The digital virtuality of the Internet is only one of several forms of virtuality present in contemporary life. Virtualization is an essential trait of globalization and of the perception of the world as a 'global village'. This is true not only for the estimated 8 million players in the online computer game World of Warcraft, but also for the anti-globalization movements activated with the help of digital media (Cere, 2007). Some critics see the trend towards virtualization as a sign of the deterioration of social bonds and community life. While distant places become close and proximate, real life relations and neighbourhoods become distant and unknown.

This digital virtuality is also having an impact on contemporary discourses about, and perceptions of, crime and punishment. In her analysis of online communication about crimes, trials and punishment Valier (2004) shows how the Internet has become a site for various forms of 'technological populism' by encouraging popular participation in web-polls and debates about crime and punishment (see discussion of penal populism in Chapter 4). The recently established 'Sun Justice' website, run by the infamous British tabloid, offers its readers 'name and shame' galleries of paedophiles and 'soft judges', an interactive map of sex offenders, a link to the Crime Stoppers' website, and CCTV footage of crime-related topics, among others. The Internet has become a forum for emotional, often hateful, discourses about crime and deviance, framing the discussions in terms of 'tabloid justice' (Valier, 2004). Through online communication the 'new punitiveness' (Pratt et al., 2005) finds an additional forum, particularly as the Internet to a large extent transcends the restrictions imposed on print and television by legal and professional journalistic standards. 'It permits anyone to act as reporter or publisher of images and information, to transmit material on any topic to a potentially global audience, as well as allowing people to participate in real-time conversations with distant others' (Valier, 2004: 97). The shift in the balance between populism and professionalism (Garland, 2001a) therefore gains an additional dimension through the mushrooming of online forums. Rather than seeing the Internet as an agent of social anomie and individualism or, on the other hand, an embodiment of the libertarian ideas of cyber-tolerance and democracy, Valier (2004: 109) points to the emerging new forms of online community and solidarity relating to issues of crime and punishment. Online communications 'bring new forms of imagined co-presence and connectedness, which question the Durkheimian association of the passion of punishment with locally or nationally based *communitas*'. In highly publicized murder cases, such as the James Bulger case, these communications may obtain a global reach and form 'transnational vengeful networks' (ibid.: 103). What is important here is that the extraterritorial nature of online communication transforms the dynamics of public penal discourse and social belonging, which has been traditionally connected to bounded local and national communities.

The Internet is therefore also a forum for creating images of 'the other' – not only criminal offenders, but also members of religious and ethnic groups, or for that matter, supporters of opposing football teams. The 'criminology of the other', discussed in Chapter 4, is in increasingly salient ways structured by the communicational environment of cyberspace. It is a telling example that the prime 'public enemies' of our time, Osama Bin Laden and his alleged network, are rendered 'real' primarily through various forms of virtually mediated reality such as videos and recorded messages posted on the Internet. Furthermore, abductions and executions of hostages in Iraq are frequently confirmed to global audiences by online videos. Despite a pervasive digital divide in the Muslim world, Bunt (2003) points out that the Internet and Cyber Islamic Environments have had a major role, in the post-9/11 context, in the development of various new forms of Muslim consciousness and activism. Online connections are nurturing offline mobilizations by evoking a language adjusted to the cultural ethos of the MTV generation. Al-Qaeda has for example created a special media production unit called Al Sahab ('The Cloud'), which routinely posts its videos online, with the realistic expectation that they will be picked up by major media outlets and other websites (Naim, 2007). Online environments are a part of the so-called global mediascapes and technoscapes (Appadurai, 1996) and are becoming essential forums for identity constitution. The Internet has been an important element in numerous contemporary political movements, not least the anti-globalization movements and political struggles of indigenous populations, such as Zapatistas in Mexico (Cere, 2007).

Contemporary web-based technologies therefore need to be understood within the broader social context of how they are inscribed into everyday life, including contemporary strategies of political struggles, crime prevention and crime control. For example, on the Megan's Law Internet site, operated by the Office of the US Attorney-General, California residents can obtain information about registered sex offenders in their community.[4] Information provided includes name, aliases, age, gender, race, physical description and photograph, as well as individuals' criminal convictions. Viewers can search the website by city, county, zip code or individual name. They can also type in the name of a park or school in a community to locate on a digital map sex offenders living in the vicinity. Importantly, the site provides home addresses of about 33,500 of the most serious offenders. Similar, more or less extensive registers are available in the majority of the US states. In this context, the virtually mediated dangers can be experienced as more 'real' than individuals' actual and concrete experiences of these dangers, thus creating a separate world of 'hyper-real' danger in the community. The Megan's Law mapping system can be seen as yet another example of the emerging surveillance society (Lyon, 2001), however it also provides an insight into the changing notions of community and danger. The system represents by no means the kind of community that first comes to mind when we think of a virtual community. Nonetheless, it is an example of how the new punitive discourse about community safety – represented by the website's motto 'Keeping children safe/parents informed' – is appropriating the surveillance potential of the latest technologies.

Online mapping of offline dangers is becoming a pervasive phenomenon. Geographic information systems (GIS) are gradually becoming a standard item of police equipment. Besides being a tool for facilitating efficiency and

---

[4] See: http://www.meganslaw.ca.gov/.

effectiveness of policing and allocation of resources, these systems offer a simulated construction of community as an 'information hub'. Introducing the language of 'crime hotspots' and 'criminogenic areas' these systems provide and create images of low and high risk communities to the police and other agencies (Gundhus, 2006). Information sharing between the police and their partners, as well as the public, is a vital aspect of these strategies, as exemplified by the US Weed and Seed system where one can obtain information not only about crime-related matters, but also about the racial and ethnic composition of a community, demographic trends, as well as income, education and housing levels of the residents.[5] In this context deviance is not a normative concept but a question of collective community deviance defined through a departure from a digitally mapped statistical average. *Crime mapping* thus transforms the community from a concrete, local entity into an abstract simulation, aptly summed up in the motto of the West Midlands online system, modestly named COSMOS: 'The universe regarded as an orderly, harmonious whole'. Through the use of geographically based statistical information about crime, demography and other aspects of their work, police and other agencies are able to enter various risk minimization strategies (Gundhus, 2006). For example, Norwegian police established in 2006 a special web-page dedicated to the hunt for a serial paedopile, where the public can access CCTV footage of the man, a map of his movements and other available information.[6] The interactivity offered by the Internet is a further step in the active involvement of citizens in the governance of not only cyber- but also terrestrial crime.

Virtual communities can have a considerable impact on locally lived communities by mobilizing ideas, opinions, money and social linkages, as was indicated by the examples of penal populism, football supporters and Zapatista rebels. Cere (2007) points out that parallel to the highly publicized riots in Paris suburbs in October 2005, there was a myriad of Internet activities mobilizing local, national and global audiences. The online and offline domains are therefore not exclusive of each other. 'People who choose to enter online social spaces do not leave their offline world behind when they do so, but rather begin a process of weaving online communications and activities into their existing offline lives' (Kendall, 2002: 16). As Appadurai (1996: 195) points out when it comes to the question of virtual neighbourhoods:

> These virtual neighbourhoods seem on the face of it to represent just that absence of face-to-face links, spatial contiguity, and multiplex social interaction that the idea of a neighbourhood seems centrally to imply. Yet we

---

[5]http://www.weedandseed.info/
[6]http://www.lommemannen-kripos.no/index.html

must not be too quick to oppose highly spatialized neighbourhoods to these virtual neighbourhoods of international electronic communication. The relationship between these two forms of neighbourhood is considerably more complex.

The idea that the Internet, and globalization in general, is an antithesis of local community has shown to be a truth with many modifications. Life on the screen is not only a space of freedom from terrestrial constraints and governmental intervention but is gradually becoming an essential medium through which contemporary social mobilizations, including those related to crime and punishment, take place. Online communication has become 'an important site for the contestation of group values. Indeed, it is through this very contestation that new forms of collectivity are imagined and performed' (Valier, 2004: 93).

Cybercrime is at times seen as a criminological curiosity, a field for the especially interested, and it is only gradually beginning to penetrate the criminological mainstream. As a concluding thought, I would like to suggest that the issues of cyberspace, cybercrime and cyber-deviance touch upon some of the central transformations discussed in this book: from questions of disembedding of social relations, deterritorialization of crime and crime control, to the issues of postmodernity and plural governance. At the same time, the discussion of cyberspace brings up numerous perennial criminological and sociological concerns, such as the issues of risk and trust, anonymity of social relations, labelling processes and the social construction of crime. 'Life on the screen' may therefore be not so different and far removed from the 'real' world as its proponents and critics sometimes seem to suggest.

Summary

The Internet represents the prime example of global connectivity and disembedding of social relations. The anonymity of online environments carries a liberatory potential as well as offering possibilities for fraud and abuse. The increasing reliance of individual and institutional lives on information and communication technologies makes societies increasingly vulnerable to the exploitation and malfunctions of these systems. The chapter discussed the phenomenon of cybercrime, a concept which covers a diverse set of practices and activities associated with the use of information technology for criminal purposes. The emergence of the Internet and of cybercrime presents considerable challenges for criminologists as well as law enforcement agencies. Cyber-deviants defy the traditional notions of criminal offenders as belonging to the poorest and least educated strata of the population. Cybercrimes can span the globe and demand a considerable level of international police co-operation, as well as a high level of expertise. The responsibilization approach and pluralization of policing are therefore also vital aspects of cyber-governance. Furthermore, commercial interests and penal populist voices are making their mark in cyberspace, just as they are shaping terrestrial crime control strategies.

STUDY QUESTIONS

1   What kinds of challenge does cyberspace represent for traditional (i.e. terrestrial) criminological theories and concepts of identity?

2   What kinds of challenge does cyberspace represent for law enforcement and other regulatory agencies?

3   Discuss the concept of synopticon and its difference from Michel Foucault's concept of panopticon. What do you see as the problematic and positive sides of the viewer society?

4   Criminalization of music piracy is one example of governance through crime. Whose interests does criminalization serve? Can you think of other ways in which commercial interests shape cyberspace?

FURTHER READING

Manuel Castells's (2001) *The Internet Galaxy* provides a broad sociological account of the Internet, particularly with relation to the notions of network society. Sherry Turkle's (1995) *Life on the Screen* is a popular early account of identity in virtual interaction. My own *Sentencing in the Age of Information* (2005b) discusses the topic of information technologies and penal change. On the topic of cybercrime, David S. Wall's (2003) *Cyberspace Crime* and Doug Thomas and Brian Loader's (2000) *Cybercrime* provides a thorough overview of the debates. Majid Yar's (2006) textbook *Cybercrime and Society* is also a useful and well-informed introduction to the field. Broader issues of cyber-deviance are addressed in two recent volumes edited by Yvonne Jewkes, *Dot.Cons* (2003) and *Crime Online* (2007). Rob Shields's (2003) *The Virtual* examines the notion of the virtual and its many meanings and examples in contemporary society and culture. Interesting discussions about the changing social context of crime in contemporary technologically mediated environments can be found in the journal *Crime, Media, Culture*.

8

Criminology between the National, Local and Global

Chapter Contents

International penal policy transfers   174

Beyond 'methodological nationalism'   176

Criminological knowledge and imperialism   179

Towards a global criminology?   183

Reframing justice in a globalizing world   186

  Summary   189

  Study questions   190

  Further reading   190

OVERVIEW

Chapter 8 examines the following issues:

- Some theoretical and methodological implications of the increasing global interconnectedness, discussed in previous chapters, for criminology as a discipline.
- International penal policy transfers and their effects on national and local crime control policies and practice.
- A critique of the ethnocentric and the nation state outlook on society, crime and justice.
- Possibilities for establishing a global criminology and how a global frame might benefit the rights of globally marginalized populations.

KEY TERMS

Americanization	homogenization	policy transfers
comparative criminology	human rights	post-colonialism
ethnocentrism	hybridity	state crime
global governance	methodological nationalism	

The worldwide 'success' of New York's policing has been mentioned at several points in this book. It may seem that the NYPD is close to becoming not only a law enforcement but also a consumer brand, selling movies and TV series, as well as coffee cups, T-shirts and other paraphernalia. As a head of a security consulting company, the former New York mayor Giuliani was hired by Mexican business leaders to come up with a plan to 'clean up' Mexico City, which has the second-highest crime rate in Latin America. According to a BBC report, Mr Giuliani

> said he plans to apply the same zero-tolerance approach to crime in Mexico City as he did in New York. The former city leader is being paid $4.3m for his services. Mr Giuliani toured the city's crime-ridden districts in a convoy of a dozen armoured vehicles, accompanied by a police motorcycle escort. The former mayor said that 'although there are differences [between Mexico City and New York] ... the situation in some ways is very similar.'(BBC News, 2003)[1]

---

[1]http://news.bbc.co.uk/2/hi/americas/2659301.stm

Zero tolerance is by no means an isolated example of international penal policy transfers (Jones and Newburn, 2006). The US, Canadian and UK risk assessment instruments are other export articles. In Chapter 6 we saw also how privatization of crime control is spreading across the world. Norwegian police officials and newspaper reporters have, for example, taken study trips to the UK to learn about the alleged benefits of criminalizing Internet 'grooming', CCTV surveillance and police DNA databases.

At first glance it may appear as if we are approaching a global crime control system. The adjective 'global' would in this context mean a homogeneous and uniform system. This indeed has been a common use of the word, reflected in the various McDonaldization and Disneyfication theses discussed earlier. However, I shall proceed to argue in this chapter that the picture is more complex. Globalization is far from being a singular development leading to an integrated and homogeneous world system, even though it may appear so at times. Rather, it is better understood as a multiple set of cross-border connections that sometimes reinforce one another, but are often conflicting. We saw, for example, how the power of the nation state, although contested, is far from diminished. The local and the national have to some extent gained in importance precisely at a time of increasing global interconnectedness. We should therefore distinguish between two consequences of globalization: homogenization and interdependence, since 'interdependence does not necessarily presume or produce homogeneity' (Nelken in Chan, 2005: 341). One of the dangers of global perspectives, within criminology as well as social studies in general, is that they (consciously or unconsciously) nurture a perception of *homogenization* and radical change. History however is seldom a process of clear change, let alone progress. Looking at penal systems across the world, one of the surprising things is how little things have changed. Prisons still often resemble prisons of 100 years ago, sometimes even being housed in the same buildings. A vital task for social observers is therefore also to explain the stability and not only the mobility and fluidity of social relations; variety and difference, not just homogeneity. One of the issues we have focused on throughout this book is the dynamics of global connections and disconnections, change and resistance to change, inherent in the global transformations. In this chapter we shall summarize the findings of the previous chapters and look more specifically at the issue of penal policy and at the methodological challenges inherent in studying global transformations.

The chapter addresses a variety of issues related to comparative and transnational criminology, global criminal justice initiatives, transnational penal policy transfers, as well as the persistence of national and local differences. It will be argued that the increasing trans-border interconnectedness does not primarily presume homogenization but has far more complex, diverse and less predictable effects (see also Newburn and Sparks, 2004; Chan, 2005). Therefore, the notions not only of order and homogenization, but also of complexity and dis-order, can be useful for understanding the global transformations (Urry, 2003). Furthermore, an argument will be made that even though penal policies and systems in individual countries can no longer be understood in isolation from each other there are nevertheless substantial difficulties inherent in the global approach. How far do general criminological theories apply to individual local and national contexts? Does much of the contemporary writing about globalization encourage a certain worldview which looks for similarities and consequently also finds similarities rather than differences and varieties? One of the major weaknesses of contemporary globalization writing is that it has been somewhat 'placeless' in its concerns (Newburn and Sparks, 2004: 13). Developing an awareness of local and national variation, as well as global interconnectedness, is a vital, if perhaps an impossible, task. Finally, a question will be asked about the viability of a 'global criminology' and its potential limits and advantages.

International penal policy transfers

Scientists and other groups of professionals are increasingly organized in a post-national manner, using modern communication systems and sharing a common system of values, rewards and events (Urry, 2003). Western criminologists and criminal justice officials increasingly inhabit the global sphere and the 'space of flows', travelling to international conferences and discussing and exchanging ideas in international journals (Chan, 2005). This phenomenon can be traced back to the origins of the criminological project and criminal justice institutions in their modern forms (Newburn and Sparks, 2004). Even in 1914, Chan (2005) shows us, a criminological book could be acquired by an Australian library in the year of its publication in England. Bentham's panoptic design is still recognizable in numerous prisons and other institutions across the world. Throughout history, the spread of modern forms of criminal justice has followed the colonizing logic of Western modernity, often with detrimental consequences for the 'modernized' populations (see Cohen, 1982; Agozino, 2003 and the discussion below). In that respect, contemporary forms of penal policy transfer, and the convergence of crime control practices, represent a continuation of a long historic development.

Today, politicians across the world borrow from American style of communication about crime. Zero tolerance policing and policies such as 'three strikes and you're out' and minimum sentencing laws can be seen as examples of 'Atlantic crossings' (Jones and Newburn, 2004). However, how these *policy transfers* are used in local contexts is another question and merits detailed empirical investigation (Newburn and Sparks, 2004). Several authors have warned that 'we cannot and should not take for granted that surface similarities necessarily imply deeper convergencies' (ibid.: 11; Jones and Newburn, 2004; Melossi, 2004). Zero tolerance and 'three strikes and you're out' policies are used quite differently in the UK context than in the US, although the rhetoric may be similar (Jones and Newburn, 2004). Similarly, risk-based forms of justice employ essentially different techniques in different Western jurisdictions (O'Malley, 2004). The exclusionary tone of US actuarial justice should be distinguished from the more inclusive and welfare-oriented tones of Australian and Scandinavian risk thinking. This distinctiveness of risk is easily overlooked in the predominantly general and abstract writing about risk society and actuarial justice.

The point here is that what may at the first glance appear as globalization of penal policies needs to be contextualized and seen in specific local – or better 'glocal' – contexts. 'Punishment is deeply embedded in the national/cultural specificity of the environment which produces it' (Melossi, 2004: 84). Penal policies change their character as they move to a new cultural setting. Although politicians, criminal justice policy makers, researchers and bureaucrats may borrow from the same international vocabulary of terms, discourses and expressions, this does not mean that these words are in practice translated into similar actions. We need therefore to be aware of the cultural embeddedness of crime and punishment, and should not 'read the emerging – global – landscape too flatly' (Loader and Sparks, 2002: 100).

> For while the prospects of particular places (towns, cities, regions, nations) and their citizens *are* today structured by events and processes happening quite elsewhere, we ought not to disregard the ways in which the levels and meanings of crime, and public and official responses to it, remain constituted – at least in part – within the national political cultures and local 'structures of feeling' of different societies. (ibid.)

The authors caution us against seeing the study of global transformation as an encouragement to focus on the macro-level developments, and as 'a license for preferring the novel and the fashionable, and for sweeping over the grounded, the empirical, and the local' (Loader and Sparks, 2002: 103). The ethnographic study of culture and cultural variation therefore gains a particular importance as an antidote to the abstract nature of many theoretical claims about globalization and its impacts.

I have argued throughout this book for the need to be attuned to the complexities of the global, which means seeing global transformations through their many facets, paradoxes, limits and discontinuities. Globalization is not an either–or development, but has many modalities and can unravel at an uneven pace. For example 'globalization's effect on criminology and policy is not necessarily related to its effect on crime' (Chan, 2005: 340). And whilst new technologies such as electronic monitoring and prison security equipment can be transferred between countries in a matter of months, penal policies are slower to follow. Yet, even when it comes to technological transfers there are great variations even among Western penal systems, let alone between the West and the developing world. For example, the UK has by now installed innumerable open-street CCTV systems, Denmark, on the other hand, has none and Norway only one. Also in Germany and several other European countries attitudes towards CCTV surveillance are far more restrictive.[2] What we usually term Western penal systems cannot be treated as a unitary category due to a variety of specific national characteristics and differences. Penal policy analysis needs to capture not only the global–local dynamics, but also the persistence of the national and the nation state, as well as the often neglected regional and inter-regional variation. Here, *comparative criminology* has a lot to offer.

Beyond 'methodological nationalism'

The persistent national differences and local peculiarities have dissuaded many criminologists from venturing into the trans-national sphere. Part of the problem in introducing comparative and international perspectives is, as Bailey (1999: 4) observes, 'the perception that the differences among phenomena are so great that analysis is impossible'. Comparative is associated with foreign and tends to be seen as irrelevant. Consequently, a considerable part of criminological research still seems to be in many ways guilty of what Ulrich Beck (2002) terms *'methodological nationalism'* – equating social boundaries with state boundaries, and having a nation state outlook on society, law, justice and history. This methodological framework structures, according to its critics, the choice of research phenomena, for example statistical indicators, which are almost exclusively national in their scope.

  The affinity between criminology as a discipline and the nation state framework is partly due to the traditional connection between criminological knowledge and the nation state apparatus. Foucault's (1977) pathbreaking study pointed out the intrinsic interdependence of criminological knowledge and the state penal apparatus. Ever since its inception, criminology as a discipline has been a part of the vast bureaucratic apparatus whose 'epistemological thaw' enables the accumulation of large amounts of knowledge about crime and punishment. From official crime statistics to records on the state of prisons, we are all

---

[2]http://www.urbaneye.net/results/results.htm

indebted to the nation state's production of information. Modern states are big consumers of research and important sources of financing. Consequently, Christie (1997) blames the eager state and its voracious appetite for knowledge for the 'boringness' and irrelevance of much contemporary criminological research. The close relationship between the state and mainstream criminology represents, according to Christie (1997: 18), a danger for criminological research. 'A danger because these new state employees know what they want from research. They want help in running the state.' This administrative focus thus functions as a block against insight and prevents alternative framing and solutions to the problems of crime and punishment.

Although radical in their assumptions, the above critical voices bring up an important question of the relevance of much criminological writing beyond the immediate boundaries of its national context. Criminology still seems to be, theoretically and methodologically, somewhat badly equipped for understanding the relevance of global transformations and the emerging 'space of flows'. The critics of methodological nationalism have pointed out that the focus on the national state as the natural unit of social theory prevents it from capturing the fundamental change in social organization brought on by globalization. As Law and Urry (2004: 403–4) point out, sociological inquiry needs to develop methods that are sensitive to the complexities of the global.

> The fleeting, the ephemeral, the geographically distributed, and the suddenly proximate are of increasing importance in current senses of the social ...
>
> We shall need to alter academic habits and develop sensibilities appropriate to a methodological decentring. Method needs to be sensitive to the complex and the elusive. It needs to be more mobile. It needs to find ways of knowing the slipperiness of 'units that are not' as they move in and beyond old categories.

The transcendence of the nation state framework would, on the one hand, broaden the horizons of social science research and incorporate previously excluded topics and phenomena. On the other hand, it would fundamentally challenge the long-held distinction between 'inside' and 'outside', 'domestic' and 'foreign' relations (Beck, 2002). This shift of focus is particularly relevant when it comes to analysing the emerging new dynamics of contemporary transnational crime, policing and security, where governance to an increasing extent 'takes place in de-bounded spaces' (ibid.: 52; see Chapters 5 and 7). According to Beck (2002), social science methodology should be 'methodological cosmopolitanism' rather than nationalism.

Taking our clue from the discussions above, we can see that exploring global complexity forces us to challenge the traditional focus of criminal law and criminology on the nation state and its control of its territory. As life is increasingly lived in various transnational scapes so too are issues of crime and its control gaining new dimensions. The shift of focus towards the global therefore prob-lematizes the notion of society, which has been, in the past two centuries, the natural unit of sociological inquiry. 'Society here meant that which was ordered through a nation state, with clear territorial and citizenship boundaries and a system of governance over its particular citizens' (Law and Urry, 2004: 398). In the emerging global (dis)order, the notion of 'society' is transformed beyond recognition by the growing trans-border flows, and can no longer preserve the illusion of being a discrete and separate entity. One can no longer study, for example, Italy simply by looking at what happens inside its territory; instead, one needs to acknowledge the effects that distant conflicts and developments have on national crime and security concerns, and vice versa.

It was indicated earlier that the comparative approach could to some extent open up criminological horizons by challenging the prevailing focus on the national. According to Bailey (1999: 5), prioritizing single case national studies 'elevates parochialism to the level of scientific principle' and emphasises 'us and them' divi-sions. Similarly, Pakes (2004: 3) suggests that one of the benefits of the comparative approach is that it may prevent *ethnocentrism*. 'Ethnocentrism refers to senti-ments that regard domestic arrangements as necessarily "normal" and "right", and other cultures or customs as "weird" and "wrong".' Furthermore, if legal systems are to meet the practical challenges of regulating and controlling the burgeoning cross-border flows, co-operation and a certain level of mutual understanding are a pre-rogative (ibid.). One does however need to keep the vast intra-national differences in mind. The pervasive global disparities, discussed throughout this book, are also reflected in the nature of the various national penal systems, in the state of their prisons, the judicial system, the police, etc. While in Norway, for example, single prison cells are seen as the norm, with access to public medical care and educa-tion, in most Third World countries this is a distant dream.

The comparative approach is faced with a number of difficulties. The essen-tial relativity of the concept of crime makes international comparisons challeng-ing, although arguably also more exciting (Sheptycki, 2005). A more fundamental challenge is the objection that while comparative criminology offers numerous valuable insights into similarities and differences between var-ious criminal justice systems, it still uses the nation state as its primary point of reference. As Sheptycki (2005: 83) observes:

> Under the circumstances of transnationalisation it is possible to observe that the differences that sustain the project of comparative criminology (and comparative social sciences more generally) have given way to dif-fusely intermingled cultural differences ...It is now difficult for cultures to remain pristine in splendid isolation. This raises new methodological challenges for comparative method.

Consequently, the task of comparative criminology becomes increasingly difficult. How are we to address appropriately phenomena such as police information and communication networks, cybercrime, smuggling and trafficking, which by their nature call for a transnational, rather than simply a comparative international standpoint? Taking my own research on border controls as an example, I was faced with a similar difficulty. How does one grapple, empirically, with the concept of a border, when a border is no longer a 'wall' around a nation state territory, but rather a distributed network of a myriad of checkpoints, technologies and actors, which can be situated inside or outside a given state territory (Aas, 2005a)? From this perspective, 'it is neither possible to distinguish clearly between the national and the international, nor, in a similar way, convincingly to contrast homogenous units' (Beck, 2002: 53). The comparative approach to criminology should therefore be distinguished from global and transnational perspectives.

The objective of this book has been essentially to look at the global and transnational as an increasingly salient explanatory factor and frame of criminological reference. We have examined the crumbling boundaries of criminology – physical, virtual and conceptual – as well as the persistence of some boundaries and the limits to the global approach within criminology. The topic of globalization forces us to reach not only beyond the established boundaries of nation states, but also beyond the established boundaries of disciplines and cultures. The globalizing process leads to *hybridity* of what some decades ago appeared to be relatively stable entities, such as the nation state, culture and society. We have examined a number of these hybridities throughout this book: from the hybridity of cultural forms to the increasing hybridity of internal and external notions of security, of public and private spaces and domains, and of social and technical spheres. Holton (2005: 3) points out that

> Understanding globalization demands an approach that is both multi-disciplinary and multi-cultural: multi-disciplinary in the need to combine insights from a range of intellectual sources, and multi-cultural in the sense that human experience from all parts of the world must be drawn upon.

Achieving that, however, is a project fraught with difficulty, particularly since parallel with the domination of Western or Northern economic, political and media institutions, we are also faced with similar global inequalities when it comes to the production of academic discourse and criminological knowledge.

Criminological knowledge and imperialism

The critique of methodological nationalism may help us to address two overlapping concerns, which tend to be pointed out as major shortcomings of traditional criminology. On the one hand, a global perspective can expand the geographical scope of criminological theories and challenge the primacy of Western, particularly Anglo-American, criminological perspectives. On the other hand, a critique of methodological nationalism could shift the focus on to the types of crime, harm and security threats which tend to be overlooked due to the before-mentioned affinity between criminological knowledge and the nation state. Both of these concerns will be discussed in greater detail in this section.

In Chapter 4 we discussed the cultural hegemony that the West, particularly the US, exercises over the rest of the world. Not only material commodities but music, cinema, books, television, news, fashion and other forms of cultural production have been dominated by the United States. Many of the contemporary cultural anxieties about globalization can in fact be better understood as reactions to the impact of *Americanization* (Beck et al., 2003). The US has also a long tradition in exporting political ideas and scholarly categories. From De Tocqueville's *Democracy in America* (1835), to the Chicago School and the subcultural studies of the 1960s and 1970s, to name just a few, social studies have a long history of US influences and inspirations. However, critics have pointed out the potentially problematic nature of uncritical intellectual imports which can amount to 'intellectual imperialism' (Bourdieu and Wacquant, 1999). This imperialism presents a specific vision of the world, relating to the conditions of US society, as universal truths. Consequently, sociological concepts, for example race and 'underclass', are taken out of their historically specific social context and uncritically applied to other societies (ibid.). We saw, for example in Chapter 5, how the concept of transnational organized crime has become, according to its critics, one such US concept.

This hegemony in the field of intellectual production has also been strongly felt within the production of criminological knowledge and criminal justice policies. When talking about the globalization of crime control policies, a better word would often be Westernization and Americanization – as in the case of zero tolerance policing. Even though global interconnectedness does not necessarily produce homogeneous world systems, it clearly accelerates the impact of certain foreign influences on local developments. Consequently, local actors experience a diminished capacity to influence the terms of their existence. In the area of penal policy, politicians in Norway or the Netherlands now can look for inspiration to criminological models in the UK, Canada and the US, rather than relying on national expertise. Users of criminological knowledge have become, according to Chan (2005: 346), 'shoppers in the supermarket of ideas and arguments'. For example, in 1999, Australia's prime minister chose to consult an American FBI chief, rather than Australian drug research experts, about solutions to the heroin problem despite the fact that Australia had had considerable success in crime reduction strategies against heroin (Chan, 2005). The deterritorialization process, which we examined in the case of cultural transfers, here applies also to scientific knowledge and expert systems. Knowledge becomes decontextualized and free of the constraints of time and space (see also Giddens, 1990). Of course, not all worldviews have the same chance of achieving global recognition and a question can be asked about what happens to intellectual ideas when they become available in the 'global marketplace'. How much of their original content is preserved, and do they have to be turned into a bland product which can be 'sold' anywhere?

A broader, and potentially more fundamental, problem is the general global inequality in the production of knowledge, which has particularly marked criminology as a discipline ever since its inception. Criminology has been marked not only by the hegemony of the US and Anglophone academic production, but also by the hegemony of Western criminology and criminal justice models over the developing world. Morrison (2005) argues that criminological texts are foremost meant as conversations within a particular community, where terms such as 'contemporary society', 'modern crime control' and 'late modern society' refer to a small group of Western (primarily US and UK) audiences. One should be wary of presenting Western (particularly Anglo-American) accounts of penal change as universal 'truths'. Similarly, Jones and Newburn (2006) point out the prevailing ethnocentrism in policing studies where there is an assumption that trends in the US and Canada can be applied to the rest of the world. Muncie (2004: 154) suggests that the concept of globalization itself is essentially ethnocentric, directing our attention primarily to the developments in neo-liberal English-speaking countries. This is indeed the case if we look at the (political, media and criminological) discourse about the 'world risk society', where most of the attention is focused on security threats to the Western world and occasional tourist resorts. The statements 'We are all Americans' and 'We are all Londoners' are, after all, statements of solidarity between Western capitals, connected by mutual feelings of fear and vulnerability.

In a seminal article Stan Cohen (1982) asked the crucial question whether the export of Western crime control models to the Third World should be seen as benign or malignant. Throughout history developing countries have been at the receiving end of Western criminal justice exports, either through openly malignant colonialism, or through apparently more benign ideas of progress. Stern (2006) points out that by placing prison at the centre of their legal system many developing countries have followed models imposed from elsewhere. The development is particularly regrettable in light of the state of prisons in many of these countries and the lack of alternatives to imprisonment. Ironically, even when the West for once is importing Third World justice models, such as restorative justice, these models are often re-exported back to the Third World in a radically different guise (Cohen, 1982). Nevertheless, the flourishing of restorative justice does represent one exception where the trend has been turned around and the West is implementing ideas originating in its former colonial territories. The development has been particularly evident in the field of youth justice, where restorative justice has found practical expression in various forms such as conferencing in Australasia, healing circles in Canada and conflict resolution boards in Norway (Muncie, 2004).

A vital task for global criminology, if it is to deserve its name, is to disturb the hegemony of Western thought within criminology, and to establish, as Cain (2000) suggests, some kind of 'interactive globalization'. This is inevitably a difficult, if not an impossible task. Criminologists have, as Cohen (1982: 85) remarks, 'either ignored the Third World completely or treated it in a most theoretically primitive fashion, while the general literature on development and colonialism is remarkably silent about crime'. In a similar voice, Cain (2000) suggests that Western criminology is guilty of a double sin: of either romanticizing non-Western societies or of assuming that they are no different from the West. Several authors have pointed out the centrality of colonialism to the emergence of Western modernity and the criminological enterprise (Brown, 2002; Agozino, 2003; Morrison, 2006). According to Morrison (2006: 2) criminology has historically restricted its knowledge to the so-called 'civilised space' whose 'civilisation' and security were sustained by the various imperial projects:

> Criminology has confined itself to a supporting role for civilised space, a territorial imagination that excludes from view the uncivilised, the other, utilising strategies that are imperially effective but domestically clean.

Today, there is still a large imbalance in the production of criminological knowledge reflected in the fact that criminology is developed predominantly in the former colonial centres of authority. Few post-colonial territories have developed criminology as an institutionalised discipline. According to Agozino (2004: 351), one of the reasons for the Third World countries' lack of interest in criminology is that it tends to be perceived as an imperialist science and much of conventional criminology is seen as lacking relevance to the reality of the Third World. While *post-colonialism* is by now an established perspective within the social sciences and literature, criminological parallels are harder to find (see for example Brown, 2002; Agozino, 2003). Much contemporary criminology is still theoretically and empirically underdeveloped when it comes to the Third World, and colonial struggles and post-colonial universities are mainly reduced to importing Western courses about policing and prison administration (Agozino, 2004).

Post-colonial studies raise a similar critique against Western social studies to Beck's challenge to methodological nationalism. However, while Beck (2003) sees methodological nationalism primarily as an unproductive epistemological approach, post-colonial studies point out that ethnocentrism has been an essential tool in the historic domination of the West over its colonies. Furthermore, a closer examination of its colonial undertones might not only shed light on criminology's colonial past, but also give a certain insight into the present penal strategies of othering. Brown (2002), for example, argues that contemporary 'criminologies of the other' bear a certain resemblance to the British colonial policies of control in 19th-century India. A greater awareness of colonialism may therefore shed a new, critical light on contemporary penal strategies and criminological theories and concepts. Knowledge is seldom, if ever, free of the subjective experiences and interests of its producers. Critics have argued that due to this imbalance in the production of knowledge even what may appear as critical and progressive thinking bears a certain Western bias. Feminist approaches and critique of knowledge, for example, do not necessarily reflect the needs and perspectives of Third World women, but tend to reinforce Western concepts as an ideal of womanhood (Spivak, 1999).

> [M]any of the concepts and theories produced about women's oppression are, and have been for many years, grounded in struggles of middle-class white women and may be quite antithetical to other women's experiences, if not representative of imperialist feminist thought. (Kempadoo, 1998: 13)

We encountered some of these topics in Chapter 2, related to issues of sex work, trafficking and the 'female underside of globalization'.

Towards a global criminology?

A global perspective may open our eyes to a variety of actors, activities and human rights violations which tend to be neglected by traditional criminology. One example are detention centres for illegal immigrants. Although *de facto* prisons, these institutions are overlooked in most studies of prison life, partly due to the unclear legal status of their inmates. Furthermore, questions of torture, war crimes, **state crime** and genocide should be of equally pressing importance but tend to be neglected in most criminological textbooks. One could argue that the prevailing methodological nationalism of Western criminology has created a 'blind spot' for crimes and human rights violations committed by states themselves and state-supported agencies. Morrison (2006) notes the remarkable silence of mainstream criminology about genocide. 'Yet the figures for state-sponsored massacres or other forms of deliberate death in the *twentieth century – excluding military personnel and civilian casualties of war –* are usually regarded as between 167 and 175 million people' (ibid.: 54; italics. original). During the last 100 years far more people have been killed by their own governments than by foreign armies (Human Security Report, 2005). These crimes, however, have been excluded from the 'civilized space' of criminological discourse, which has limited its interests to the nation state criminal justice processes. There are, for example, no official statistics on political violence. While international organizations collect statistics from governments on health, education, environment, etc., there are no official data on human rights abuses, political and state violence (ibid.).

The main point here is that by maintaining the national methodological research frame, one loses sight of enormous global injustices and inequalities. Beck (2003: 50) points out that the 'fragmentation of the world into nation states removes accountability for global inequalities'. Paraphrasing Cohen (2002), nation states are to that extent also 'states of denial' about the enormous social inequalities and suffering on the global scale. Seen in this view, a global perspective presents itself not only as a valuable scientific approach but also as an ethical imperative. If social science research is not only descriptive, but also *constitutive* of the phenomena it addresses, then a question can be asked about the ethical implications of our choice of research phenomena.

Several authors have presented an argument for moving beyond the nation state definitions of crime and deviance to incorporate the wide spectrum of acts and harm which tend to be overlooked due to the narrowness of the state-defined concept of crime. We saw in Chapter 1 how the unclear and problematic nature of the concept of crime represents an inherent difficulty in the criminological project. Consequently, attempts have been made to transcend the conceptual boundaries presented in the state's own definitions of crime. As Skolnick (1969 in McLaughlin, 2001: 285) argues:

> Less dramatic but equally destructive processes may occur well within the routine operation of 'orderly' social life…indifference, inaction, and slow decay that routinely afflict the poor are far more destructive than the bomb in the night. High infant mortality rates or rates of preventive disease, perpetuated through discrimination, take a far greater toll than civil disorder.

On a similar note, Hillyard et al. (2004) suggest that criminology should move 'beyond criminology' (i.e. the study of crime) and define itself as a study of social harm. By focusing only on criminalized forms of harm, the authors argue, a wide range of damaging and potentially more dangerous forms of harm are neglected. The concept of harm is thus much broader than crime as it includes a wide array of acts and phenomena, such as work-related accidents and deaths, the harmful consequences of poverty and pollution, state crime and human rights violations. The broadness of the concept of harm may be potentially too wide, particularly for establishing notions of responsibility, yet according to its proponents this broadness enables us to address 'the social wreckage of neo-liberal globalization' (ibid.: 3), which tends to be neglected and uncensored by the nation state penal systems.

A further broadening of the traditional boundaries has been also proposed by the growing field of so-called green or environmental criminology, which has put issues of environmental justice on the criminological agenda (see for example Lynch and Stretsky, 2003). This approach demands not only the broadening of the concept of crime, but also a simultaneous view of global and local levels in the production of environmental damage. It then becomes obvious that local harm is a product of a long chain of geographically often dispersed and un-bounded events and actions. We have seen several examples of this global interconnectedness throughout this book: migration is an intricate result of push and pull factors, rather than simply individual decisions; local security concerns are influenced by global threats and perceptions of threats, and the security of the global North is inevitably connected to development and social justice issues in the global South. The transcendence of the national methodological framework does not mean that global aspects are by definition vital in explaining local and national phenomena. It does mean, however, that they should be looked to as a possibility.

Also the shifting terms of recent political and scholarly debates about security – from state to human security – reflect the inadequacy of the traditional nation state frame of understanding. This shift is based on the acknowledgement that there are essential differences between human and state security: 'secure states do not automatically mean secure people' (Human Security Report, 2005). The focus of human security is on the protection of individuals rather on the protection of states. The nation state view of security is nevertheless still strongly held in the field of migration studies, where the predominant approaches frame migration as a security threat leading to the progressive securitization of migration and militarization of borders (see Chapter 2). By comparison, the insecurity of migrating individuals is far more seldom discussed. Several thousand people reportedly die every year trying desperately to climb the walls of 'fortress continents'. As recently as 2006, 2,000 people were estimated to have died on the shores of the Spanish Canary Islands, although the exact numbers are hard to establish. Nevertheless, the prevailing discussions of migration envision migration first and foremost as a security threat to the Western nation states. Similarly, Pickering (2005) argues that we need to see migration, particularly forced migration, as a humanitarian rather than a criminal concern. The disparity between human security and state security becomes obvious here as the former suffers at the expense of the latter. Migrant populations are vulnerable precisely because of their exclusion from the nation state security concepts. For example, while Britain and other European countries were sending warships to evacuate their citizens from Beirut, during Israeli attacks in the summer of 2006, 11,000 migrant workers, mainly domestic servants, were left stranded.[3]

---

[3] http://newsvote.bbc.co.uk/mpapps/pagetools/print/news.bbc.co.uk/2/hi/in_depth/6183803.stm

Reframing justice in a globalizing world

The globalizing process nevertheless not only demands new methods and frames of understanding, but significantly, also offers new possibilities for social justice and political action, particularly with regard to those social groups and issues which nation states are unwilling or unable to accommodate. We saw in Chapter 6 that the provision of security is being pluralized, moving below, above and beyond the state. Increasingly, this dispersal and pluralization of governance is also viewed as an opportunity for creating alternative ideologies and modes of achieving justice to the traditional state focus on punishment and criminalization. Restorative justice initiatives are aiming to replace the state-focused justice models with solutions which aim to solve conflicts and build peace within the communities (Christie, 2004; Wood and Shearing, 2007a). Criminology in the new global order has therefore not only a crime-fighting and war-making potential but, crucially, also offers peacemaking possibilities (Barak, 2005). This is particularly important in cases where the crisis of state sovereignty fails to provide for the security needs of local communities (see Chapter 6), or where the criminal law approach is impotent and inappropriate for establishing the responsibility of powerful actors (as was the case of South Africa and its Truth and Reconciliation Commission).

Furthermore, various types of **global governance** seek to establish mechanisms for responsibilization of states and corporations when it comes to human rights violations. In Chapter 5 we saw how the European Court of Human Rights has become a forum for establishing responsibility: for example, of Russia for human rights violations in Chechnya. The international criminal tribunals for the former Yugoslavia and Rwanda have aimed to establish the responsibility of states and state actors for human rights violations and war crimes, albeit under much criticism and with varying success. The so-called 'corporate social responsibility' initiatives aim to achieve the compliance of business with international human rights and environmental standards. Transnational mobilization has been central in combating certain types of crimes such as corruption. Traditionally, governments perceived the problem of combating corruption as a matter of national sovereignty. Now, on the other hand, with NGOs such as Amnesty International and Transparency International, action on the global level is making an impact and becoming an important motor of national change. It is now possible to put an issue on 'the global agenda', even though nation states are unwilling to put it on the national agenda. The acknowledgement that 'justice must transcend the territorial limits it has operated within modernity' (Morrison, 2006: 2) has driven a series of social mobilizations against environmental crime, state crime and human rights violations. Social movements and NGOs, such as Amnesty International, Human Rights Watch, Transparency

International, Greenpeace and many more, have in important ways preceded the state-sanctioned legal forms of action, as well as criminological knowledge.

This of course is by no means a historical novelty. In the late 1700s, anti-slavery campaigns found people in Britain, and later other countries, politically engaging in issues at the far side of the world at a time when the meaning of distance was much greater. Interestingly, the campaigners used some distinctly modern forms of political pressure and mobilization, such as political lobbying, celebrity endorsements and consumer boycotts of sugar, thus revealing an awareness of the intertwining of global issues and local actions. Today, international mobilizations have had an impact on numerous criminologically relevant domains from global anti-domestic violence campaigns and struggles for better prison conditions to anti-death penalty activism, to name just a few. For example, the 1995 Beijing Conference on Women provided a global platform for debating women's issues, including discrimination, poverty, human rights and violence against women. Participants included 189 governments, representatives of 2,100 NGOs and nearly 30,000 individuals. Globalization therefore also offers empowerment opportunities to nationally marginalized groups to be more connected, to create transnational connections and new forms of social and political action.

A vital generator in the process of transnationalization of justice has been transnationalization of law. In this book we encountered examples of cyber-crime, terrorism, trafficking and smuggling which have been defined on the international level and then incorporated into national law. For a long time, the power of criminalization has been primarily vested in the nation state as a prerequisite of its sovereignty. Now, however, the power to put definitions of criminality on the agenda is moving to transnational and international actors (the UN and its accompanying entourage of diplomats, bureaucrats and lobbyists, human rights organizations and other NGOs). These actors operate on the international stage, and even though they may frequently be representing national and local interests, they contribute to the 'normative convergence' (Chan, 2005: 342) of contemporary criminal justice. Transnationalization of law is also evident in the progressive evolution of international criminal law and its system of tribunals. The International Criminal Court is the first ever global public court with universal jurisdiction among signatory countries.

The proliferation of the international **human rights** discourse and instruments has been a vital element in the emerging sphere of global justice, although it is by no means a historic novelty. The language of human rights provides an antidote to the nation-state-based system of rights and entitlements. The 'right to have rights' does not depend on one's citizenship status but belongs to individuals in their capacity as human beings. Hudson (2003: 223) suggests that the universalism of human rights can represent a vital counter-discourse to the utilitarianism of risk society and its production of folk devils, by maintaining that 'all persons, not just members of one's own community, not just members in good standing in any community, have rights that each of us is morally obliged to uphold'. The language of human rights, furthermore, represents one of the few counterpoints to the growing demands for security in the present world order. It therefore has the potential for establishing limits to national and international trends towards securitization and militarization. The issue is by no means without tension. While the proponents of the human rights approach see its universalism as a major strength, critics have pointed out that it contradicts local notions of justice and experiences of injustice. The discourse of human rights has been described as a Western project, insensitive to local traditions and definitions of justice.

Globalization is therefore changing the way we think and should think about justice (Benhabib, 2004; Fraser, 2005a). In the heyday of what has been termed the Westphalian frame (i.e. the territorial nation state) there was a sharp distinction between 'domestic' and 'international' space. Looking at the examples presented above, we can see that today, disputes about justice often transcend the nation state frame. 'No longer addressed exclusively to national states or debated exclusively by national publics, claimants no longer focus solely on relations among fellow citizens' (Fraser, 2005a: 72). Justice today is increasingly 'abnormal' in the sense that it no longer addresses one's fellow citizens in a bounded community and that participants no longer share some common assumptions about justice. The global is gradually becoming the site of collective action for disempowered actors and not only for international elites. According to Fraser (2005a: 81), when the major sources of injustice belong to the space of flows, 'they cannot be made answerable to claims of justice that are framed in terms of the state-territorial principle'. This should apply to a variety of issues discussed in this book, such as migration, the global criminal economy, corruption, cybercrime, environmental crime, as well as the 'war on drugs', secret rendition flights and other methods used in the war on terror. In the post-Westphalian worldview conflicts are no longer territorialized – now new units emerge, using the trans-national, regional and sub-national stage for making claims about justice. Fraser points out that within this new framework it is no longer clear what the scope of justice is and who counts as the subject of justice. Before, in the post-war social democratic societies, the 'who of justice' was the citizenry of the territorial state. Now, on the other hand, the question of boundaries becomes crucial. Sayla Benhabib's (2004) book *The Rights of Others* forcefully outlines the importance of boundaries, as they define some as members and others as aliens. This boundary drawing and frame setting excludes some people as non-members who do not even have 'the right to have rights'. The nation state frame of justice can therefore be a source of injustice in itself due to 'the injustice of mis-framing' (Fraser, 2005a). Through this mis-framing some are excluded from making claims (for example, asylum seekers and 'enemy combatants'), while some actors are shielded from critique and from the reach of justice because they operate outside the national space (exemplified by tax havens and state crime).

A key point here is that sharp distinctions between domestic and international matters are in themselves becoming a major source of injustice. A vital question for critical criminology is therefore whether, in the face of global transformations, to defend the embattled territorial nation state, or whether to transcend the nation state order and to include in its repertoire of outsider the 'global others'. As Hogg (2002: 209) asks: 'To whom are we obliged and what is the scope of the "social contract" – the "imagined community" – to which we belong in an increasingly global world?' What is to be the scope of our knowledge about crime, (in)justice and social exclusion? Fraser (2005a), for example, suggests that in a globalizing world, the subject of a justice discourse should be anyone who is affected, regardless of their citizenship status. Issues of national justice can no longer be separated from issues of global justice.

It may be appropriate to conclude this volume on an optimistic note by pointing out the liberating possibilities of global interconnections. These possibilities should be kept in mind together with the otherwise rather pessimistic accounts of globalization. The global is not the exclusive domain of powerful international actors, but is gradually also becoming a facilitator of new forms of empowerment and resistance. However, it remains to be seen whether the heavily guarded boundaries of Western nation states are to remain the boundaries of the criminological imagination. Will our knowledge, as criminological scholars and students, continue to be defined by the nation state, or will we dare to move beyond (above and below) its sphere of interests?

Summary

This final chapter located the main transformations and challenges that the increasing global connectedness poses for criminology as a discipline. Transnational flows, networks and movements fundamentally transform the meaning of society, forcing us to re-examine our theoretical and methodological approaches to crime and crime control. The central role previously vested in the nation state now no longer seems self-evident and the national methodological focus should be complemented by more diverse and cosmopolitan perspectives. Governance of security, and responses to crime, are no longer shaped only within nation states, but have moved above and below the national level. The transcendence of the nation state frame of understanding enables us to see a variety of harms which tend to be unnoticed (and unsanctioned) by individual national justice systems, such as state crime, genocide, environmental crime and corruption. A global framework, furthermore, enables us to expand the conceptual limits of community to include those 'global others' who have been excluded from having rights in individual national justice systems.

STUDY QUESTIONS

1 How are penal policy transfers affecting your national criminal justice system? Can you think of examples of homogenization, Americanization, Europeanization, etc.?

2 What are the methodological challenges in studying transnational and geographically distributed social phenomena?

3 How has the criminological focus on crimes, as defined by states and committed *within* states, produced blind spots for other types of harm?

4 What are the advantages and drawbacks of criminological knowledge reaching beyond nation state boundaries?

FURTHER READING

Piers Beirne and D. Nelken's (1997) comprehensive edited volume *Issues in Comparative Criminology* and Frances Pakes's (2004) *Comparative Criminal Justice* reveal the challenges and the potential of the comparative approach. Ali Wardak and James Sheptycki's (2005) *Transnational and Comparative Criminology* is another informed recent contribution to the field. The issue of state crime has been the subject of several recent books, such as Penny Green and Tony Ward's (2004) *State Crime*, while Wayne Morrison's (2006) *Criminology, Civilisation and the New World Order* looks at the criminological silence about genocide. Denials of atrocities are also the subject of Stan Cohen's (2001) acclaimed book *States of Denial: Knowing about Atrocities and Suffering*. Biko Agozino's (2003) *Counter-Colonial Criminology* provides a powerful critique of criminological imperialism. The broadening of the boundaries of our political communities, justice and understanding is the subject of Seyla Benhabib's (2004) influential book *The Rights of Others*. Updated reports on the status of human rights across the world are provided by NGOs and activists such as Amnesty International, Human Rights Watch and Transparency International. A comprehensive long-term analysis of the threats to human security is provided by *Human Security Report*, published by the Human Security Centre (http://www.humansecuritycentre.org/).

References

Aas, K. F. (2005a) '"Getting ahead of the game": border technologies and the changing space of governance', in E. Zureik and M. Salter (eds) *Global Surveillance and Policing*: *Borders, Security, Identity*, Cullompton: Willan

Aas, K. F. (2005b) *Sentencing in the Age of Information*: *From Faust to Macintosh*, London: Glasshouse Press

Aas, K. F. (2006) '"The body does not lie": Identity, risk and trust in technoculture', *Crime, Media, Culture*, 2 (2): 143–58

Aas, K. F. (2007) 'Beyond "the desert of the real": crime control in a virtual(ised) reality', in Y. Jewkes (ed.) *Crime Online*, Cullompton: Willan

Abraham, I. and van Schendel, W. (2005) 'Introduction: The making of Illicitness', in I. Abraham and W. van Schendel (eds) *Illicit Flows and Criminal Things*: *States, Borders, and the Other Side of Globalization*, Bloomington and Indianapolis: Indiana University Press

Agamben, G. (2005) *State of Exception*, Chicago: University of Chicago Press

Adey, P. (2004) 'Secure and sorted mobilities: examples from the airport', *Surveillance and Society*, 1 (4): 500–19

Agozino, B. (2003) *Counter-Colonial Criminology*: *A Critique of Imperialist Reason*, London: Pluto Press

Agozino, B. (2004) 'Imperialism, crime and criminology: towards the decoloniasation of criminology', *Crime, Law & Social Change*, 41: 343–58

Albrecht, H. -J. (2000) 'Foreigners, migration, immigration and the development of criminal justice in Europe', in P. Green and A. Rutherford (eds) *Criminal Policy in Transition*, Oxford and Portland: Hart

Albrow, M. (1996) *The Global Age*, Cambridge: Polity Press

Altman, D. (2001) *Global Sex*, Chicago and London: University of Chicago Press

Amin, A. (2005) 'Local community on trial', *Economy and Society*, 34 (4): 612–33

Amnesty International (2005) *'They Come in Shooting'*: *Policing Socially Excluded Communities*; report available at: http://web.amnesty.org/library/index/engamr190252005

Andreas, P. (2000) *Border Games*: *Policing the US–Mexico Divide*, Ithaca, NY: Cornell University Press

Andreas, P. and Nadelmann, E. (2006) *Policing the Globe*: *Criminalization and Crime Control in International Relations*, Oxford: Oxford University Press

Andrejevic, M. (2006) 'Interactive (in)security: the participatory promise of ready.gov', *Cultural Studies*, 20 (4–5): 441–58

Appadurai, A. (1996) *Modernity at Large*: *Cultural Dimensions of Globalization*, Minneapolis: University of Minneapolis Press

Aronowitz, A. (2003) 'Trafficking in human beings: an international perspective', in D. Siegel et al. (eds) *Global Organized Crime: Trends and Developments*, Dordrecht, Boston and London: Kluwer Academic

Auge, M. (1995) *Non-places: Introduction to an Anthropology of Supermodernity*, London: Verso

Bailey, D. H. (1999) 'Approaches to Comparative Analysis: The Impossibility of becoming an expert on everywhere' in R. I. Mawby (ed.) *Policing Across the World: Issues for the Twenty-First Century*, London: UCL Press

Baker, E. and Roberts, J. V. (2005) 'Globalization and the new punitiveness', in J. Pratt et al. (eds) *The New Punitiveness: Trends, Theories, Perspectives*, Cullompton: Willan

Bales, K. (1999) *Disposable People: New Slavery in the Global Economy*, Berkeley: University of California Press

Bales, K. (2003) 'Because She Looks Like a Child' in B. Ehrenreich and A. R. Hochschild (eds) *Global Woman: Nannies, Maids and Sex Workers in the New Economy*, London: Granta Books

Barak, G. (2005) 'A Reciprocal Approach to Peacemaking Criminology: Between Adversarialism and Mutualism', *Theoretical Criminology*, vol 9 (2):131–52

Barber, B. (2003) *Jihad vs. McWorld*, New York: Corgi Books

Barry, A. (2002) *Political Machines: Governing a Technological Society*, London and New York: Athlone Press

Bauman, Z. (1997) *Postmodernity and its Discontents*, Cambridge: Polity

Bauman. Z. (1998) *Globalization: The Human Consequences*, Cambridge: Polity Press

Bauman, Z. (2000) *Liquid Modernity*, Cambridge: Polity Press

Bauman, Z. (2002) *Society under Siege*, Cambridge: Polity Press

Bauman, Z. (2004) *Wasted Lives: Modernity and its Outcasts*, Cambridge: Polity Press

Beck, U. (1992) *Risk Society: Towards a New Modernity*, London: Sage

Beck, U. (1999) *World Risk Society*, Cambridge: Polity Press

Beck, U. (2002) 'The terrorist threat: world risk society revisited', *Theory, Culture & Society*, 19 (4): 39–55

Beck, U. (2003) 'The analysis of global inequality: from national to cosmopolitan perspective', in M. Kaldor et al. (eds) *Global Civil Society*, London: Centre for the Study of Global Governance (Yearbook)

Beck, U., Sznaider, N., and Winter, R. (eds) (2003) *Global America? The Cultural Consequences of Globalization*, Liverpool: Liverpool University Press

Benhabib, S. (2004) *The Rights of Others: Aliens, Residents and Citizens*, Cambridge: Cambridge University Press

Bierne, P. and Nelken, D. (eds) (1997) *Issues in Comparative Criminology*, Aldershot: Ashgate

Bigo, D. (2000a) 'When two become one: internal and external securitisation in Europe', in M. Kelstrup and M. C. Williams (eds) *International Relations Theory and the Politics of European Integration*, London and New York: Routledge

Bigo, D. (2000b) 'Liaison officers in Europe: new officers in the European security field', in J. W. E. Sheptycki (ed.) *Issues in Transnational Policing*, London and New York: Routledge

Bigo, D. and Guild, E. (2004) 'Distancering af de fremmede – logikken i Schengenvisumet', *Tidsskriftet Politikk*, 7 (3): 23–33

Bigo, D. and Guild, E. (2005) *Controlling Frontiers: Free Movement into and within Europe*, Aldershot: Ashgate

Bjørgo, T. (1997) *'Racist and right-wing violence in Scandinavia: patterns, perpetrators, and responses'*, PhD thesis, Rijksuniversiteit te Leiden

Bjørgo, T. (ed.) (2005) *Root Causes of Terrorism: Myths, Reality and Ways Forward*, London: Routledge

Bjørgo, T. and White, R. (eds.) (1993) *Racist Violence in Europe*, Basingstoke: Macmillan

Blakely, E. J. and Snyder, M. G. (1999) *Fortress America: Gated Communities in the United States*, Washington, DC: Brookings Institution Press

Borja, J. and Castells, M. (1997) *Local & Global: Management of Cities in the Information Age*, London: Earthscan

Bottoms, A. E. (1995) 'The Philosophy and Politics of Punishment and Sentencing' in C. Clarkson and R. Morgan (eds) *The Politics of Sentencing Reform*, Oxford: Clarendon Press

Bottoms, A. E. and Wiles, P. (2002) 'Environmental criminology', in M. Maguire et al. (eds) *The Oxford Handbook of Criminology*, 3rd edn, Oxford: Oxford University Press

Bourdieu, P. (1980) *The Logic of Practice*, Stanford: Stanford University Press

Bourdieu, P. (1999) 'Site Effects' in P. Bourdieu et al. (eds) *The Weight of the World: Social Suffering in Contemporary Society*, Cambridge: Polity Press

Bourdieu, P. and Wacquant, L. (1999) 'On the cunning of imperialist reason', *Theory, Culture & Society*, 16 (1): 41–58

Bourgois, P. (2003) *In Search of Respect: Selling Crack in El Barrio*, 2nd edn, Cambridge: Cambridge University Press

Braithwaite, J. (2000) 'The new regulatory state and the transformation of criminology', *British Journal of Criminology*, 40 (2): 222–38

Braithwaite, J. (2004) 'Methods of Power for Development: Weapons of the Weak, Weapons of the Strong', *Michigan Journal of International Law*, vol. 26: 297–330

Brennan, D. (2003) 'Selling sex for visas: sex tourism as a stepping-stone to international migration', in B. Ehrenreich and A. R. Hochschild (eds) *Global Woman: Nannies, Maids and Sex Workers in the New Economy*, London: Granta Books

Brenner, N. and Keil, R. (2006) *The Global Cities Reader*, London and New York: Routledge

Brenner, S. W. (2007) *'Cybercrime:* re-thinking *crime control strategies'*, in Y. Jewkes (ed.) *Crime Online*, Cullompton: Willan

Brown, M. (2002) 'The politics of penal excess and the echo of colonial penality', *Punishment & Society*, 4 (4): 403–23

Brown, M. (2005) '"Setting the conditions" for Abu Ghraib: the prison nation abroad', *American Quarterly*, Sept.: 973–97

Bryman, A. (2004) *The Disneyization of Society*, London, Thousand Oaks and New Delhi: Sage

Bunt, G. (2003) *Islam in the Digital Age: E-Jihad, Online Fatwas and Cyber Islamic Environments*, London and Sterling, VA: Pluto Press

Burchell, G., Gordon, C. and Miller, P. (eds) (1991) *The Foucault Effect: Studies in Governmentality*, Chicago: University of Chicago Press

Cain, M. (2000) 'Orientalism, Occidentalism and the Sociology of Crime', *British Journal of Criminology*, 40: 239–60

Caldeira, T. (2000) *City of Walls: Crime, Segregation and Citizenship in São Paulo*, Berkeley: University of California Press

Calhoun, C., Price, P. and Timmer, A. (2002) 'Introduction', in C. Calhoun et al. (eds) *Understanding September 11*, New York: The New Press

Castells, M. (1996) *The Rise of the Network Society*, Oxford: Blackwell

Castells, M. (2000) *End of Millennium*, 2nd edn, Oxford: Blackwell

Castells, M. (2001) *The Internet Galaxy*, Oxford: Oxford University Press

Castells, M. (2004) *The Power of Identity*, 2nd edn, Oxford: Blackwell

Castles, S. and Miller, M. J. (2003) *The Age of Migration: International Population Movements in the Modern World*, Basingstoke: Palgrave Macmillan

Cere, R. (2007) 'Digital undergrounds: alternative politics and civil society', in Y. Jewkes (ed.) *Crime Online*, Cullompton: Willan

Chan, J. (2005) 'Globalisation, reflexivity and the practice of criminology', in J. Sheptycki and A. Wardak (eds) *Transnational and Comparative Criminology*, London: Glasshouse Press

Chapkis, V. W. (2005) 'Soft glove, punishing fist: The Trafficking victims protection Act of 2000', in E. Bernstein and L. Schaffner (eds) *Regulating Sex: The Politics of Intimacy and Identity*, New York and London: Routledge

Chow, E. N. (2003) 'Gender matters: studying globalization and social change in the 21st century', *International Sociology*, 18 (3): 443–60

Christie, N. (1986) 'Suitable enemy', in H. Bianchi and R. van Swaaningen (eds) *Abolitionism: Toward a Non-repressive Approach to Crime*, Amsterdam: Free University Press

Christie, N. (1997) 'Four blocks against insight: notes on the oversocialization of criminologists', *Theoretical Criminology*, 1 (1): 13–23

Christie, N. (2000) *Crime Control as Industry: Towards Gulags, Western Style*, 3rd edn, London: Routledge

Christie, N. (2004) *A Suitable Amount of Crime*, London: Routledge

Clarke, R. A. (2003) 'Dataveillance – 15 Years on', at http://www.amu.edu.au/people/Roger.clarke/DV/DVNZ03.html

Cohen, R. and Kennedy, P. (2000) *Global Sociology*, Basingstoke: Palgrave Macmillan

Cohen, S. (1982) 'Western Crime Control Models in the Third World: benign or Malignant?' *Research in Law, deviance and Social Control*, 4: 85–119

Cohen, S. (2002) *Folk Devils and Moral Panics: The Creation of the Mods and Rockers*, Third edition, London: Routledge

Cohen, S. (2006) 'Neither honesty nor hypocrisy: the legal reconstruction of torture', in T. Newburn and P. Rock (eds) *The Politics of Crime Control: Essays in Honour of David Downes*, Oxford: Oxford University Press.

Cole, D. (2004) *Enemy Aliens: Double Standards and Constitutional Freedoms in the War on Terrorism*, New York and London: The New Press

Coleman, R. (2004) *Reclaiming the Streets: Surveillance, Social Control and the City*, Cullompton: Willan

Computerworld (2005) 'NSW Police eye roadside fingerprint biometrics' (14 Oct.), at http://www.computerworld.com.au/

Connell, R. W. (1995) *Masculinities*, Berkeley: University of California Press

Coyle, A. (2005) 'On being a prisoner in the United Kingdom in the 21st century', *Prison Service Journal*, 162: 41–7

Crawford, A. (2006) 'Networked governance and the post-regulatory state?', *Theoretical Criminology*, 10 (4): 449–79

Cunneen, C. and Stubbs, J. (2004) 'Cultural criminology and engagement with race, gender and post-colonial identities', in J. Ferrell et al. (eds) *Cultural Criminology Unleashed*, London, Sydney and Portland: GlassHouse Press

Currie, E. (1997) 'Market, Crime and Community: Toward a Mid-Range Theory of Post-Industrial Violence', *Theoretical Criminology*, Vol 1 (2): 147–72

Currie, E. (1998) 'Crime and market society: lessons from the United States', in P. Walton and J. Young (eds) *The New Criminology Revisited*, Basingstoke: Macmillan

Curry, M. R. (2004) 'The profiler's question and the treacherous traveler: narratives of belonging in commercial aviation', *Surveillance and Society*, 1 (4): 475–99.

Davidson, Julia O'Connell (2005) *Children in the Global Sex Trade*, Cambridge: Polity Press.

Davis, M. (1998) *The City of Quartz: Excavating the Future of Los Angeles*, London: Pimlico

Davis, M. (1999) *Ecology of Fear: Los Angeles and the Imagination of Disaster*, New York: Vintage Books

Davis, M. (2006) *Planet of Slums*, London and New York: Verso

della Porta, D., Peterson, A. and Reiter, H. (eds) (2006) *The Policing of Transnational Protest*, Aldershot: Ashgate

Deflem, M. (2002) *Policing World Society: Historical Foundations of International Police Cooperation*, Oxford: Oxford University Press

Deflem, M. (2004) *Terrorism and Counter-terrorism: Criminological Perspectives*, Amsterdam: Elsevier

Di Eugenio, K. (2005) 'Rethinking criminology: the capital of barrios', unfinished manuscript.

Dikeç (2006) 'Badlands of the Republic? Revolts, the French state, and the question of banlieues', *Environment and Planning D: Society and Space*, 24 (2): 159–63

Diken, B. and Laustsen, C. B. (2005) *The Culture of Exception: Sociology facing the Camp*, London and New York: Routledge

DiMarco, H. (2003) 'The electronic cloak: secret sexual deviance in cybersociety', in Y. Jewkes (ed.) *Dot.Cons: Crime, Deviance and Identity on the Internet*, Cullompton: Willan

Ditton, J., Short, E., Philipps, S., Norris, C. and Armstrong, G. (1999) *The Effect of Closed Circuit Television on Recorded Crime Rates, and on the Fear of Crime in Glasgow*, Edinburgh: Central Research Unit, Scottish Office

Doezema, J. (1999) 'Loose women or lost women? The re-emergence of the myth of "white slaver" in contemporary discourses of trafficking in women', *Gender Issues*, 18 (1): 23–50

Duclos, D. (2005) 'Everyone under control: on the cultivation of fear', http://www.eurozine.com/authors/duclos.html

Durkheim, E. (1933) *The division of Labor in Society*, trans. George Simpson, New York: The Free Press

Edwards, A and Gill, P. (eds) (2003) *Transnational Organised Crime: Perspectives on Global Security*, London: Routledge

Ehrenreich, B. and Hochschild, A. R. (eds) (2003) *Global Woman: Nannies, Maids and Sex Workers in the New Economy*, London: Granta Books

Ericson, R. (2007) *Crime in an Insecure World*, Cambridge: Polity Press

Ericson, R. and Haggerty, K. H. (1997) *Policing the Risk Society*, Toronto: University of Toronto Press

Ericson, R. and Stehr, N. (2000) 'The ungovernability of modern societies: states, democracies, markets, participation, and citizens', in R. Ericson and N. Stehr (eds) *Governing Modern Societies*, Toronto: University of Toronto Press

Feeley, Malcolm M. and Simon, J. (1992) 'The new penology: notes on the emerging strategy of corrections and its implications', *Criminology*, 30 (4): 449–73

Ferrell, J. (1996) *Crimes of Style: Urban Graffiti and Politics of Criminality*, Boston: Northeastern University Press

Ferrell, J. (2001) *Tearing Down the Streets: Adventures in Urban Anarchy*, Basingstoke: Palgrave Macmillan

Ferrell, J., Greer, C. and Jewkes, Y. (2005) 'Hip hop graffiti, Mexican murals and the war on terror', *Crime, Media, Culture*, 1 (1): 5–9

Finch, E. (2007) 'The problem of stolen identity and the Internet', in Y. Jewkes (ed.) *Crime Online*, Cullompton: Willan

Findlay, M. (1999) *The Globalization of Crime*, Cambridge: Cambridge University Press

Findlay, M. (2003) *The Globalization of Crime: Understanding Transnational Relationships in Context*, Cambridge: Cambridge University Press

Flyghed, J. (2005) 'Crime-control in the post-wall era: the menace of security', *Journal of Scandinavian Studies in Criminology and Crime Prevention*, 6: 165–82

Foucault, M. (1977) *Discipline and Punish: The Birth of the Prison*, trans. Alan Sheridan, New York: Vintage Books

Franklin, A. (2003) 'The tourist syndrome: an interview with Zygmunt Bauman', *Tourist Studies*, 3 (2): 205–17

Frantzsen, E. (2006) *Narkojakt på gateplan. Om politikontroll av narkotika på Vesterbro*, København: Københavns Universitet

Fraser, N. (2005a) 'Reframing justice in a globalizing world', *New Left Review*, Nov–Dec.: 69–88

Fraser, N. (2005b) 'Transnationalizing the public sphere', http://www.republicart.net/disc/publicum/fraser01_en.htm

Friedman, J. (1986) 'The World City Hypothesis', *Development and Change*, 17: 69–83

Furedi, F. (2002) *Culture of Fear: Risk-taking and the Morality of Low Expectations*, London: Continuum

Galeotti, M. (2004) 'Introduction: global crime today', *Global Crime*, 6 (1): 1–7

Garland, D. (1990) *Punishment and Modern Society*, Oxford: Clarendon Press

Garland, D. (2001a) *The Culture of Control: Crime and Social Order in Contemporary Society*, Oxford: Oxford University Press

Garland, D. (ed.) (2001b) *Mass Imprisonment: Social Causes and Consequences*, London, Thousand Oaks and New Delhi: Sage

Giddens, A. (1990) *The Consequences of Modernity*. Cambridge: Polity Press

Giddens, A. (1998) *The Third Way. The Renewal of Social Democracy*, Cambridge: Polity Press

Giddens, A. (2000) *Runaway World*, New York: Routledge

Goffman, E. (1961) *Asylums: Essays on the Social Situation of Mental Patients and Other Inmates*, New York: Anchor Books

Goldsmith, A. (2003) 'Policing Weak States: Citizen Safety and State Responsibility', *Policing and Society*, vol. 13 (1) 3–21

Goodey, J. (2005) 'Sex trafficking in the European Union', in J. Sheptycki and A. Wardak (eds) *Transnational and Comparative Criminology*, London: Glasshouse

Grabosky, P. N. (2001) 'Virtual criminality: old wine in new bottles? *Social & Legal Studies*, 10 (2): 243–9

Graham, S. and Marvin, S. (2001) *Splintering Urbanism: Networked Infrastructures, Technological Mobilities and the Urban Condition*, London: Routledge

Green, P. and Ward, T. (2004) *State Crime: Governments, Violence and Corruption*, London: Pluto Press

Greenberg, K. J. (2006) *The Torture Debate in America*, New York: Cambridge University Press

Greenberg, K. J. and Dratel, J. L. (2005) *The Torture Papers: The Road to Abu Ghraib*, New York: Cambridge University Press

Gundhus, H. (2006) *For Sikkerhets Skyld: IKT, yrkeskulturer og kunnskapsarbeid I politiet*, Oslo: University of Oslo

Gupta, A. and Ferguson, J. (2002) 'beyond "Culture": Space, Identity, and the Politics of Difference' in J. X. Inda and R Rosaldo (eds) *The Anthropology of Globalization: A Reader*, Oxford: Blackwell

Haggerty, K. D. and Ericson, R. V. (2000) 'The surveillant assemblage', *British Journal of Sociology*, 51: 605–22

Haggerty, K. D. and Ericson, R.V. (2006) *The New Politics of Surveillance and Visibility*, Toronto: University of Toronto Press

Hall, S. (1995) 'New cultures for old', in D. Massey and P. Jess (eds) *A Place in the World? Places, Cultures and Globalization*, Milton Keynes: Open University Press

Hall, S. (2006) 'Cosmopolitan promises, multicultural realities', in R. Scholar (ed.) *Divided Cities*, Oxford: Oxford University Press

Hall, S. and Winlow, S. (2005) 'Anti-nirvana: crime, culture and instrumentalism in the age of insecurity', *Crime, Media, Culture*, 1 (1): 31–48

Hallsworth, S. (2005) *Street Crime*, Cullompton: Willan

Hamnett, C. (2003) *Unequal City: London in the Global Era*, London: Routledge

Hannerz, U. (2005) 'The withering away of the nation?' in B. Mazkish and A. Iriye (eds) *The Global History Reader*, New York and London: Routledge

Harcourt, B. E. (2001) *Illusion of Order: The False Promise of Broken Windows Policing*, Cambridge, MA and London: Harvard University Press

Harding, R. (1997) *Private Prisons and Public Accountability*, Buckingham: Open University Press

Hardt, M. and Negri, A. (2000) *Empire*, Cambridge, MA Harvard University Press

Harvey, D. (1990) *The Condition of Postmodernity: An Enquiry into the Origins of Cultural Change*, Oxford: Blackwell

Hayes, B. (2004) 'From the Schengen Information System to SIS II and the Visa Information System (VIS): the proposals explained', *Statewatch analysis*, www.statewatch.org/news/2004/feb/summary-sis.reprt.htm

Hayward, K. (2004) *City Limits: Crime, Consumer Culture and the Urban Experience*, London: Glasshouse Press

Hayward, K. and Morrison, W. (2002) 'Locating "Ground Zero": caught between the narratives of crime and war', in J. Strawson (ed.) *Law after Ground Zero*, London: Glasshouse Press

Held, D. (1995) *Democracy and the Global Order*, Cambridge: Polity Press

Held, D. (2000) 'The changing contours of political community', in R. Ericson and N. Stehr (eds) *Governing Modern Societies*, Toronto: University of Toronto Press

Held, D. (2005) *Democracy and the Global Order*, Cambridge: Polity Press

Held, D. and McGrew, A. (eds) (2003) *The Global Transformations Reader*, 2nd edn, Cambridge: Polity Press

Held, D., McGrew, A. Goldblatt, D. and Perraton, J. (2003) 'Rethinking globalization', in D. Held and A. McGrew (eds) *The Global Transformations Reader*, 2nd edn, Cambridge: Polity Press

Hillyard, P., Pantazis, C. Tombs, S. and Gordon D. (eds) (2004) *Beyond Criminology: Taking Crime Seriously*, London: Pluto Press

Hirst, P. Q. and Thompson, G. (1996) *Globalization in Question*, London: Polity Press

Hirst, P. Q. and Thompson, G. (1999) *Globalization in Question: The International Economy and the Possibilities of Governance*, Cambridge: Polity Press

Hobbs, D. and Dunnighan, C. (1998) 'Glocal organized crime: context and pretext', in V. Ruggiero et al. (eds) *The New European Criminology: Crime and Social Order*, London: Routledge

Hochschild, A. R. (2003) 'Love and gold', in B. Ehrenreich and A. R. Hochschild (eds) *Global Woman: Nannies, Maids and Sex Workers in the New Economy*, London: Granta Books

Hoffman, B. (2005) 'What is terrorism?' in B. Mazlish and A. Iriye (eds) *The Global History Reader*, New York and London: Routledge

Hogg, R. (2002) 'Criminology Beyond the Nation State: Global Conflicts, Human Rights and "the New World Diosorder"' in C. Karrington and R. Hogg (eds) *Critical Criminology: Issues, Debates, Challenges*, Cullompton: Willan

Holton, R. J. (2005) *Making Globalization*, Basingstoke and New York: Palgrave Macmillan

Høigård, C. (2002) *Gategallerier*, Oslo: Pax Forlag

Hudson, B. (2003) *Justice in the Risk Society: Challenging and Re-affirming Justice in Late-Modernity*, London: Sage

Human Security Report (2005) *War and Peace in the 21st Century*, The University of British Columbia, Canada: Human Society Centre

Huntington, S. P. (1996) *The Clash of Civilizations and the Remaking of World Order*, New York : Simon & Schuster

Huysmans, J. (2006) *The Politics of Insecurity: Fear, Migration and Asylum in the EU*, London and New York: Routledge

Hylland Eriksen, T. (2003) *Globalisation: Studies in Anthrophology*, London: Pluto Press

Inda, J. X. (2006) *Targeting Immigrants: Government, Technology and Ethics*, Oxford: Blackwell

Inda, J. X. and Rosaldo, R. (2002) 'Introduction: A World in Motion' in J. X. Inda and R. Rosaldo (eds) *The Anthropology of Globalization: A Reader*, pp. 1–34. Oxford: Blackwell

Iyer, P. (2000) *The Global Soul: Jet Lag, Shopping Malls and the Search for Home*, London: Bloomsbury

Jamieson, R. (ed.) (2003) 'War, crime and human rights', special issue of *Theoretical Criminology*, 7 (3).

Jess, P. and Massey, D. (eds) (1995) *A Place in the World? Places, Cultures and Globalization*, Milton Keynes: Open University Press

Jewkes, Y. (ed.) (2003) *Dot.Cons: Crime, Deviance and Identity on the Internet*, Cullompton: Willan

Jewkes, Y. (2004) *Media and Crime*, London: Sage

Jewkes, Y. (2007) '"Killed by the Internet": cyber homicides, cyber suicides and cyber sex crimes', in Y. Jewkes (ed.) *Crime Online*, Cullompton: Willan

Jewkes, Y. and Andrews, C. (2007) 'Internet child pornography: international responses', in Y. Jewkes (ed.) *Crime Online*, Cullompton: Willan

Jewkes, Y. and Sharp, K. (2003) 'Crime, deviance and the disembodied self: transcending the dangers of corporeality', in Y. Jewkes (ed.) *Dot.Cons: Crime, Deviance and Identity on the Internet*, Cullompton: Willan

Johansen, P. O. (2001) 'Kriminalitetens global økonomi', Retfoerd vol. 24 (4): 3–14

Johnston, L. and Shearing, C. (2003) *Governing Security: Explorations in Policing and Justice*, New York: Routledge

Jones, T. and Newburn, T. (1998) *Private Security and Public Policing*, Oxford: Clarendon Press

Jones, T. and Newburn, T. (2004) 'The convergence of US and UK crime control policy: exploring substance and process', in T. Newburn and R. Sparks (eds) *Criminal Justice and Political Cultures*, Cullompton: Willan

Jones, T. and Newburn, T. (2006) *Plural Policing: A Comparative Perspective*, London: Routledge

Kelling, G. L. and Coles, C. M. (1996) *Fixing Broken Windows: Restoring Order and Reducing Crime in our Communities*, New York: The Free Press

Kempadoo, K. (1998) 'Globalizing sex workers' rights', in K. Kempadoo and J. Doezema (eds) *Global Sex Workers: Rights, Resistance, and Redefinition*, New York and London: Routledge

Kendall, L. (2002) *Hanging Out in the Virtual Pub: Masculinities and Relationships Online*, Berkeley, Los Angeles and London: University of California Press

Kimmel, M. S. (2003) 'Globalization and its mal(e)contents', in *International Sociology*, 18 (3): 603–20

Klein, N. (2000) *No Logo: Taking Aim at the Brand Bullies*, London: Flamingo

Klein, N. (2003) 'Fortress continents: the US and Europe are both creating multi-tiered regional strongholds', http://www.thenation.com/doc/20030203/klein

Kyle, D. and Koslowski, R. (eds) (2001) *Global Human Smuggling: Comparative Perspectives*, Baltimore: John Hopkins University Press

Laguerre, M. S. (2000) *The global Ethnopolis: Chinatown, Japantown and Manilatown in American Society*, Basingstoke, Macmillan; New York: St Martin's Press

Laqueur, W. (2001) *The New Terrorism: Fanaticism and the Arms of Mass Destruction*, London: Phoenix Press

Lash, S. and Urry, J. (1994) *Economies of Signs & Space*, London: Sage

Law, J. amd Urry, J. (2004) 'Enacting the Social', *Economy and Society*, 33 (3): 340–410

Lea, J. and Young, J. (1993) *What is to be Done about Law and Order? Crisis in the Nineties*, London: Pluto Press

Lemke, T. (2002) 'Prison industry goes global', *Insight on the News*, http://www.findarticles.com/p/articles/mi_m1571/is_14_18/ai_84971439

Lessig, L. (1999) *Code and Other Laws of Cyberspace*, New York: Basic Books

Letherby, G. and Marchbank, J. (2003) 'Cyber-chattels: buying brides and babies on the Net', in Y. Jewkes (ed.) *Dot.Cons: Crime, Deviance and Identity on the Internet*, Cullompton: Willan

Loader, I. (1999) 'consumer culture and the commodification of policing and security', *Sociology* 33 (2): 373–92

Loader, I. (2002) 'Governing European policing: some problems and prospects', *Policing & Society*, 12 (4): 291–305

Loader, I. (2004) 'Policing, securitisation and democratisation in Europe', in T. Newburn and R. Sparks (eds) *Criminal Justice and Political Cultures: National and International Dimensions of Crime Control*, Cullompton: Willan

Loader, I. and Sparks, R. (2002) 'Contemporary landscapes of crime, order and control', in M. Maguire et al. (eds) *The Oxford Handbook of Criminology*, Oxford: Oxford University Press

Loader, I. and Walker, N. (2001) 'Policing as public good: reconstructing the connections between policing and the state', *Theoretical Criminology*, 5 (1): 9–35

Lomell, H. M. (2007) *Det selektive overblikk: En studie av videoovervåkingspraksis*, Oslo: Universitetsforlaget

Low, S. (2003) *Behind the Gates: Life, Security and the Pursuit of Happiness in Fortress America*, New York and London: Routledge

Lynch, M. J. and Stretsky, P. B. (eds) (2003) special issue of *Theoretical Criminology*, 7 (2)

Lyon, D. (2001) *Surveillance Society: Monitoring Everyday Life*, Maidenhead: Open University Press

Lyon, D. (2003a) *Surveillance after September 11*, Cambridge: Polity Press

Lyon, D. (2003b) 'Surveillance as social sorting: computer codes and mobile bodies', in D. Lyon (ed.) *Surveillance as Social Sorting: Privacy, Risk and Digital Discrimination*, London and New York: Routledge

Lyon, D. (2005) 'The border is everywhere: ID cards, surveillance, and the other', in
E. Zureik and M. Salter (eds) *Global Surveillance and Policing: Borders, Security, Identity*,
Cullompton: Willan

Lyon, D. (ed.) (2006) *Theorizing Surveillance: The Panopticon and Beyond*, Cullompton: Willan

McArdle, A. and Erzen, T. (2001) *Zero Tolerance: Quality of Life and the New Police Brutality
in New York City*, New York and London: New York University Press

McCahill, M. (2002) *The Surveillance Web: The Rise of Visual Surveillance in an English city*,
Cullompton: Willan

McKenzie, E. (1994) *Privatopia: Homeowner Associations and the Rise of Residential Private
Government*, New Haven, Conn.: Yale University Press

McLaughlin, E. (2001) 'Political violence, terrorism and states of fear', in J. Muncie and
E. McLaughlin (eds) *The Problem of Crime*, 2nd edn, London: Sage

Mathiesen, T. (1997) 'The viewer society: Michel Foucault's "Panopticon" revisisted',
Theoretical Criminology, 1 (2): 215–34

Mathiesen, T. (2003) 'The rise of the surveillant state in times of globalisation', in
C. Sumner (ed.) *The Blackwell Companion to Criminology*, Maiden, Oxford, Victoria and
Berlin: Blackwell

Mathiesen, T. (2006) '*Lex Vigilatoria* – towards a control system without a state?' in
S. Armstrong and L. McAra (eds) *Perspectives on Punishment*, Oxford: Oxford University
Press

Melossi, D. (2003) '"In a peaceful life": migration and the crime of modernity in
Europe/Italy', *Punishment & Society*, 5 (4): 371–97

Melossi, D. (2004) 'The cultural embeddedness of social control', in T. Newburn and
R. Sparks (eds) *Criminal Justice and Political Cultures: National and International
Dimensions of crime control*, Cullompton: Willan

Merton, R. (1938) 'Social structure and anomie', *American Sociological Review*, 3: 672–82

Mitchell, D. (2003) *The Right to the City: Social Justice and the Fight for Public Space*,
New York: Guilford Press

Morley, D. (2000) *Home Territories: Media, Mobility and Identity*, London and New York:
Routledge

Morrison, W. (1995) *Theoretical Criminology: From Modernity to Post-modernism*, London:
Cavendish

Morrison, W. (2005) 'Rethinking narratives of penal change in global context', in J. Pratt
et al. (eds) *The New Punitiveness: Trends, Theories, Perspectives*, Cullompton: Willan

Morrison, W. (2006) *Criminology, Civilisation and the New World Order: Rethinking
Criminology in a Global Context*, London: Glasshouse Press

Muncie, J. (2004) 'Youth justice: globalisation and multi-modal governance', in
T. Newburn and R. Sparks (eds) *Criminal Justice and Political Cultures: National and
International Dimensions of Crime Control*, Cullompton: Willan.

Murdoch, G. (2004) 'Democracy in digital times', paper given at The Materiality of
Mediated Communication Conference, 17–18 May, Bergen, Norway.

Mythen, G. and Walkate, S. (2006a) 'Criminology and terrorism: which thesis? Risk
Society or governmentality?' *British Journal of Criminology*, 46 (3): 379–98

Mythen, G. and Walkate, S. (2006b) 'Communicating the terrorist risk: harnessing a
culture of fear', *Crime, Media, Culture*, 2 (2): 123–42

Nadelmann, E. (1993) *Cops across Borders: The Internationalization of US Criminal Law
Enforcement*, Pennsylvania: Pennsylvania State University Press

Naim, M. (2006) *Illicit: How Smugglers, Traffickers and Copycats are Hijacking the Global Economy*, New York: Anchor Books

Naim, M. (2007) 'The You Tube Effect' in Foreign Policy, viewed at: http://www.foreign-policy.com/story/cms.php?story_id = 3676

National Commission on Terrorist Attacks Upon the United States (2004) *The 9/11 Report*, New York: St Martin's Press

Newburn, T. and Jones, T. (2005) 'Symbolic politics and penal populism: the long shadow of Willie Horton', in *Crime, Media, Culture*, 1 (1): 72–87

Newburn, T. and Sparks, R. (eds) (2004) *Criminal Justice and Political Cultures: National and International Dimensions of Crime Control*, Cullompton: Willan

Nightingale, C. (1993) *On the Edge*, New York: Basic Books

Nikolic-Ristanovic, V. (1998) 'War and crime in the former Yugoslavia', in V. Ruggiero et al. (eds) *The New European Criminology*, London and New York: Routledge

Nordstrom, C. (2000) 'Shadows and sovereigns', *Theory Culture & Society*, 17 (4): 35–54

Norris, C. and Armstrong, G. (1999) *The Maximum Surveillance Society: The Rise of CCTV*, Oxford: Berg

Ohmae, K. (1990) *The Borderless World: Power and Strategy in the International Economy*, London: Collins

O'Malley, P. (2004) 'Globalising risk? Distinguishing styles of "Neoliberal" criminal justice in Australia and the USA', in T. Newburn and R. Sparks (eds) *Criminal Justice and Political Cultures: National and International Dimensions of Crime Control*, Cullompton: Willan

Outshoorn, J. (ed.) (2004) *The Politics of Prostitution: Women's Movements, Democratic States and the Globalization of Sex Commerce*, Cambridge: Cambridge University Press

Pakes, F. (2004) *Comparative Criminal Justice*, Cullompton: Willan

Papastergiadis, N. (2000) *The Turbulence of Migration*, Cambridge: Polity Press

Park, R. E., Burgess, E. W. and McKenzie, R. D. (1925) *The City*, Chicago: University of Chicago Press

Passas, N. (2000) 'Global anomie, dysnomie, and economic crime: hidden consequences of neoliberalism and globalization in Russia and around the World', *Social Justice*, 27 (2): 16–43

Passas, N. (ed.) (2003) *International Crimes*, Aldershot: Ashgate

Passas, N. and Agnew, R. (eds) (1997) *The Future of Anomie Theory*, Boston, MA: Northeastern University Press

Perrons, D. (2004) *Globalization and Social Change: People and Places in a Divided World*, London and New York: Routledge

Philipps, C. and Bowling, B. (2002) 'Racism, ethnicity, crime and criminal justice', in M. Maguire et al. (eds) *The Oxford Handbook of Criminology*, Oxford: Oxford University Press

Pickering, S. (2005) *Refugees and State Crime*, Sydney: The Federation Press

Pickering, S. and Lambert, C. (eds) (2004) *Global Issues, Women and Justice*, Sydney: Sydney Institute of Criminology

Polet, F. (ed.) (2004) *Globalizing Resistance: The State of Struggle*, London: Pluto Press in assoc. with CETRI, Louvain-la-Neuve, Belgium

Policing & Society (2002) Special issue on police accountability in Europe, 12 (4).

Poynting, S. and Noble, G. (2004) *Bin Laden in the Suburbs*, Sydney: Institute of Criminology

Pratt, J. (2000) 'The return of the Wheelbarrow Man', *British Journal of Criminology*, 40: 127–45

Pratt, J. (2002) 'Critical criminology and the punitive society: some new "visions of social control"', in K. Carrington and R. Hogg (eds) *Critical Criminology: Issues, Debates, Challenges*, Cullompton: Willan

Pratt, J. (2007) *Penal Populism*, London: Routledge

Pratt, J., Brown, D. Brown, M. Hallsworth, S. and Morrison, W (eds) (2005) *The New Punitiveness: Trends, Theories, Perspectives*, Cullompton: Willan

Prieur, A. (2004) *Balansekunstnere*, Oslo: Pax Forlag

Rasmussen, T. (2000) *Social Theory and Communication Technology*, Aldershot: Ashgate

Reich, R. (1991) *The Work of Nations*: Preparing Ourselves for 21st-Century Capitalism. New York: Alfred A. Knopf.

Reich, R. (2005) 'The New Rich-Rich Gap' published December 12, 2005 at http://www.commondreams.org/views05/1212-20.htm

Rigakos, G. S. (2002) *The New Parapolice. Risk Markets and Commodified Social Control*, Toronto, Buffalo and London: University of Toronto Press

Ritzer, G. and Liska, A. (1997) '"McDisneyization" and post-tourism': complementary perspectives on contemporary tourism', in C. Royek and J. Urry (eds) *Touring Cultures: Transformations of Travel and Theory*, London: Routledge

Robertson, R. (1995) 'Glocalization: time-space and homogeneity – heterogeneity?' in M. Featherstone, S. Lash and R. Robertson (eds) *Global Modernities*, London: Sage

Rose, N. (1999) *Powers of Freedom: Reframing Political Thought*, Cambridge: Cambridge University Press

Rose, N. (2000) 'Government and control', *British Journal of Criminology*, 40: 321–39

Ruggiero, V. (1997) 'Criminals and service-providers: cross-national dirty economies', *Crime, Law & Social Change*, 28: 27–38

Ruggiero, V. (2003) 'Terrorism: cloning the enemy', *International Journal of the Sociology of Law*, 31 (1): 23–34

Said, E. (1978/1985) *Orientalism*. London: Penguin Books

Sanghera, J., Pattanaik, B. and Kempadoo, K. (2005) *Trafficking and Prostitution Reconsidered: New Perspectives on Migration, Sex Work, and Human Rights*, Boulder, CO: Paradigm

Sassen, S. (1998) *Globalization and its Discontents*, New York: The New Press

Sassen, S. (2001) *The Global City: New York, London, Tokyo*, 2nd edn, Princeton: Princeton University Press

Sassen, S. (2003) 'Global cities and survival circuits', in B. Ehrenreich and A. R. Hochschild (eds) *Global Woman: Nannies, Maids and Sex Workers in the New Economy*, London: Granta Books

Saul, B. (2006) *Defining Terrorism in International Law*, Oxford: Oxford University Press

Sayad, A. (2004) *The Suffering of the Immigrant*, Cambridge: Polity Press

Scheper-Hughes, N. (2005) 'The last commodity: post-human ethics and the global traffic in "Fresh" organs', in A. Ong and S. J. Collier (eds) *Global Assemblages: Technology, Politics and Ethics as Anthropological Problems*, Oxford: Blackwell

Scholar, R. (ed.) (2006) *Divided Cities*, Oxford: Oxford University Press

Sennett, R. (1974) *The Fall of the Public Man*, Cambridge: Cambridge University Press

Sennett, R. (1998) *The Corrosion of Character: The Personal Consequences of Work in the New Capitalism*, New York: W. W. Norton

Sennett, R. (2000) 'Cities without Care or Connection', *New Statesman*, June 5th 2000 at http://www.newstatesman.com/200006050018

Sernhede, O. (2002) *AlieNation is my Nation: Hiphop och unga mans utanforskap I Det Nya Sverige*, Stockholm: Ordfront forlag

Shaw, C. R. and McKay, H. D. (1942) *Juvenile Delinquency and Urban Areas*, Chicago: University of Chicago Press.

Shearing, C. (2004) 'Thoughts on sovereignty', *Policing & Society*, 14 (1): 5–12

Shearing, C. and Stenning, P. (1981) 'Modern private security', in M. Tonry and N. Morris (eds) *Crime and Justice: An annual review of research*, Chicago: University of Chicago Press

Shearing, C. and Stenning, P. (1985) 'From the Panopticon to Disney World: The development of Discipline' In A. Doob and E. Greenspan (eds) *Perspectives in Criminal Law*, Ontario: Canada Law Books

Sheptycki, J. W. E. (ed.) (2000a) *Issues in Transnational Policing*, London: Routledge

Sheptycki, J. W. E. (2000b) 'The "drug war": learning from the paradigm example of transnational policing', in J. Sheptycki (ed.) *Issues in Transnational Policing*, London: Routledge

Sheptycki, J. (2002a) 'Accountability across the policing field: towards a general cartography of accountability for post-modern policing', *Policing & Society*, 12 (4): 323–38

Sheptycki, J. (2002b) *In Search of Transnational Policing*: Towards a Sociology of Global Policing. Aldershot: Ashgate

Sheptycki, J. (2004) 'Organizational pathologies in police intelligence systems', *European Journal of Criminology*, 1 (3): 307–32

Sheptycki, J. (2005) 'Relativism, transnationalisation and comparative criminology', in J. W. E. Sheptycki and A. Wardak (eds) *Transnational & Comparative Criminology*, London: Glasshouse Press

Shields, R. (2003) *The Virtual*, London and New York: Routledge

Siegel, D., Bunt, H. and Zeitich, D. (eds) (2003) *Global Organized Crime: Trends and Developments*, Dordrecht, Boston and London: Kluwer Academic

Simmel, G. (1964) *The Sociology of Georg Simmel*, trans., ed. and with an introduction by Kurt H. Wolff, New York: The Free Press

Simon, J. (1997) 'Governing through crime', in L. Friedman and G. Fisher (eds) *The Crime Conundrum: Essays in Criminal Justice*, Boulder, CO: Westview Press

Simon, J. (2000) 'The "society of captives" in the era of hyper-incarceration', *Theoretical Criminology*, 4 (3): 285–308

Simon, J. and Feeley, M. M. (1995) 'True crime: the new penology and public discourse on crime', in T. G. Bloomberg and S. Cohen (eds) *Punishment and Social Control: Essays in Honor of Sheldon L. Messinger*, New York: Aldine de Gruyter

Singer, P. W. (2003) *Corporate Warriors: The Rise of the Privatized Military Industry*, New York: Cornell University Press

Skilbrei, M. -L. and Polyakova, I. (2006) *'My Life Is Too Short; I Want to Live Now'*, Oslo: University of Oslo

Skilbrei, M. -L., Tveit, M. and Brunovskis, A. (2006) *Afrikanske drømmer på europeiske gater*, Fafo rapport 525, Oslo: Fafo

Smith, R. G. (2007) 'Biometric solutions to identity-related crime', in Y. Jewkes (ed.) *Crime Online*, Cullompton: Willan

Spalek, B. (2002) *Islam, Crime and Criminal Justice*, Cullompton: Willan

Sparks, R. and Hope, T. (eds) (2000) *Crime, Risk and Insecurity: Law and Order in Everyday Life and Political Discourse*, New York: Routledge

Spivak, G. C. (1999) *A Critique of Postcolonial Reason: Toward a History of the Vanishing Present*, Cambridge, Mass.: Harvard University Press

Stalder, F. and Lyon, D. (2003) 'Electronic identity cards and social classification', in D. Lyon (ed.) *Surveillance as Social Sorting: Privacy, Risk and Digital Discrimination,* London and New York: Routledge

Stern, V. (2006) *Creating Criminals: Prisons and People in a Market Society,* London and New York: Zed Books

Stiglitz, J. (2002) *Globalization and its Discontents,* London: Penguin Books

Thomas, D. and Loader, B. (eds) (2000) *Cybercrime: Law Enforcement, Security and Surveillance in the Information Age,* London: Routledge

Thomson, J. E. (1994) *Mercenaries, Pirates and Sovereigns: State Building and Extraterritorial Violence in Early Modern Europe,* Princeton NJ: Princeton University Press

Thorbek, S. and Pattanaik, B. (eds) (2002) *Transnational Prostitution: Changing Patterns in a Global Context,* London: Zed Books

Torpey, J. (2000) *The Invention of the Passport: Surveillance, Citizenship and the State,* Cambridge: Cambridge University Press

Turkle, S. (1995) *Life on the Screen: Identity in the Age of the Internet,* London: Phoenix

UN-Habitat (2003) *The Challenge of Slums*: Global Report on Human Settlements 2003. London and Sterling, VA: Earthscan

UNODOC (2007) United Nations Office on Drugs and Crime, Annual report, available at: http://www.unodc.org/unodc/annual_report_2007.html

Urry, J. (2000) *Sociology beyond Societies: Mobilities for the Twenty-first Century,* London: Routledge

Urry, J. (2002a) 'The global complexities of September 11th, *Theory, Culture & Society,* 19 (4): 57–69

Urry, J. (2002b) *The Tourist Gaze,* 2nd edn, London: Sage

Urry, J. (2003) *Global Complexity,* Cambridge: Polity Press

Valier, C. (2003) 'Foreigners, crime and changing mobilities', *British Journal of Criminology,* 43: 1–21

Valier, C. (2004) *Crime and Punishment in Contemporary Culture,* London and New York: Routledge

Van Creveld, M. (1991) *The Transformation of War,* New York: The Free Press

Virilio, P. (2000) *The Information Bomb,* London: Verso Books

Wacquant, L. (1999) 'Suitable enemies', *Punishment & Society,* 1 (2): 215–22

Wacquant, L. (2001) 'Deadly symbiosis: when ghetto and prison meet and mesh', *Punishment & Society,* 3 (1): 95–134

Wacquant, L. (2003) 'Towards a dictatorship over the poor? Notes on the penalization of poverty', *Punishment & Society,* 5 (2): 197–205

Waddington, P. A. J. (2005) 'Slippery slopes of civil libertarian pessimism', *Policing & Society,* 15 (3): 353–75

Wakefield, A. (2003) *Selling Security: The Private Policing of Public Spaces,* Cullompton: Willan

Walker, N. (2003) 'The pattern of transnational policing', in T. Newburn (ed.) *Handbook of Policing,* Cullompton: Willan

Wall, D. (ed.) (2001) *Crime and the Internet: Cybercrimes and Cyberfears,* London: Routledge

Wall, D. S. (ed.) (2003) *Cyberspace Crime,* Aldershot: Ashgate

Wall, D. (2007, forthcoming) *Cybercrimes: The Transformation of Crime in the Information Age.* Cambridge: Polity Press

Walters, W. (2004) 'Secure borders, safe haven, domopolitics', *Citizenship Studies*, 8 (3): 237–60

Wardak, A. and Sheptycki, J. (eds) (2005) *Transnational and Comparative Criminology*, London: Cavendish

Weber, M. (1948) *From Max Weber: Essays in Sociology*. London: Routledge and Kegan Paul

Weber, L. (2002) 'The detention of asylum seekers – 20 reasons why criminologists should care', *Current Issues in Criminal Justice: Special Issue – Refugee Issues and Criminology*, 14 (1): 9–30

Welch, M. and Schuster, L. (2005a) 'Detention of asylum seekers in the UK and USA: deciphering noisy and quiet constructions', *Punishment & Society*, 7 (4): 397–417

Welch, M. and Schuster, L. (2005b) 'Detention of asylum seekers in the US, UK, France, Germany and Italy', *Criminal Justice*, 5 (4): 331–55

Welmsley, R. (2006) *World Prison Population List*, 7th edn, available at: http://www.kcl.ac.uk/depsta/rel/icps/home.html

Whyte, D. (2007) 'The Crimes of Neo-Liberal Rule in Occupied Iraq', *The British Journal of Criminology*, vol. 47 (2): 177–95

Whyte, W. F. (1943) *Street Corner Society: The Social Structure of an Italian Slum*, Chicago: University of Chicago Press

Wilson, J. (1987) *The Truly Disadvantaged: The Inner City, the Underclass, and Public Policy*, Chicago: University of Chicago Press

Wilson, J. Q. and Kelling, G. L. (1982) 'Broken windows', *Atlantic Monthly*, March: 29–38

Witte, G. (2005) 'Private security contractors head to Gulf', www.washingtonpost.com

Wood, D. M. (ed.) (2006) *A Report on the Surveillance Society: For the Information Commissioner by the Surveillance studies Network*, available at http://www.ico.gov.uk/about_us/news_and _views/current_topics/Surveillance_society_report.aspx

Wood, J. and Shearing, C. (2007a) *Imagining Security*, Cullompton: Willan

Woodwiss, M. (2003) 'Transnational organized crime: the global reach of an American concept', in A. Edwards and P. Gill (eds) *Transnational Organised Crime: Perspectives on Global Security*, London and New York: Routledge

Woolgar, S. (ed.) (2002) *Virtual Society? Technology, Cyberbole, Reality*, Oxford: Oxford University Press

World Health Organization (2002) *World Report on Violence and Health*, Geneva, available online: http://www.who.int/violence_injury_prevention/violence/world_report/en/

Wykes, M. (2007) 'Constructing crime: stalking, celebrity, "cyber" and media', in Y. Jewkes (ed.) *Crime Online*, Cullompton: Willan

Yar, M. (2006) *Cybercrime and Society*, London: Sage

Yar, M. (2007) 'Teenage kicks or virtual villainy? Internet piracy, moral entrepreneurship and the social construction of a crime problem', in Y. Jewkes (ed.) *Crime Online*, Cullompton: Willan

Yesil, B. (2006) 'Watching ourselves: video surveillance, urban space and self-responsibilization', *Cultural Studies*, 20 (4–5): 400–16

Young, J. (1999) *The Exclusive Society*, London: Sage

Young, J. (2003) 'Merton with energy, Katz with structure', *Theoretical Criminology*, 7 (3): 388–414

Yuval-Davis, N. (1997) 'Ethnicity, Gender Relations and Multiculturalism' in P. Werbner and T. Modood (eds) *Debating Cultural Hybridity: Multicultural Identities and the Politics of Anti-Racism*. London: Zed Books.

Zarembka, J. M. (2003) 'America's dirty work: migrant maids and modern-day slavery', in B. Ehrenreich and A. R. Hochschild (eds) *Global Woman: Nannies, Maids, and Sex Workers in the New Economy*, London: Granta Books

Zedner, L. (2000) 'The pursuit of security', in T. Hope and R. Sparks (eds) *Crime, Risk and Insecurity*, London and New York: Routledge

Zedner, L. (2002) 'Dangers of Dystopia in Penal Theory', *Oxford Journal of Legal Studies*, Vol 22 (2): 341–66

Zedner, L. (2003) 'Too much security?', *International Journal of the Sociology of Law*, 31: 155–84.

Zedner, L. (2004) *Criminal Justice*, Oxford: Oxford University Press

Zedner, L. (2006) 'Policing before and after the police: the historical antecedents of contemporary crime control', *British Journal of Criminology*, 46: 78–96

Zizek, S. (2002) *Welcome to the Desert of the Real! Five Essays on September 11 and Related Dates*, London and New York: Verso

Zureik, E. and Salter, M. (eds) (2005) *Global Surveillance and Policing: Borders, Security, Identity*, Cullompton: Willan

Glossary

actuarial justice – a form of justice which relies on the application of statistical methods within criminal justice. A term popularized by Malcolm M. Feeley and Jonathan Simon (1992) to describe a development towards more risk-oriented forms of justice, which put priority on management of dangerous groups rather than doing justice in individual cases.

Americanization – a term used to describe the influence that the United States exerts over the culture and politics of other countries. Sometimes cultural consequences of globalization are equated with Americanization (alternatively described as Cocacolonization and Disneyfication).

anomie – a concept describing a state of normlessness. Originating from Emile Durkheim and further developed by Robert Merton, who described anomie as a condition which occurs when desires go beyond what can be obtained in socially accepted ways.

biometrics – from the ancient Greek words *bios* (life) and *metron* (measurement). Today, the term denotes computerized identification and authentication systems which rely on measurement of individuals' unique physical characteristics, such as fingerprints, retinas, irises, palms or even voice and gait.

CCTV – closed-circuit television. The term refers to the use of video cameras to transmit visual images to a set of monitors and/or recording devices. The cameras can be used for surveillance of public spaces (open street surveillance), or more commonly, private and semi-private spaces such as shops and shopping malls, banks, airports, etc.

Chicago School – The Chicago School of Human Ecology refers to a group of researchers loosely associated with the University of Chicago, which in the 1920s and 1930s pioneered the field of ethnographic urban sociology and criminology. Criminologically, the most influential representatives were Robert E. Park, Ernest Burgess, Clifford R. Shaw and H. D. McKay. After the Second World War came the second Chicago School, heavily influenced by symbolic interactionism.

clash of civilizations – a popular thesis developed by Samuel Huntington (1996), which sees the contemporary world as divided into competing civilizations that are based on irreconcilable differences in culture and religion.

commodification – the process by which something (a non-commodity) is turned into a commodity (i.e. is assigned economic value and evaluated in monetary terms).

consumerism – a term popularly used to describe the cultural focus on material consumption, particularly the emphasis on brand names and status-enhancing products.

cosmopolitanism – an outlook on politics, culture, society and justice which aims to encompass all the world; also meaning free of local, national and provincial attachments and prejudices.

crime – a violation of the law which can be subject to prosecution and punishment. Which harmful acts are defined as criminal, and the nature of their sanctions, is to some extent culturally and historically relative. Acts become defined as criminal through a social process of **criminalization.**

crime mapping – a form of crime analysis which relies on the use of Geographic Information Systems (GIS) in order to detect patterns of crime and 'hot spots' and to identify problem areas.

criminology of the other – a form of discourse about crime which relies on various forms of **othering** and sees offenders as essentially different from the rest of society, as 'evil' and, ultimately, as incorrigible.

cultural criminology – a recent criminological approach which emphasises the cultural construction of crime and crime control, and the role of image, style, representation, consumption, pleasure and performance among deviant subcultures (Jewkes, 2004: 223).

cybercrime – crime committed through the use of networks of information and communication technologies such as the Internet.

dataveillance – a form of surveillance which focuses on the collection and analysis of data and electronic records rather than on direct observation.

digital divide – a condition of social inequality with regard to access to, and the skills of operating, the new information and communication technologies, particularly the Internet.

Disneyization – a term popularized by Alan Bryman (2004) which describes how the principles of Disney theme parks are spreading throughout society. Related terms are McDonaldization and McDisneyization.

essentialism – a belief that identity is determined by some underlying essence.

ethnocentrism – originates from the Greek *ethno*, meaning people. It is a perspective which sees one's own community as a superior model against which all others have to be judged.

failed state – an expression for a weak state which to a large extent fails to exercise sovereignty over its territory. This is a controversial term, which is often used in a pejorative way, with potential political and military implications.

feminism – a broad term used to denote social theories and political movements concerned with the political and economic inequality between the sexes. In criminology, feminist approaches critically explore the relationship of sex/gender to crime and criminal justice.

fortress continents – a term denoting prosperous Western continents with closed and heavily policed borders. The concept of Fortress Europe is a particularly frequently used expression to describe the European Union's attempts to exclude non-EU citizens, goods and businesses.

gated communities – residential communities with controlled entrances and fortified boundaries in the form of gates, walls, security guards, **CCTV**, and other technologies.

global city theory – originally **world city theory**, has been developed by urban geographers to describe the new spatial organization of global capitalism, where large cities and urban regions (rather then nations) are the most important units of economic and social life.

global governance – this refers to attempts at solving problems on a global level, organized either by state-supported institutions such as the UN, the IMF and the World Bank, or by private actors such as NGOs, private business entities and civil society movements.

globalism – the perception of the world as connected. It can be visible in several aspects: political, cultural, economic, environmental, etc.

glocalization – a term popularized by Robertson (1995) describing how global phenomena conform to local conditions.

governmentality – a mode of governance originally described in the later work of the French philosopher Michel Foucault, and influentially developed in the 1990s by authors such as Nikolas Rose (1999, 2000) and others. In Foucault's view, power is not limited to the state alone, but is without a centre and dispersed throughout the social body, where its members play an active role in their own self-government (see **responsibilization strategy**).

homogenization – a process by which phenomena that were once different come to resemble and become essentially alike.

human rights – a set of rights which are universal and fundamental to human beings, regardless of jurisdiction or other factors, such as ethnicity, nationality or sex. Legally, the international body of human rights is most notably outlined in the United Nations Universal Declaration of Human Rights.

hybridity – refers principally to the process of creation of mixed phenomena, such as hybrid cultures and identities.

late modernity – perception of the present age societies as a continuation of **modernity** (i.e. post-feudal societies marked by a pursuit of material, techno-logical and social progress, industrialization, urbanization and a strong nation state).

Marxism – a theoretical approach, originally developed by Karl Marx and Friedrich Engels, framing its analysis in terms of class struggles and criticising the exploitative nature of capitalism. The term covers a wide range of academic theoretical schools, social movements and political positions.

masculinity – a set of cultural norms, ideas and social expectations associated with being a man.

mass private property – large commercial complexes, such as shopping malls and amusement parks, where the private sector assumes the monopoly on secu-rity governance and policing.

methodological nationalism – a methodological research framework which 'equates societies with nation state societies, and sees states and their govern-ments as the cornerstones of a social science analysis' (Beck, 2002: 51).

migration – movement of a person or persons, whether within a country (inter-nal migration), or across national borders (international migration).

militarization – a development in which social relations are redefined through the convergence of militaristic, police and penal contexts.

moral panic – a term popularized by Stan Cohen (2002), describing a dispro-portionate social reaction towards a perceived threat (a crime, group, person or a subculture), usually fuelled by sensationalist media reports.

neo-liberalism – an economic and political doctrine which gives priority to free market forces and competition and emphasises minimal state intervention.

ontological insecurity – the opposite of ontological security, described by Giddens (1990: 92) as 'the confidence that most human beings have in the continuity of their self-identity and in the consistency of the surrounding social and material environments of action'.

Orientalism – denotes a set of beliefs about the nature and peculiarity of the Oriental people. The term was popularized by Edward W. Said's (1978) analysis of deep-seated Western cultural prejudices about Asia and the Middle East.

panopticon – a prison design, created in the 19th century by Jeremy Bentham, based on a principle that enables few observers to watch the many. It was used as a blueprint for numerous prisons and became a symbol of surveillance and social control.

penal populism – describes 'the notion of politicians tapping into, and using for their own purposes, what they believe to be the public's generally punitive stance' Bottoms (1995: 40).

people smuggling – describes the facilitation of illegal cross-border movements for financial gain. At the point of arrival, the smuggled person is usually free to go. The relation between the smuggler and the client is primarily a financial transaction, which distinguishes smuggling from **human trafficking** which also involves various degrees of the use of force and/or violence.

policy transfer – a process of policy convergence in which policies, administrative arrangements, institutions and ideas in one (national) political setting are used in another political setting.

post-colonialism – a set of theories in philosophy, film and literature that critically analyse the Western colonial rule. Edward W. Said's (1978) work on **Orientalism** is a particularly influential contribution.

post-Fordism – an economic system where workers are mostly employed on a temporary basis and have limited influence over employers. The systems marks a shift from the previously stable, standardized (Fordist) modes of industrial production.

private authority – various forms of non-government authority which fill the void left by the demise of **state sovereignty**. They can be legal, such as private companies policing the spaces of mass private property, or illegal and **illicit**, for example paramilitary forces, guerrillas, gangs and organized crime groups, whose influence is visible particularly in the case of **failed states**.

racism – a belief in the superiority (biological, cultural) of one's own ethnic group. A related term is **xenophobia** – hatred and fear of foreigners. Racism has been a motivating factor in social discrimination, racial segregation and violence.

regulatory state – a term describing a mode of governance characteristic of neo-liberalism, where the state is 'steering' rather than directly 'rowing' the state affairs. The state directs, while the provision of services is left to other actors, principally market mechanisms (see **responsibilization strategy**).

relative deprivation – a concept describing how individual and group experiences of deprivation are defined through comparison to others. Poverty is not just a question of satisfying basic needs (absolute deprivation), but is essentially a feeling of deprivation which emerges when people feel deprived of goods and privileges enjoyed by other members of society.

responsibilization strategy – a mode of governance marked by a tendency to transfer the responsibility for governance (of crime and security) to other non-state actors (local communities, individual citizens and businesses).

restorative justice – an alternative approach to justice, which puts emphasis on non-punitive solutions to conflicts, on victim–offender reconciliation and on the rebuilding of relationships within communities. It is today used in a variety of settings such as youth justice, criminal justice, community problem solving and large-scale peacemaking tribunals, such as the Truth and Reconciliation Commissions in South Africa.

risk society – a term popularized by Ulrich Beck (1992), describing organization of society which is in a systematic way preoccupied with dealing with various risks and insecurities, which are a by-product of **modernity**.

Schengen Information System (SIS) – a computerized information network which allows police and other agents from Schengen Member States to access and enter a variety of data on specific individuals, vehicles and objects.

securitization – a political and discursive process by which the language of security becomes the organizing principle of social relations.

sex tourism – travel (by men or women) to engage in commercial sexual activities, typically undertaken internationally by tourists from wealthier countries.

sex work – a variety of commercial sexual activities, such as stripping, erotic massage, phone sex and prostitution; sometimes also used as an alternative term for prostitution.

social construction of crime – a criminological perspective which sees **crime** as a relative category, whose meaning is not an intrinsic quality of certain acts, but is constructed through a series of social, cultural and political processes of definition.

space of flows – a new spatial organization of society, described by Castells (1996), where information technologies transform space and time, enabling synchronic, real time interaction without physical proximity. It is the opposite of spatially rooted social organization – 'the space of places'.

state of exception – a term popularized by Georgio Agamben (2005), describing exceptionalism from the normal as a dominant paradigm for governing in contemporary politics, particularly in the post-9/11 climate.

state sovereignty – the right of a state to exercise a monopoly of legal and coercive power over a given territory. For our purposes, sovereignty is defined as the entitlement of a state to rule over its territory (Held, 1995).

surveillant assemblage – a term coined by Kevin Haggerty and Richard Ericson (2000) to describe intensification of surveillance, which is achieved by the merging of various surveillance technologies and institutions.

synopticon – or a **viewer society**, where the many watch the few and which functions as the opposite of the panoptic principle (Mathiesen, 1997).

technological determinism – describes the relationship between technology and society, in which technological change is seen to condition social change.

terrorism – politically motivated violence or other forms of harm, whose definitions are intensely contested and debated. Includes a variety of types: state terrorism as a form of **state crime**, international terrorism, domestic terrorism, etc.).

time–space compression – a term, generally attributed to David Harvey (1990), which describes processes that seem to accelerate the experience of time and reduce the significance of distance

transnational organized crime – the cross-border activities of organized crime groups, arguably exploiting to their advantage increasing global interconnectedness.

urbanization of poverty – the concentration of poor populations within cities and metropolitan regions, usually in spaces of exclusion termed slums, ghettos, favellas and *banlieues*.

virtual communities – at-a-distance forms of community established on the basis of non-corporeal presence, particularly in cyberspace.

zero tolerance policing – or so-called 'quality of life policing' is an aggressive style of policing primarily directed at minor offences perceived to degrade the city's visual image.

Index

Abacha, S. 23
Abu Ghraib 103, 110, 118, 119–20
accountability
　private security 23
　transnational policing 146
actuarial justice 20, 207
Agamben, G. 117–18
airports/airlines 33–4, 135, 136
Albrecht, H.-J. 86
Albrow, M. 5
al-Qaeda 109, 117–18, 167
Altman, D. 44
Americanization 5, 120–1, 180, 207
Amin, A. 70
Andrews, C. 160
anomie 92, 122, 207
anonymity, cyberspace 157, 158
anti-globalization protests 5, 165
Appadurai, A. 8, 54, 90, 147, 168–9
armpit smugglers 125
Armstrong, G. 59, 60, 61
asylum seekers 34, 36–40, 79–82, 83, 91
　bogus 85
　detention centres 86–8
asymmetric warfare 105, 118

Bailey, D. H. 178
banlieue 66, 67, 68–9
Barber, B. 95, 108
Barlow, J. P. 161–2
Bauman, Z. 11, 17, 20–1, 29, 31, 62, 67, 73,
　82, 103, 144, 157
Beck, U. 12, 13–14, 16, 110–11, 112–13, 176,
　177, 182, 184
Beijing Conference on Women 187
Benhabib, S. 188
Bentham, J. 60, 174
Big Brother metaphor 61, 113–16, 127
Bigo, D. 104
biometrics 34, 35, 157, 207
Black, C. 118
Blackwater 142
Blair, T. 88–9, 132
Blakely, E. J. 70, 71
border controls 31–6, 179
borderless world 31

Borja, J. 17, 95
boundaries 105, 188
Bourdieu, P. 63, 68–9, 82, 96
Bourgois, P. 67, 92, 96
Bratton, W. 64, 65
Brennan, D. 44–5
broken windows thesis 64
Brown, M. 119, 183
Bunt, G. 167
bureaucracy, transnational policing 145
Bush, G. 106, 118

Cain, M. 182
Calhoun, C. 103
care deficit 42
Carnivore 164
Castells, M. 9–10, 11, 17, 29, 57, 58, 90, 95,
　103, 123–5, 154, 155, 163
Castles, S. 30, 36, 41–2
CCTV 59–62, 63, 73, 135, 138, 168, 173,
　176, 207
Chan, J. 174
Chernobyl disaster 24
Chicago School 53–5, 69, 207
child sex tourism 46
Chow, E. N. 42–3
Christie, N. 12, 20, 22, 29, 69, 84, 137,
　140, 177
cities 49–74, 209
civil liberties 115, 117
clash of civilizations 84, 95, 108, 110, 207
class 42, 95–8
Cohen, S. 84–5, 118–19, 181, 182, 184
Cole, D. 117–18
commercialization, cyberspace 162
commodification 41, 138–9, 140, 208
commodities 136–8, 158
communitas 166
comparative criminology 178–9
concentric zone theory 53–4
Connell, R. W. 96
consumerism 19, 62, 73, 92, 140, 208
Convention Against Transnational Organized
　Crime 37, 38
Corrections Corporation of America 137
corruption 186

cosmetic fallacy 66
cosmopolitan citizenship 98
cosmopolitanism 208
COSMOS 168
    see also geographic information systems
Council of Europe's Convention on
        Cybercrime 164
Coyle, A. 86
Crawford, A. 143–4
crime mapping 53, 168, 208
crime wars 24, 101–28
    see also war on drugs; war on terror
criminalization 78, 83, 113, 120–1
cultural capital 96
cultural criminology 62, 208
cultural dynamics 88–98
cultural hybridity 93
culture of control 21
culture of exception 65–8
culture of fear 111–12
Cunneen, C. 158
Currie, E. 18–19
cyber-chattels 158
cybercrime 158–61, 163–5, 169–70, 173, 208
cyberdeviance 159, 160, 169
cyber-environments 157, 161
cyber-libertarians 161
cyber-regulation 161–5
cyberspace, control 151–70

data doubles 36, 114
data gathering 163
data-mining 114
data protection 115
dataveillance 164, 208
Davidson, J. 30, 39, 45, 46
Davis, M. 53, 56, 63, 67, 122
Deflem, M. 145
deindustrialization 56, 67, 68
de Menezes, J. C. 83
democratic deficit 146
Department of Homeland Security 114, 115
deregulation 132
detention centres 86–8
    Abu Ghraib 103, 110, 118, 119–20
    Guantanamo Bay 13, 103, 117–18, 119–20
deterritorialization 90, 102, 160, 180–1
deviant immigrants 32
Di Eugenio, K. 69
difference, living with 93–5
digital divide 154, 166–7, 208
DiMarco, H. 158
disembedded identity 157

Disneyization 47, 173, 208
Disney World 139
domestic violence 43
drugs 18, 56, 92, 180
    ghetto 67–8
    social marginalization 96
    war on 24, 120–5, 145
dual cities 57–8
Dublin Convention 34
Dunnighan, C. 6
Durkheim, E. 80, 122

ECHELON system 147
ecology of fear 53, 72–3
economy
    global 9
    global criminal 123–6
    illicit 11, 40
    market economies 39–41
    neoliberalism 17
elusive societies 21
environmental criminology 185
Ericson, R. 113, 117, 147
essentialism 93–6, 208
ethnicity 95–8
ethnocentrism 178, 181, 209
ethnoscapes 54, 68
Eurodac 34
Eurojust 146
European Court of Human Rights 186
European Union 82, 146, 148
    black list 32
    SIS 34
    terrorism 107, 113
Europol 146, 147
exclusive societies 21
extraordinary renditions 13

failed states 11, 125, 133, 141, 209
fear
    capitalism of 138
    of crime 14–16, 70–3, 111–12, 138
    culture 111–12
    ecology of 53, 72–3
Feeley, M. M. 20
feminism 42, 183, 209
feminization of migration 41–3
folk devils 84–5
Fordism 10
fortress continents 31–4, 70, 135, 185, 209
Foucault, M. 10, 36, 45, 60, 78, 113, 116,
        117, 134, 176
Fraser, N. 188, 189

Friedman, J. 56
Frontex 146

Garland, D. 20, 21, 79, 84, 99, 133–4, 135, 144
gated communities 70–3, 138, 140, 209
gated towns 72
gender
  Beijing Conference on Women 187
  female oppression 183
  Internet commodities 158
  migration feminization 41–3, 48
General Motors 32–3
Geneva Conventions 117–18
genocide 23, 183
geographic information systems (GIS) 53, 167–8
  see also COSMOS
ghettos 66–70, 73, 90, 91, 96, 122
Giddens, A. 3, 4–5, 6, 7, 14, 15, 25, 132
Giuliani, Mayor 64, 65, 172
global cities 49–74
global city theory 56–7, 209
global governance 121, 148, 186, 209
globalism 5, 209
globalization juggernaut 11
global village 17, 25, 165
glocalization 6, 94, 175, 209
Goffman, E. 120
Golden Age 16, 80
Goodey, J. 37, 38
governance
  cyberspace 161–5
  global 121, 148, 186, 209
  nodal 136
governmentality 134, 209
Grabosky, P. N. 159
Graham, S. 58
green criminology 24, 185
Green, P. 23
grooming 163–4, 173
Group 4 Securicor 137, 139
Guantanamo Bay 13, 103, 117–18, 119–20

Haggerty, K. H. 147
Hall, S. 54, 93, 94
Hallsworth, S. 62
Hannerz, U. 90
Harvey, D. 7
Hayes, B. 34
Hayward, K. 24, 62
Held, D. 4
Hillyard, P. 184
Hobbs, D. 6

Hoffman, B. 107
Hogg, R. 81, 189
Holton, R. J. 179
homogenization 173–4, 210
Hope, T. 15
Hudson, B. 72, 84, 116
human organs, traffic 41
human rights 187–8, 210
  violations 183, 186
human security 24–5
  see also security
Huntington, S. 95, 108
Hurricane Katrina 133, 142
Hussein, S. 152, 155
Huysmans, J. 112
hybridity 93, 105, 179, 210
Hylland Eriksen, T. 6–7
hyperghetto 67
hyperglobalism 132
hyperincarceration 20

ID cards 35, 157
identity 62
  cyberspace 156–8
  masculinity 96–7
  production 19
  theft/fraud 156–7
illegal immigrants 33, 36–40
illicit economy 11, 40
illicit flows 123–6
illicit private authority 126, 141
immigrants
  see also asylum seekers
  deviant 75–100
  female labour 42–3, 48, 59
  gated communities 71–2
  illegal 33, 36–40
immobilization 20
imperialism 180
industrialization 52, 53
industrial revolution 9–10
inequality 17–19, 25, 40, 57–9
information exchange 146–7
information revolution 9–10
insecurity 14–17, 25, 110–12
  ontological 15, 210–11
interdependence 173
international criminal tribunals 186
international mobilizations 187
Internet
  cybercrime 158–61, 163–5, 169–70, 173, 208
  cyberspace control 151–70

Internet *cont.*
 data doubles 114
 marriage 158
 sex trade 43, 44
 surveillance 114–15
 terrorists 110
 vengeful networks 85
Interpol 145
Iraq 23, 142–3
Islam 83–4, 95
Iyer, P. 58

Jewkes, Y. 15, 155, 160
Johnston, L. 72, 140
Jones, T. 181

Kelling, G. L. 64
Kempadoo, K. 183
Kimmel, M. S. 96–7

Laqueur, W. 108
Lash, S. 10
law, transnationalization 187
Law, J. 177
Lessig, L. 162
Loader, I. 80, 147
local 171–90
 multicultural society 68–70
 transformation 6
London terrorist attacks 2, 89
Low, S. 71
Lyon, D. 33, 35–6, 114

McClintock, 44
McDonaldization 5, 109, 173
McLuhan, M. 154
McWorld 95, 108
market economies, limits 39–41
market society 18–19
Marvin, S. 58
Marxism 18–19, 53, 210
Marx, K. 10, 18, 78
masculinity 96–8, 210
mass private property 60, 140, 210
Mathiesen, T. 107, 146, 147, 155
mediascapes 109
megacities 52
Megan's Law 167
mercenaries 142–3
Merton, R. 92, 122
methodological nationalism 176–7, 179–80,
 182, 183–4, 210

migration 27–48, 185, 210
 see also immigrants
 border controls 31–4
 deviant immigrants 75–100
 feminization 41–3
 urbanization 54
migration industry 36
militarization 24, 33, 63–5, 73,
 106, 210
Miller, M. J. 30, 36, 41–2
Milgram, S. 120
mobility 27–48
 risk society 14
 urbanization 54–5
modernity 25
 ghetto 67
 late 4–5, 14, 19–20, 21–2,
 113, 210
 liquid 11, 15, 29, 31, 157
 moral panic 84–5, 210
Morley, D. 89
Morrison, W. 23, 24, 104, 120, 181,
 182, 183
multiculturalism 55, 68–70, 93
Mythen, G. 16, 24, 84

Nadelmann, E. 120–1
Naim, M. 124
national 171–90
nationalism 94
 methodological 176–7, 179–80, 182,
 183–4, 210
neo-conservatism 144
neo-Fascism 94
neo-liberalism 10–13, 17–18, 123, 132,
 134–6, 144, 210
neo-Marxism 18
network society 9–10, 17, 57–8, 154
neutralization technique 95
Newburn, T. 181
Nightingale, C. 91
nodal governance 136
no-go zones 63
normative issues, privatization 140–3
Norris, C. 59, 60, 61
nowherevilles 47, 58

Oklahoma City bombing 108
Olympics 46
ontological insecurity 15, 210–11
Orientalism 84, 211
Orwell, G. 113

other
  criminology of the 77–8, 79, 84, 99, 166,
    183, 208
  Internet 166
  Oriental 84
  tourism 47

Pakes, F. 178
Palermo protocols 37
panopticon 36, 59–62, 113, 116, 174, 211
Papastergiadis, N. 30
passports, biometrics 35
Pelican Bay 20
penal policy transfers 5, 65, 173, 174–6, 211
penal politics 134
penal populism 81, 134, 166, 170, 211
people smuggling 36–9, 47–8, 211
people trafficking 27–48
Pickering, S. 185
plural policing 136, 165, 170
Police Chiefs Operational Task Force 146
policy transfers 5, 65, 173, 174–6, 211
politicization, migration 32
pornography 159–60, 164
post-colonialism 182–3, 211
post-Fordism 10, 61, 62, 63, 73, 211
post-industrialism 10
postmodernism 15
post-scepticism 132–3
poverty
  drug trade 121
  dual cities 57–8
  inequality 18–19
  risk society 16
  urbanization of 52, 213
Pratt, J. 81
prisons 20–1, 67, 78
  foreigners 86
  panopticon 60
  population growth 21, 143, 149
  privatization 136–8, 141
  punitiveness 20, 21
  supermax 20, 119
privacy 115, 116
private authority 141, 211
private policing 138–9, 140–2
private security 12, 23, 138–42, 148–9
privatization 11–13, 132, 136–8, 140–3, 148–9, 173
  normative issues 140–3
prostiturismo see sex tourism
prostitution 18, 44
  see also sex slaves/tourism/work

pull factors 39, 48
punishment 80–1
  culture 175
push factors 39, 40

quality of life crimes 64

race
  CCTV 61
  gated communities 71–2
  prisoners 86
  underclass thesis 91
  war on terror 83
racism 94, 97, 211
Rasmussen, T. 155
regulatory state 135, 211–12
Reich, R. 56
relative deprivation 19, 92, 96, 212
responsibility, cybercrime 160–1
responsibilization 116, 135, 138, 149,
    170, 186, 212
restorative justice 134, 181–2, 186, 212
risk assessment instruments 173
risk communication 147
risk society 13–14, 16, 26, 110–13, 127, 138,
    147, 181, 212
  see also world risk society
Robertson, R. 5, 6, 94
Russia, pillage 11–12

Al Sahab 167
Said, E. 84
Sanghera, J. 38
Sassen, S. 42, 43, 51
scapegoat society 16
scepticism 132
Schengen Agreement 34, 146
Schengen Information System (SIS) 34, 146,
    147, 212
Scheper-Hughes, N. 41
Schmitt, C. 117
Securitas Group 139
securitization 32, 33, 35, 36, 112–13,
    116, 212
security
  airports 33–4
  deficit 141
  limits 116
  private 12, 23, 138–42, 148–9
  quest for 14–16
  risk society 110–13, 127
  tourism 46–7

security *cont.*
  transnational crime 103–6
  see also human security; interpendence
Sennett, R. 55, 72
September 11th 3, 24, 34–5, 82, 103–4, 109
Sernhede, O. 93
sex slaves 28, 37, 38–9, 43
sex tourism 44, 45–7, 212
sex trade 43–5
sex work 40, 44–5, 48, 212
Shearing, C. 69, 72, 139, 140
Sheptycki, J. W. E. 121, 178
Simmel, G. 55, 78
Simon, J. 20, 33, 113
Sirene System 147
Skolnick, 184
Snyder, M. G. 70, 71
social capital 69
social construction of crime 22, 106–7,
  163, 212
social exclusion 17, 19, 20, 21, 59, 62, 63, 66,
  68, 71–3, 78
social inclusion 19, 78
social marginalization 96
social sorting 36, 114
solidarity 2–3, 80
space of flows 9, 29, 50, 57, 73, 90, 103, 154,
  174, 188, 212–13
space of places 90
Sparks, R. 15, 80
spatial exclusion 68–9, 73, 76, 90
spatial relations, cities 63
state 188
  crime 23–4, 183–4, 186
  illicit flows 125
  role 11–13, 25
  sovereignty 11–12, 121, 129–50, 213
  terror 107
state of exception 116–20, 213
Stenning, P. 139
stereotyping, terrorists 83
Stiglitz, J. 18
strain theory 122
stranger fear 55, 78–9, 83
Stubbs, J. 158
suitable enemy 84, 121
Sun Justice 166
surveillance 13
  border controls 33, 34–6
  CCTV 59–62, 63, 73, 135, 138, 168, 173,
    176, 207
  cyberspace 163–4

surveillance *cont.*
  Megan's Law 167
  post 9/11 113–16, 117, 127, 143
surveillance society 36
surveillant assemblage 36, 113–14, 213
symbolic politics 81
synoptic societies/synopticon 155, 213

Tampa incident 81
Tampare Summit 146
technological determinism 154, 155, 213
technological populism 166
technology 12–13
  see also Internet
  cyberspace control 151–70
  government 134
  transnational policing 146–7
technoscapes 147
territoriality 31
terrorism 79, 102–4, 213
  London bombs 2, 89
  new 106–10, 116
  postmodernism 15
  risk society 110–13
  September 11th 3, 24, 34–5, 82,
    103–4, 109
  state of exception 116–20
  tourism 46
  war on terror 12, 13, 24, 82–5, 116–17,
    120, 126–7
Thatcher, M. 80
third way 132–3
time-space compression 7, 25, 29, 50,
  103–6, 213
Toronto airport 136
torture 118–19, 120, 183
Total Information Awareness Program 114
tourism, sex trade 44, 45–7, 212
tourist gaze 45–7
tourists 31
transnational crime 101–28
transnationalization 4, 40
  of law 187
transnational networks 33, 123–4
transnational organized crime 79, 121,
  123–6, 213
transnational policing 145–8
  see also Europol; Interpol; Schengen
    Information System
transplant tourism 41
trickle-down effect 18
turbo-capitalism 11

underclass thesis 91
United Nations 37, 38, 52, 142, 148, 187
urban apartheid 63
urban criminology 49–74
urban ecology 53
urbanization 30, 52, 213
urban warfare 66
Urry, J. 8–9, 10, 45, 109, 110, 177

vagabonds 31
Valier, C. 85, 166, 169
van Creveld, M. 105
victimization 112
viewer society 115, 155, 161
Virillio, P. 29
virtual communities 165–9, 213
virtualization 165
visa information system (VIS) 34

Wackenhut Corporation 130, 131
Wacquant, L. 17, 66, 67, 86
Walkate, S. 16, 24, 84
Walker, N. 145–6
war 24, 105–6
  on drugs 24, 120–5, 145
  privatization 142–3
  on terror 12, 13, 24, 82–5, 116–17, 126–7
    Abu Ghraib 103, 110, 118, 119–20
    Guantanamo Bay 13, 103, 117–18, 119–20

Ward, T. 23
Weber, M. 131, 145
Weed and Seed system 168
welfare state 19–20, 69, 78, 144
Westernization 5, 180
Westphalian frame 188
Whyte, D. 23
Whyte, W. F. 69
Wilson, J. Q. 64
withering away thesis 11, 12, 25, 93, 126,
  132–3, 143–5
Wood, J. 69
Woodwiss, M. 121, 124
world in motion 3
world risk society 13–14, 110–11, 181
  see also risk society

Yar, M. 159, 160, 163
Young, J. 15–16, 19, 21, 24, 66, 91–2, 94–5
YouTube 115, 155–6
Yuval-Davis, N. 94

Zedner, L. 21, 22, 112, 140, 141–2
zero tolerance policing 5, 6, 64–6, 172–3,
  174–5, 213
  see also penal policy transfers
Zimbardo, P. 120